Visions of the Press in Britain, 1850–1950

Visions of the Press in Britain, 1850–1950

MARK HAMPTON

University of Illinois Press
URBANA AND CHICAGO

© 2004 by the Board of Trustees
of the University of Illinois
All rights reserved
Manufactured in the United States of America
C 5 4 3 2 1

∞ This book is printed on acid-free paper.

Library of Congress Cataloging-in-Publication Data
Hampton, Mark, 1970–
Visions of the press in Britain, 1850–1950 / Mark Hampton.
p.   cm.
Includes bibliographical references and index.
ISBN 0-252-02946-1 (alk. paper)
1. Press—Great Britain—History—19th century. 2. Press—Great Britain—History—20th century. 3. Journalism—Great Britain—History—19th century. 4. Journalism—Great Britain—History—20th century.   I. Title.
PN5117.H27   2004
070'.09'034—dc22   2004004966

Contents

Acknowledgments *vii*

Introduction *1*

1. The Press in Britain, 1850–1950 *19*
2. Imagining the Press, 1850–80: The Educational Ideal Ascendant *48*
3. The Educational Ideal of the Press in the Era of the New Journalism, 1880–1914 *75*
4. "Representing the People": The Press as a "Fourth Estate," 1880–1914 *106*
5. Persuasion or Propaganda? Thinking about the Press in Britain, 1914–50 *130*

Epilogue: The First Royal Commission on the Press (and Beyond) *173*

Bibliography *181*

Index *215*

Acknowledgments

I wish to thank several colleagues and institutions for their generous help as I wrote this book. The history department at Vanderbilt University provided much of the funding for this book's initial research through a Leland Sage dissertation year fellowship and multiple Blanche and Henry Weaver and William J. Binkley grants. Margo Todd went out of her way to help me secure this funding. In addition, the Vanderbilt University Graduate School provided a Dissertation Enhancement Fellowship. Wesleyan College has provided Faculty Development grants for three consecutive summers; I am grateful to Interim Dean Hilary Kight and Dean Delmas Crisp.

Material scattered in chapters 2, 3, and 4 originally appeared in journal articles: "'Understanding Media': Theories of the Press in Britain, 1850–1914," *Media, Culture, and Society* 23 (March 2001): 213–31; "Liberalism, the Press, and the Construction of the Public Sphere: Theories of the Press in Britain, 1830–1914," *Victorian Periodicals Review* 37 (Spring 2004): 72–92. Chapter 5 originally includes material originally published in "Censors and Stereotypes: Kingsley Martin Theorizes the Press," *Media History* 10 (April 2004): 17–28. Quotations from the Mass-Observation Archive are reproduced with permission of Curtis Brown Group Ltd., London, on behalf of the Trustees of the Mass-Observation Archive (Copyright © Trustees of the Mass-Observation Archive). The David Low cartoon "Seeing Red" is reproduced by permission of Atlantic Syndication. Quotations from the *Manchester Guardian* Archive are reproduced by courtesy of the librarian and director of the John Rylands University Library of Manchester. References from the Lord Beaverbrook Papers are reproduced by permission of the clerk of the records, House of Lords Record Office, acting on behalf of the Beaverbrook Foundation. I am also grateful to the National Union of Journalists for permission to cite material from its archive at the Modern Records Centre, University of Warwick, and to the Manchester Central Library for permission to cite the Robert Blatchford Papers. Numerous librarians and archivists provided valuable assistance, particularly at the British Library, the House of Lords Record Office, the University of Sussex Special Collections, Cambridge University's Churchill College, and the Public Record Office. Above all, I wish to thank Catherine Lee, head librarian at Wesleyan College, who has helped me tirelessly (in many cases even securing for me loans of material that is "not lent"). I am also grateful to everyone at the University of Illinois Press, particularly Robert McChesney and my editor, Kerry Callahan.

Jim Epstein directed the dissertation from which chapters 3 and 4 and part of chapter 1 originated. I could not have asked for a better mentor: he knew when to challenge me and when to be supportive, and he inspired me with his own matchless scholarship. Since that time, he has continued to read virtually every manuscript I have written and to answer my neverending barrage of questions. Michael Bess, Matthew Ramsey, and Helmut Smith offered probing, insightful suggestions as I wrote the dissertation and friendship and encouragement since. In addition, Michael has taught me much about the relationships between scholarship and (for lack of a better term) real life. Rohan McWilliam gave careful readings to numerous versions of this book's argument, introduced me to the historical profession in London, and generally showed me what it means to be a historian. David Steiner, Phil Harling, James Vernon, Antony Taylor, and Dror Wahrman commented helpfully on portions of the manuscript at an early and formative stage. Jeff Jackson and Joe Roidt gave crucial nonspecialist readings to various chapters; both, moreover, have constantly inspired me with their character and personal commitments. David Karr has provided theoretically sophisticated critiques of everything I have sent him, but even more importantly he has been a remarkable friend for several years. Joel Wiener and Aled Jones both read the entire manuscript, offering helpful criticisms large and small. In addition, both have given me tremendous encouragement, welcoming me into a research field that they have done much to build. All of my Wesleyan colleagues, but above all Regina Oost, Marcile Taylor, and Barbara Donovan, have provided a supportive environment and responded creatively to my numerous unpolished ideas.

I was fortunate to share my London postgraduate research pilgrimage with several engaging fellow pilgrims, including Andrew Jacobson, Isaac Land, Mary Conley, Lydia Murdoch, Brenda Assael, and Elizabeth Buettner. I am grateful for their friendship during exciting yet anxious times. Roger Cooter, Karen Harvey, and Harry Cocks helped me to forget that I was far from home.

I owe a debt to my parents and sister: Larry, Kay, and Allysa Hampton. They have provided love and guidance as long as I can remember. Finally, Ring Mei Han Low has been my companion and my joy since we met in Manchester in the summer of 1996. She has never ceased to challenge me, to comfort me, and to make me better than I am. This book is for her.

Introduction

In 1995, a poster advertising *The Spectator*, a conservative political weekly journal, boasted the following:

> Something our writers won't do is send you to sleep. Their politics range from right to left, their circumstances from high life to low life. They offer a quality and originality of argument not to be had in any other weekly magazine. Our in-depth political commentary and colourful reporting are complemented by expert coverage of the arts and literature and spiced with the wit of Britain's funniest cartoonists. But sometimes we are deadly serious. The truth as we tell it has led to the resignation of a KGB contact from a national newspaper, parliamentary debates, and even a cabinet reshuffle. And then you find that what we said yesterday the newspapers say tomorrow.
> *The Spectator*, every week. Why wait?[1]

Lively writing and speed combine with impartiality, depth, expertise, and seriousness to produce a watchdog that monitors the powerful. As inherently desirable as all of these qualities may seem, their appeal did not arise accidentally but as the result of what the historian Aled Jones has called a "long argument" over the meanings and nature of the modern press.[2] This book analyzes the ways in which British elites conceptualized the press between 1850 and 1950, examining the debates that helped to lead the British to the point where informing readers and toppling governments, and never in a boring fashion, could appear as the appropriate function of journalism.

British historians recognize the cultural centrality of the press in the late nineteenth and early twentieth centuries, and many make extensive use of the newspapers of the period as primary sources, yet they often fail to pay adequate attention to the ways in which the press itself was situated in British culture. Although press history has become a growth industry in the past three decades, most studies of the period considered here fall into one of two groups. Many fine content analyses of newspapers or periodicals illuminate a particular analytical category, such as gender or nationalism, while a voluminous assortment of studies chronicle the almost daily workings of particular journals or journalists. Very few studies address the press itself as a category, over a substantial chronological period, whether to examine its economic structure, readership, or role within culture, society, and politics.[3] This book is an attempt to do so.

This book also belongs within the context of intellectual history: It treats the press as a focus of inquiry and discussion, much as other studies treat themes such as political or social thought or concepts such as altruism or honor.[4] Unlike many works of intellectual history, however, the present study does not focus primarily on a set of formally structured works by canonical thinkers, if only because throughout this period such works on the press were in very short supply. Rather, it focuses on discussions of the press wherever they can be found—journalists' memoirs, novels, periodical literature, parliamentary debates, and occasionally in unpublished documents. Moreover, it considers extended arguments along with quick asides and slogans. How the press was discussed and understood in the nineteenth and twentieth centuries has received little scholarly attention.[5]

Finally, this study is influenced by the recognition that media studies in Britain typically pays inadequate attention to historical research. James Curran, whose work stands as a notable exception to this generalization, has called historical scholarship the "neglected grandparent of media studies."[6] Although Curran's point is that our own understanding of the media needs a firm historical footing, it is also clear that understandings of the media are themselves situated in historical contexts. This is an important point to make within the field of media studies. As Ralph Negrine has argued, the dominant twentieth-century arguments about the media derived, in many cases, from theories originally worked out in the nineteenth century.[7] This means that contemporary theories of the mass media are often anachronistic, both because they are heavily based on discussions of exclusively print media, and because they fail to account for changes in media ownership over the past century. To take only one example, libertarian arguments that originally attacked an authoritarian state now are used to defend the prerogatives of international conglomerates that can be equally undemocratic.[8] At the same time, many popular contemporary conceptions of the media are unduly alarmist, forgetting that many of their concerns are far from new. This study attempts to negotiate the space between media studies and British history.

This book will tell the story of the changing conceptions of the press in Britain between approximately 1850, when the debate over the "taxes on knowledge" was gathering steam, and 1950, just after the Royal Commission on the Press responded to allegations that the ownership of the media had become unduly concentrated. During this century, the newspaper press moved into the center of British political culture, the political order changed dramatically, becoming (on the surface at least) much more democratic, the media became a respectable topic for academic inquiry, and modern electronic media emerged to break the press's monopoly on news. Not surprisingly, this period is extremely rich in discussions of the press's role in society and politics.

* * *

The mass media sits at the center of the political process in modern democracies. For this reason, the meaning of the mass media is contested terrain. This is in part a conflict over whose values or political views are supported in print and broadcast media. Conservatives and leftists both decry the biases in media content, though their arguments differ. Conservatives tend to see an army of left-leaning journalists seeking to impose their values on audiences, while leftist critics tend to emphasize the corporate ownership of the mass media, the dominance of media content by powerful institutions armed with well-funded public relations departments able to offer "information subsidies" to overworked journalists, and career-oriented journalists' internalization of routine practices that reinforce the existing social and political order. At the same time, conservatives often emphasize the possibility that audiences will emulate what they see in the mass media, whereas leftists tend to emphasize the ways that a narrowly defined media reality deprives citizens of information necessary for functional democracies.[9]

In Britain and the United States, there is a growing concern over the constricted ownership of the media; in particular, critics question whether a "free" press is compatible with a concentrated ownership.[10] Such critics argue that censorship can be understood more broadly than simply government policy. If the corporate ownership of the mass media prevents certain perspectives from being expressed, then censorship has occurred, regardless of how free the media is under the law. The resulting narrow range of opinions available in the media has negative consequences for democracy; taken to its logical conclusion, this large-scale concentration of ownership forestalls proper debate and allows the mass media to become the outlet for the "selling of the president."[11]

Ownership patterns are not the only nonstate source of censorship. Organized groups exert increasing pressure to alter media content, especially in films, if that content includes negative portrayals of religion, gender, or sexual orientation.[12] Apart from pressure groups attempting to "censor" the media, moreover, critics have shown concern over the way that certain "values" are embodied in the media. Throughout the 1990s, politicians struck a populist chord by railing against sex and violence on television, in movies, and in video games, while leftist critics have pointed to the ways in which stereotypes of race, gender, and sexuality are perpetuated in the media.[13] The media is seen as central not only to the political process, narrowly construed, but also to the more broadly political contest over images, ideas, and values.

In the midst of these long-standing contests over the concentration of ownership and the content of the media, several critics have focused instead on the technological and communicative biases inherent in particular media. Marshall McLuhan first popularized the notion that the "medium is the message," although he had precursors in medium theory.[14] Broadly speaking, McLuhan and those influenced by him have argued that the structure of a medium constrains the type of content that can be conveyed through it and shapes the general character of thought and discourse communicated through it. In its different manifestations, medium theory has been employed to argue that Americans are losing their ability to distinguish between reality and fantasy and that public discourse (including education and election campaigns) has been "dumbed down."[15] For Todd Gitlin, the most salient bias in our media environment is the bias in favor of media: "The media have been smuggling the habit of living with the media." Moreover, Gitlin argues that this "supersaturation" is not a recent product of television or the Internet but is several centuries in the making.[16] Perhaps most ambitiously, Ronald Deibert has argued persuasively that the current world political order, including the primacy of nation-states, may not "fit" with the emerging "hypermedia" environment and may be forced to adapt accordingly.[17]

The more deeply mediated our lives become, the more controversy the mass media provokes. Critics from both the Right and the Left invest the mass media with the power of either undermining or saving democratic politics: it can educate citizens or turn them into idiots—or at least into people who think in "nonlinear" ways. It can create leftists or "secular humanists" or inhibit thinking beyond the status quo.[18] Most of these arguments are united, however, in that they center around those members of the media audience whose lack of knowledge, real or imagined, prevents them from withstanding the media onslaught. Most discussions of the media therefore create an implied critical audience. To take only one example, when Vice President Dan Quayle famously complained in 1992 about the television character Murphy Brown's influence on "family values," he was not imagining that *he* would be tempted to have a child out of wedlock; nor was he suggesting that "you, the good audience member who will be as concerned about this as I am," would be tempted to emulate Murphy Brown. It was an imprecisely defined "impressionable" group that worried him. This observation holds true at different analytical levels and across the political spectrum, for scholars as well as politicians, priests, and pundits. Debates about media's effects imply other, less discerning audiences than those engaging in the debate.

Who makes up this group? To different writers and speakers, the culprits may differ. The high school dropout? The "underclass"? In nineteenth- and early twentieth-century Britain, such an implied group lay behind discussions of the press; this group, broadly speaking, comprised the popular classes. To put it more plainly, discussions of the press between 1850 and 1950 generally were products of elite culture, and they focused on the effects of the press on the behavior of the nonelite.

The precise concerns of those who discussed the press in this period differed from contemporary concerns, but the general patterns of the debates were remarkably similar. The debates centered on how accessible the press should be, whether the press influenced or reflected society, the press's impact on culture and politics, and, especially after World War I, who owned the press. Behind each of these questions, a broader theme can be found: what role were the popular classes going to play in a rapidly changing British society?

During the course of the nineteenth and early twentieth centuries, the expansion of the reading public—and with it, the growth and increased circulation of the daily press—coincided with the expansion of the electorate. These twin processes met with optimism and anxiety on the part of elite segments of British society. For some observers, the expanding press and franchise represented a more inclusive political nation, a development that was desirable in itself and was consonant with the image of England as a progressive nation. Indeed, one of the great benefits attributed to newspaper reading was its ability to educate new or future voters, making them worthy of their solemn electoral duty. For many among the elites, however, political developments constituted not a desirable liberalization but a descent into a frightening mass society, age of the crowd, or rule by the "half-educated." The more optimistic view predominated into the 1880s, before giving way to the more pessimistic view. This transformation was reflected in an important alteration in the language used by elite commentators in discussing the press.

"Elite" is a purposefully vague term, but it is well suited to the present study, and not only because it sidesteps the debate on the appropriateness of "class" as a category of modern British history.[19] The subjects of this book are defined in the first instance not by their relationship to the means of production, nor even to the "experience" of class-consciousness. Rather, the subjects are overwhelmingly those who wrote in mainstream periodicals and books, participating in a self-selected "conversation" about the press from the assumed perspective of insiders. Whatever conclusions these authors drew about the role of the press vis-à-vis the popular classes, as either writers or readers, *their own* inclusion was never in doubt. Similarly, most of the commentaries analyzed in this book were written by people who would have qualified for the vote even in 1850. Rather than refer to these writers in "traditional" class terms, I employ Stuart Hall's distinction between dominant and popular culture and, derivatively, the elite (or dominant) and the popular (or dominated) classes.[20]

This book's central argument is that elite discussions of the press constituted an attempt to understand and perhaps to control the emerging mass society. This is particularly true in the distinctions made between the "quality" and burgeoning popular newspapers of the day. In Hall's terms, prevailing theories of the press were part of "a continuous and necessarily uneven and unequal struggle, by the dominant culture, constantly to disorganise and reorganise popular culture; to enclose and confine its definitions and forms within a more inclusive range of dominant forms."[21] Moreover, these efforts were quite natural and understandable given the gulf that separated elite and popular worldviews.

There was, of course, another side to this "struggle": the response of the popular classes. A full consideration of this topic is beyond the scope of this book; indeed, it deserves its own study.[22] Still, it bears mentioning that the popular classes were not passive objects of study but active readers and letter writers. Popular tastes could shape newspaper content, and readers of all classes could approach the press with skepticism. In addition, numerous scholars have noted that consumption is not a passive process; it is not contained within the moment of purchase.[23] Rather, readers assign diverse meanings to texts. These caveats, however, should not distract us from the structures of dominance that Hall has identified. The recent emphases on multivalence and consumer sovereignty risk masking class-based inequalities in access to media products.[24] Moreover, counterhegemonic readings, even "subversive" readings, are ultimately "dependent rather than originating."[25]

While the effort to understand frightening new forms of popular culture helped to shape the debates on the press, this was not the whole story. Theories of the press also reflected a fascination with a relatively new medium that seemed indicative of the "speed" of modern life and an attempt by journalists to gain social recognition for their endeavors. The first of these themes can await treatment in a subsequent chapter. It is essential to address at the outset, however, the fact that most of the sources analyzed in this book were produced by people who were, at least to some extent, associated with journalism and who thus had an essential stake in how the press was understood by society. Unlike a contemporary academic media scholar, for example, a nineteenth-century commentator, who in most cases was a journalist, could not be expected to downplay the importance of the press.

Laurel Brake has demonstrated that it was only in the late nineteenth century that journalism and literature became distinguished as separate fields of endeavor and that this separation was largely brought about by literary scholars seeking professional recognition for their own field.[26] Two related points should be noted. First, in the mid-nineteenth century there was no hard and fast distinction between the broad categories of journalist, politician, and scholar: Prime Minister William Gladstone is only the most obvious example of overlap that comes to mind. This means that for much of the period studied here virtually *every* writer had *some* connection with journalism. Second, even as literary (and other) scholars made claims for their distinct status, journalists, too, articulated various competing claims about their own professional distinction.[27] The discourse analyzed here was therefore often intended not only to make sense of an important aspect of mass society but also to promote the professional recognition of journalists. Even beyond this purpose, many of the sources, such as journalists' memoirs, were produced by impoverished former journalists trying to capitalize on the public's fascination with the romance of Fleet Street.

This realization cautions us against taking the sources' claims simply at face value. Indeed, one might even ask whether we can take seriously "theories" of the press that were produced under such circumstances. This difficulty shapes the way we must read the sources, but it is not an insurmountable problem—nor is it one from which any historian is exempt. True, the discussions of the press examined here involved posturing as much as investigation. Given their character as *public* posturing, however, these discussions drew on themes and images that their authors expected would resonate with their audiences. In other words, in their representations of the relationships between the press and readers, the press and politics, or the press and social transformations, the writings analyzed here were necessarily constrained by the broader store of prevailing and acceptable ideas.

* * *

While elite discussions of the press have tended to constitute a means of exerting imaginative control over the "unwashed masses," they have at the same time played a prominent part in efforts to delimit an imagined "public sphere." Although this term has perhaps become hackneyed in the past decade, since the translation into English of Jürgen Habermas's 1962 book *The Structural Transformation of the Public Sphere*,[28] Habermas's own depiction of a rational space between individuals and the state neatly captures an ideal that permeated mid-Victorian elite society. This ideal, which H. C. G. Matthew has called the "liberal ethos," might also be called an ideal of politics by public discussion.[29] This ideal emphasized the free exchange of ideas, the persuasion of opponents, and the valiant effort to step outside of one's limited perspective in order to reason "from the point of view of the universe."[30] To someone who held this ideal, the desired end was a consensus around the "truth" or the "common good." This end, of course, remained more of a focus than a reachable goal, and barring consensus, or even if consensus was attained, public discussion was seen as a necessity.

Even in the mid-nineteenth century this ideal achieved only predominance, not hegemony. Still, much of the story told in this book is the story of its waning. Naturally, this ideal contained elements of "social control"; like free trade itself, the free trade of ideas was generally put forth by those confident that their own self-evidently true beliefs would prevail.[31] This observation does not alter the fact that the liberal ideal exerted a powerful attraction over the mid-Victorian imagination.

This part of my argument derives substantially from Alan J. Lee's pathbreaking study.[32] In reading Lee's book, however, one gets the impression that following the mid-Victorian "golden age," in which journalism in practice mostly lived up to this high ideal, the commercialism of the late nineteenth century robbed the press of any ideals whatsoever. In this telling, a handful of liberals and radicals continued to pine after an increasingly anachronistic vision of the press, even as the practice of journalism became little more than a cynical race for profits. At this point my interpretation parts from Lee's. Although it is undeniable that the conditions of the "New Journalism" ran counter to midcentury ideals, cynicism and anachronism never became the only options. The press remained a topic of serious debate, and its importance to a democratic political culture was seldom challenged.

In the period from 1850 to 1950, the debates over the role of the British press focused on questions of press accessibility and ownership and the relationship between the press and public opinion—that is, whether the press influenced or reflected public opinion. In these debates, two main analytical traditions surfaced. Most convergent with the "liberal ethos," or politics by public discussion, an ideal of the press developed that I have called the "educational ideal": the press was regarded as a powerful agent for improving individuals. Used properly, newspapers could fulfill two related and overlapping educational functions. First, they could "influence," "inform," or "elevate" readers, bringing them into possession of certain supposedly established truths, such as the scientific basis of political economy and the wonders of the British constitution. This is the aspect of the educational ideal that has struck scholars as an exercise in "social control." Second, however, in the most idealized version, newspapers were seen as creating an arena for public discussion on the "questions of the day." In this view, nothing could be more natural than for newspapers to offer a highly partisan rendering of political questions, in the expectation that conscientious readers would, as Lord Roseberry famously did, read newspapers of several different perspectives every day. Whether many readers ever lived up to this ideal is questionable; still, it exerted a potent hold over many mid-Victorian thinkers. Broadly speaking, this ideal held sway from roughly the 1850s into the 1880s.

The second major tradition to emerge in this period I call the "representative ideal" of the press.[33] In this view, the press did not influence readers or public opinion but reflected them. In this rendering, newspapers conveyed the opinions, wants, or needs of readers, crystallizing them into a powerful form that could bring pressure to bear on Parliament. This version of the press is most nearly conveyed in the press's label as the "Fourth Estate": the press was the champion of the people, in the most ambitious telling even replacing the House of Commons as the "chamber of initiative."

This motif, which began to predominate in the 1880s, recalled the radical critique of "old corruption" of the pre-Reform era as well as the rich "liberty of the press" tradition. Both of these deployments were ironic in that the representative ideal emerged in a period in which old-fashioned censorship had been largely eradicated and the newly enfranchised working class would seem to be less in need of a "representative" press than previously. This irony can be better understood, however, when one considers that the representative ideal effectively removed the "masses" from a politics by public discussion. Rather than seeking to involve the mass readers in a discussion or seeking to persuade these readers, those who articulated the representative ideal offered to speak on their behalf. This theory offered some comfort in a period in which many among the elites anxiously observed the apparent emergence of a mass democracy.

Why did the educational ideal yield to the representative ideal in the 1880s? First, it is important to note that this change was only relative, not absolute. The educational ideal did not vanish but merely receded in prominence.[34] In the late nineteenth century and throughout the period studied here, the educational ideal tended to wind up on the Left, among socialists such as Robert Blatchford or "forward" liberals such as C. P. Scott and his *Manchester Guardian* writers. This continued commitment to an educational ideal of the press remained part of a broader commitment to a program of elevation for the working class, a program that included "liberal summer schools" and "rational recreation."[35]

Still, the educational ideal did retreat considerably. This decline reflected developments in the British press and British society more generally. Lee's thesis of a mid-Victorian "golden age" of the penny press is somewhat overstated but not entirely inaccurate. Compared to later developments, ownership of the press was fairly dispersed and editorial independence relatively more secure. To be sure, even at that point an editor could not afford to neglect the commercial bottom line. Still, newspaper ownership was diffused widely enough and the spectrum of political views was diverse enough that the educational ideal could seem plausible. Moreover, that ideal meshed well with evangelical notions such as self-help: what could be more comforting than the idea of a working-class autodidact reading healthy newspapers at the same time that he worked and saved for the future? In Gladstone's view, such a combination helped make a certain segment of the working class "fitter and fitter" to join the electorate.[36]

In the late nineteenth century, by contrast, and particularly beginning in the 1880s, newspaper ownership became increasingly concentrated. This concentration occurred largely because of the emergence of a mass readership, the reliance on ever more expensive machines, and the increasing dominance of advertising revenue. In this environment, few independent proprietors could persevere. At the same time, the emergence of a mass readership—commonly but inaccurately attributed to the 1870 Education Act—contributed to the introduction of headlines, shorter stories (the column giving way to the paragraph), a simplification of prose, and eventually photography. From an early twenty-first-century perspective, of course, even the *Daily Mail* of 1896 appears sober and restrained.[37] To commentators accustomed to the mid-Victorian press, however, these modest developments seemed ominous. In this newspaper environment, the educational ideal appeared more and more chimerical.

At the same time, broader cultural developments made the educational ideal less appealing or resonant. For example, the years 1873 to 1896, often referred to as the "great depression," saw the so-called age of equipoise give way to a less consensual political atmosphere. As casual labor expanded, many among the social and political elites became less willing to think of workers becoming "fitter and fitter" to join the political nation; instead, these years saw the expansion of the imagined "residuum," that segment of the popular classes that was "beyond the pale."[38] At the same time, the 1880s brought the "New Unionism," a unionization that was more militant than the older version and one that extended to unskilled labor. Some historians may have exaggerated the level of consensus in the mid-Victorian years; nonetheless, it is difficult to deny that the 1880s and later brought a new (or revived) radicalization among workers.

This radicalization included political as well as economic organization. In 1884, the Third Reform Bill vastly increased the number of workers in the electorate, and the 1918 Representation of the People Act completed universal male suffrage.[39] Even this observation does not exhaust the extent of political transformation, because it is obvious that many among the elites *experienced* the 1884 act as a major change, a perception that is attested to by "Lib-Labism" among Liberals in weak constituencies and a redefinition of the Conservative party to include business as well as landed elites.[40] Politicians began to consider various welfare measures, even if only as the "ransom" that property must pay for its security.[41] Even the Conservative party's employment of jingoist themes can be seen as part of its attempt to co-opt the transformed electorate.

Even the redefinition of the two parties to attract new constituencies could not prevent the emergence of a Labour party. Although most historians no longer accept a simple relationship between the expansion of the electorate and the eventual triumph of the Labour party, contemporaries can perhaps be excused for having imagined such a link.[42] Moreover, the expansion of the electorate, the persistence of the great depression, and the emergence of militant unions, socialist thinkers, and working-class politicians could easily have struck elite observers as being all of a piece. No clear consensus prevailed on how to respond to these changing social conditions. The changes themselves, though, seemed undeniable, and thus it is not surprising that elite optimism about selectively integrating the popular classes into the political nation gave way to a late nineteenth-century anxiety. In this environment, representing the people seemed less risky than inviting them to participate in public discussion.

The emphasis on representing readers rather than educating them and engaging them in discussion also fit well with an emerging late nineteenth-century concept of the managed society. As the scramble for empire and industrial competition reached dizzying new levels of intensity, questions of "national efficiency" took on a greater urgency. The complex problems of industrial society appeared less amenable to individualist (or moralist) solutions, and many thinkers began to call upon "professionals" to address these problems, especially poverty. In this atmosphere, the mid-Victorian ideals of self-help and self-reliance, while by no means disappearing, lost some of their credibility. In place of a British version of "Ragged Dick," elite opinion favored the social scientist.[43]

Gender and imperial anxieties also figured in the late nineteenth-century transformation of press ideals, though frequently in implicit ways. Numerous scholars have emphasized the gendered basis of the nineteenth-century public sphere.[44] Concepts such as work, rationality, and citizenship often implied masculinity. By the 1880s, the emergence of the "New Woman" and the suffrage movement, combined with related attacks on masculinity, called these gendered concepts into question.[45] Midcentury theories of the press tended to employ such gendered language; educational newspapers and educable readers were implicitly cast in masculine terms. The shift to the representative ideal accompanied an emphasis on newspaper coverage of "domestic" or "feminine" topics. This point blends well with Bill Schwarz's observation that late-Victorian middle-class commentators tended to attribute feminine characteristics to the working classes.[46]

The imperial context rarely figures explicitly in this study. As with other aspects of British cultural history, however, understandings of the press depended on concepts of Britishness that derived from comparisons to non-British "others."[47] During the late 1850s, for example, even as campaigners pushed for the repeal of the final tax on knowledge, the British state imposed further restrictions on the Indian press. This action, part of the reaction to the Sepoy Mutiny, presumed that nonwhite civilizations remained, in John Stuart Mill's famous words, in their "nonage." Despotic forms of government were suitable to these subjects.[48] The mid-Victorian idealized newspaper reader thus had masculine, European, and middle-class attributes. In the 1880s, anxieties about "new" readers who did not share these attributes helps to account for the shift from the educational to the representative ideal.[49]

Finally, while the prevailing conditions of the press made the educational ideal less convincing, and while political and social conditions made that ideal less attractive, even the prevailing understanding of communication seemed to undermine the educational ideal. That ideal depended upon an individual reader's ability to choose rationally between competing ideas, and in the late nineteenth century, the number of thinkers who continued to believe in this ability declined. Instead, an "organic" view prevailed, in which opinion was seen as a product not of individual choice but deep, impersonal forces. In this atmosphere, when commentators considered whether the press influenced or reflected public opinion, it is not surprising that they decided upon the latter.

The yielding of the educational ideal to the representative ideal was, we might say, overdetermined. As pointed out above, this intellectual transformation was by no means complete. Not only did some, particularly on the Left, continue to embrace the educational ideal, but a kind of synthesis emerged by the early twentieth century in which sophisticated writers such as R. A. Scott-James and George Binney Dibblee essentially adopted the educational ideal when speaking of the elite press and the representative ideal when speaking of the popular press. At this point, the idealized public sphere had bifurcated—which is to say, it had ceased to exist as a genuinely inclusive *public* sphere.

During the interwar years, the debates continued to develop within the framework already outlined. At this point, however, the terrain became more complicated, and the categories became somewhat redefined. In the first place, electronic media emerged, and contemporaries attributed to these media many of the same qualities that had been originally linked to the Victorian press. For example, John Reith, the director of the BBC, brought an ideology of "elevating" the masses to the corporation that was, in some important respects, an adaptation of the educational ideal.[50] By the end of this period, similar hopes were held out for television.

The terrain also became more complicated as the mass media became a respected topic of academic investigation. At the same time, by the First World War, the lines between scholarship, journalism, and politics had become less fluid. At this point, it was more conceivable (though by no means certain) that a statement about the press could lack a directly self-interested agenda. As the intervention of academic writers and the emergence of new media complicated the arena of discussion, the categories changed somewhat. In particular, the link between influence and education was decisively broken, and "influence" mostly lost its positive connotation. By the 1920s, observers tended to link "influence" to "propaganda" and to see it as nonrational rather than rational. Propaganda theory emerged independently in Britain, in response to government actions in the First World War, but not surprisingly, this line of debate was significantly shaped in the 1930s by developments in Nazi Germany. Propaganda can include a wide range of media, especially government-owned media. By the end of the period studied here, however, the currently widespread view that the mainstream, privately owned mass media engages in propaganda (a term now understood pejoratively) had become prevalent.

* * *

The organization of this book is straightforward. Chapter 1 provides a brief, synthetic overview of the position of the press in British society in the late nineteenth and early twentieth centuries. Chapter 2 outlines the development of the educational ideal in the mid-Victorian period, paying particular attention to the debates on the "taxes on knowledge" that led to their repeal in the years between 1853 and 1861. Chapter 3 analyzes the educational ideal during the period between the 1880s and 1914, as the ideal adapted to the changing conditions of journalism and transformations in British culture more broadly. Chapter 4 focuses on the same period, examining the emergence and "triumph" of the representative ideal. Chapter 5 traces the debates on the role of the press into the period between 1914 and 1950, focusing particularly on the tensions between a long-standing resistance to state interference in the press and recognition that private monopoly might be replacing the state as the greatest threat to press freedom. A brief epilogue examines the first Royal Commission on the Press and makes a few tentative links to contemporary debates.

The mass media is contested territory—often bitterly contested. This book traces the contest in Great Britain between 1850 and 1950 over the way the press would be conceptualized and, correspondingly, the role it ought to play. As stated before, this contest was often not merely over the press but also over popular culture—the promising or frightening new mass reader. In one sense, this book is the story of the long decline of the educational ideal of the press—the hope that newspapers could teach readers and could integrate an ever greater number into a politics by public discussion. Yet the story told here is also about the continuing appeal of this ideal and its continuing vitality as a norm against which contemporary developments can be judged.

It is worth noting that my own reading of the evidence has been influenced by my reaching maturity, as a member of the "popular classes," in the United States during the last decades of the twentieth century. For my generation, the idea of speaking from the point of view of the universe has come to seem hopelessly naïve. "Opinion," as conveyed in the media, has become the public-relations product of well-funded think tanks. Worse still, the popular ideal of argument has become, in Christopher Lasch's words, "a clash of rival dogmas, a shouting match in which neither side gives any ground." I hope that in some modest way this book can help to rehabilitate what Lasch calls "the lost art of argument."[51]

Notes

1. This poster was widely displayed in the London Underground in the fall of 1995.
2. Jones, *Powers of the Press.*
3. For this reason, British historians wishing to generalize about the press in this period still most often turn to the pathbreaking works of Alan Lee, Lucy Brown, and Stephen Koss, all of which were published between 1976 and 1985. See Lee, *Origins of the Popular Press in England,* Brown, *Victorian News and Newspapers,* and Koss, *Rise and Fall of the Political Press in Britain.* Three more recent works that provide sophisticated, broader interpretations of the press in this period are Jones, *Powers of the Press,* Chalaby, *Invention of Journalism,* and Conboy, *Press and Popular Culture.*
4. Recent trends in British intellectual history are expertly summarized by Bevir, "Long Nineteenth Century in Intellectual History."
5. The most notable exception is Jones, *Powers of the Press.* See also O'Malley, "History of Self-Regulation," and Boyce, "Fourth Estate." See Siebert, Peterson, and Schramm, *Four Theories of the Press,* for an international perspective.
6. Curran, "Rethinking the Media as a Public Sphere," 27.
7. Negrine, *Politics and the Mass Media in Britain,* 20.
8. Curran and Seaton, *Power without Responsibility,* 5–108; Keane, *Media and Democracy.*
9. For arguments about the institutionalized conservative bias of the mass media, see Chomsky and Hermann, *Manufacturing Consent,* Chomsky, *Necessary Illusions,* Parenti, *Inventing Reality,* and Gans, *Democracy and the News.* For an important recent critique of this radical scholarship set in the British context, see Davis, *Public Relations Democracy.* Davis shows that corporate control of press content, via public relations, tends to occur in very specific circumstances and is more concentrated in financial news than in other parts of the press. In addition, he shows that public relations can often serve "outsiders" well. Despite these caveats, Davis's book qualifies rather than undermines radical scholarship. For the charge of "liberal bias" in the American context, see, for example, Maddoux, *Free Speech or Propaganda?* and Goldberg, *Bias.* As pertains to *political* liberalism, this charge is increasingly difficult for serious people to credit. Eric Alterman has recently shown that many of the most prominent conservatives no longer believe in the "liberal bias" thesis but admit to articulating it nonetheless in an attempt to "work" journalists. See Alterman, *What Liberal Media?* The charge remains more convincing when applied to *cultural* liberalism (which is itself attractive to much of the business and political elite). Indeed, C. John Sommerville claims that the bias of periodicity is inherently a "liberal media bias"; the demands of periodicity contribute to a "permanent revolution" in cultural matters, though not in the deeper structures of politics and economics. See Sommerville, *News Revolution in England,* 10, 160–70.

10. Parenti, *Inventing Reality*; Curran and Seaton, *Power without Responsibility*; McChesney, *Rich Media, Poor Democracy*; Gans, *Democracy and the News*; Franklin, *Newszak and News Media*; Barnett and Gaber, *Westminster Tales*; McNair, *Sociology of Journalism*.

11. Jamieson, *Packaging the Presidency*. For a British example, see Harris, *Good and Faithful Servant*.

12. See Lyons, *New Censors*.

13. See Todd Gitlin's perceptive comments on the "content critic" in Gitlin, *Media Unlimited*, 135–42. See also Braham, "How the Media Report Race," Zoonen, "Tyranny of Intimacy?" and Douglas, *Where the Girls Are*. See also Bruce, *Pray TV*, for an argument about how evangelical Christianity employs the mass media in the United States.

14. The two foundational works by McLuhan are *The Gutenberg Galaxy* and *Understanding Media*. For the history of medium theory before McLuhan, see Heyer, *Communication and History*.

15. Mitroff and Bennis, *Unreality Industry*; Postman, *Amusing Ourselves to Death*. See also Gitlin, "Bites and Blips." Benjamin Barber has argued that the "videology of McWorld" engineers consensus in a subrational manner around lifestyles of pleasure and consumption. See Barber, *Jihad vs. McWorld*. For a critique of this tendency to lament the "death of print," see Stephens, *Rise of the Image the Fall of the Word*.

16. Gitlin, *Media Unlimited*, 4.

17. Deibert, *Parchment, Printing, and Hypermedia*. Deibert's concept of hypermedia is borrowed from Jean Baudrillard. See also Hardt and Negri, *Empire*, 321–24. Borrowing from Guy Debord's idea of the "society of the spectacle," Hardt and Negri see the major media's "something approaching a monopoly over what appears to the general population" as an important component of Empire's postmodern constitution.

18. These analyses have to be read alongside studies that suggest limitations to the mass media's power to shape values and influence behavior. See Seaton, "Sociology of the Mass Media," and Corner, "'Influence.'"

19. For an introduction to this debate, see Epstein, *In Practice*, 15–56, and McWilliam, *Popular Politics in Nineteenth-Century England*, 53–70.

20. Hall, "Notes on Deconstructing 'the Popular.'" Hall argues that the terms "class" and "popular" are "deeply related but they are not absolutely interchangeable" (240). The "elites" in this study consist largely of the same types of people as D. L. LeMahieu's "cultivated élites" and the people that Richard Hoggart's working-class subjects would recognize as "them." See LeMahieu, *Culture for Democracy*, and Hoggart, *Uses of Literacy*, 72–101.

21. Hall, "Notes on Deconstructing 'the Popular,'" 233.

22. For a masterful assessment of the broader intellectual history of the working classes, see Rose, *Intellectual Life of the British Working Classes*.

23. For an excellent synthesis of these questions, see Clarke, "Pessimism versus Populism." See also Conboy, *Press and Popular Culture*, 5–22, and Beetham, *Magazine of Her Own?* 10–13.

24. Murdock, "Reconstructing the Ruined Tower."

25. Clarke, "Pessimism versus Populism," 40.

26. Brake, *Subjugated Knowledges*, xi–xiv.

27. Hampton, "Journalists and the 'Professional Ideal' in Britain."

28. See Calhoun, ed., *Habermas and the Public Sphere,* and Mah, "Phantasies of the Public Sphere" (see 153–54 n.3 for an extensive bibliography of statements on the use of Habermas by historians).

29. Matthew, "Rhetoric and Politics in Great Britain."

30. Collini, *Public Moralists,* 57.

31. Curran, "Press as an Agency of Social Control."

32. Lee, *Origins of the Popular Press in England.*

33. Both of these labels are my own inventions; no journalist in 1885 would have said, "I used to believe in the educational ideal, but lately I am more persuaded by the representative ideal." The words "education" and "represent" were used extensively, however, along with related words like "influence," "reflect," "elevate," and "mirror." The idea of one ideal giving way to another naturally involves a degree of oversimplification and depends upon an impressionistic rather than scientific examination of the evidence. Yet this impression reflects hundreds of sources, and I hope that the development of my argument displays more nuance than can be conveyed in the introduction.

34. I am borrowing Raymond Williams's concepts of "dominant, residual, and emergent" cultural practices. See Williams, *Marxism and Literature,* 121–41.

35. Waters, *British Socialists and the Politics of Popular Culture.*

36. Gladstone, *Speeches on the Great Questions of the Day,* 26–27.

37. See LeMahieu, *Culture for Democracy,* 26–32, for a comparison of the *Daily Mail, Daily Express,* and *The Times* in the early twentieth century.

38. Jones, *Outcast London.*

39. Even with some 40 percent of adult males excluded under the 1884 franchise, this restriction disproportionately excluded upper-class males, not workers. See Tanner, "Rise of Labour in England and Wales."

40. Clarke, *Lancashire and the New Liberalism;* Bernstein, *Liberalism and Liberal Politics in Edwardian England;* Green, *Crisis of Conservatism;* Cornford, "Transformation of Conservatism in the Late Nineteenth Century."

41. Perkin, *Rise of Professional Society,* 140.

42. See Cronin, "Class, Citizenship, and Party Allegiance."

43. Searle, *Quest for National Efficiency;* Perkin, *Rise of Professional Society,* 155–70; Yeo, *Contest for Social Science.* See also Goldman, *Science, Reform, and Politics in Victorian Britain.*

44. Kent, *Gender and Power in Britain;* Vickery, "Golden Age to Separate Spheres?"

45. Kent, *Gender and Power in Britain,* 229–55.

46. Schwarz, "Politics and Rhetoric in the Age of Mass Culture," 129–31. On the press and gender, see Boyd, *Manliness and the Boys' Story Paper in Britain,* Beetham, *Magazine of Her Own?* Brake, *Subjugated Knowledges,* Flint, *Woman Reader,* and Tusan, "Making of the Women's Political Press."

47. See Hall, "Rethinking Imperial Histories."

48. Mill, *On Liberty,* 9–10. For explicit treatments of the relationship between press and empire, see de Nie, *Eternal Paddy,* Kaul, *Reporting the Raj,* and Startt, *Journalists for Empire.*

49. This shift parallels the roughly contemporaneous fluctuations in French visions of imperialism between "assimilation" and "association." The British popular classes were,

in the minds of elite commentators, fit subjects for colonization; arguments thus centered on whether or not the former could join the political nation. See Betts, *Assimilation and Association in French Colonial Theory.*

50. LeMahieu, *Culture for Democracy,* 141–53, 179–89, 273–92.

51. Lasch, *Revolt of the Elites and the Betrayal of Democracy,* 161–75.

1. The Press in Britain, 1850–1950

Before tracing the changes in the ways that the British thought about the press, it might be helpful to provide, by way of context, a synthetic overview of the press's economic and social structure, its legal basis, and its role in politics and society. Broadly, the period that is the subject of this book represents the peak of the press's influence. Throughout this period the press's influence and expansion grew steadily, and by the interwar period it had become arguably the most important medium of political communication and cultural influence. This position was reflected in the growing scale of the debates about the newspaper's function and purpose. In addition, the press became steadily more commercialized and its ownership steadily more concentrated.

To the Great War

Throughout this period, the press was a central political and cultural artifact. It would be difficult to overstate the importance and ubiquity of the press in Victorian and Edwardian Britain. As Lucy Brown has written, "In the second half of the nineteenth century the newspaper became established as part of the normal furniture of life for all classes." Aled Jones has concurred, arguing that from competing with other media, such as platform, periodical, and sermon, the newspaper became the dominant medium by the end of the century.[1] This centrality, confirmed by historians, was well noted by contemporaries. *The Economist* claimed in 1852 that the press was part of the daily lives "'of all the people'" and was "'indispensable to civilisation.'" Even when abroad, at the scene of battles during the Crimean War, the Scottish Jamaican nurse Mary Seacole, "mixing medicines or making good things in the kitchen of the British Hotel," first learned of the details of many of the battles, "perhaps, from the newspapers which came from home."[2] J. Thackray Bunce, editor of the *Birmingham Daily Post,* observed in 1893: "The journals are in every house, in every hand, amongst all classes—from the castle to the cottage, from the club to the village reading-room; in the factories of towns, in the country tap-rooms, wherever, indeed, men come together for business or pleasure, there, in one or other of its varieties, you find the newspaper." In a similar vein, J. D. Symon claimed in 1914, "There is no escaping the creature. It is at the door before the householder, bathed and shaved, has descended to the breakfast room. During the morning meal, it interferes seriously, and amid protest, with the attention he ought to pay to the remarks of his wife."[3]

Nor were observers content merely to comment on the *presence* of the daily press. Such fervent newspaper reading, commentators perceived, altered readers' primary mental categories. For example, William Somerset Maugham's Philip Carey observed the power of the press in shaping the reader's language. He wondered "whether what [Mildred] said had any meaning for her: perhaps she knew no other way to express her genuine feelings than the stilted language of the *Family Herald.*"[4] During the course of the nineteenth century, references to newspapers' influence over readers' minds became a staple in novels. In Joseph Conrad's *The Secret Agent,* published in 1907, the press is by no means a central focus, yet it asserts itself frequently as a primary motivation of the main protagonists. In the aftermath of a terrorist bombing, Chief Inspector Heat's decision to arrest a none-too-certain suspect results, at least in part, from the possible reaction of the newspapers: "it seemed to him an excellent thing to have that man in hand to be thrown down to the public should it think fit to roar with any special indignation in this case. It was impossible to say yet whether it would roar or not. That in the last instance depended, of course, on the newspaper press." In making this statement, Heat claims no particular insight; in his opinion, newspapers' power to shape a public outcry is "of course" common knowledge. Unfortunately, however, his suspect had been made famous two years earlier "by some emotional journalists in want of special copy." Not that this would prevent Heat from making the arrest. Arresting the ex-convict was perfectly legal, "and the journalists who had written him up with emotional gush would be ready to write him down with emotional indignation."[5]

Joseph Conrad's imagination does not offer conclusive evidence of the link between crime fighting and a press-driven public frenzy in Edwardian Britain. In the present context, two points are significant. First, an important

(a)

By the late nineteenth century, newspapers were "part of the normal furniture of life." In figures (a) through (c), we see the prevailing image of a man keeping current in public affairs, while his wife distracts him with trivial banter. In (d), his wife has been replaced with his dog, and the newspaper joins tobacco as an important component of civilized relaxation. From (a) *Punch*, 1 May 1884; (b) *Punch*, 27 March 1880; (c) *Punch*, 9 June 1883; (d) *Illustrated London News*, 18 May 1907.

(b)

novelist found it plausible to imagine a police chief attributing to the press the ability to shape public opinion. Second, alongside evidence of the ubiquity of newspapers in British life, we see the press's high place in Britain's imaginative life: one could not read a novel such as *The Secret Agent* without encountering "the power of the press" as a stock character.

Even when not figuring as a motivating power, newspapers regularly appeared in novels as background props. It would be easy to collect dozens of examples; a few will suffice to illustrate this point. In Thackeray's *Pendennis* (1864), when Major Pendennis comes to the country to set straight his nephew, Arthur Pendennis, Thackeray presents leaving London as a great sacrifice: "He gave up London in May—his newspapers and his mornings." The sac-

(c)

rifice's enumeration continues for several lines; newspapers come first. Given his place in society, the major's sacrifice leaves him twice afflicted; not only will he miss reading his newspapers, he will miss seeing his name in the *Morning Post* on the day after each of the "great London entertainments." In an example set much lower in the social scale, the title character in Elizabeth Gaskell's *Mary Barton* (1848), in dreaming of her rescue from poverty by a fortuitous marriage, envisions living in a "grand house, where her father should have newspapers, and pamphlets, and pipes, and meat dinners, every day." Later in the same novel, following Jem's alleged murder of Harry Carson, Sally Leadbitter visits Mary in hopes of learning some gossip-worthy details about Jem's faithful lover. Interestingly, this young woman's pleasure in gossiping—in being the conveyor of news—is compared to the production of a newspaper: Gaskell notes that "such particulars [as Mary's dress, hair, and accessories] would make Sally into a Gazette Extraordinary the next morning at the workroom."[6]

Newspapers appear in Victorian novels as objects of great importance: as the daily staple that one misses most when leaving London; as the chief example of luxury in the mind of an impoverished Chartist-era working-class

Many a man considered his tobacco as good until he tried Gallaher's Two Flakes.

We are willing to rest our whole case on the smoking qualities of Two Flakes.

But remember you must ask for Gallaher's Two Flakes. There are many ordinary tobaccos called Two Flakes which are not at all like Gallaher's.

Packed in 1-oz., 2-oz. and 4-oz. decorated tins; also in 2-oz. and 4-oz. air-tight tins.

Made by Gallaher, Ltd., of Belfast.
We belong to no ring or combine.

(d)

woman; as a metaphor for knowingness and gossip. By the twentieth century, newspaper reading had become considerably more widespread. In E. M. Forster's *Howard's End,* published in 1910, the newspaper appears as a manifestation of respectability or decency in addition to serving as a source of information. Witness the exchange between Leonard Bast and Mr. Cunningham on a "question of the day":

"Very serious thing, this decline of the birth-rate in Manchester," repeated Mr. Cunningham, tapping the Sunday paper, in which the calamity in question had just been announced to him.

"Ah, yes," said Leonard, who was not going to let on that he had not bought a Sunday paper.[7]

By the 1930s, George Orwell (in a journalistic account) was able to name newspapers as one of the cheap luxuries that were available to the impoverished workers of Wigan and to say of an unemployed Scottish miner, "Like so many unemployed men he spent too much time reading newspapers, and if you did not head him off he would discourse for hours about such things as the Yellow Peril, trunk murders, astrology, and the conflict between religion and science."[8]

Newspapers attained a prominent place in British society between 1850 and 1950. The primary sources cited throughout this book constitute evidence of the importance of the press in the minds of British educated elites in this period. The circulation figures conveyed below reveal that the press had emerged as a leading industry by the twentieth century. Finally, the *Punch* cartoons and Gallaher's Tobacco advertisement illustrate the pervasiveness of the newspaper as a cultural icon by the late nineteenth century. Even when the press was not an illustration's primary focus, it appeared, in Brown's phrase, as "part of the normal furniture of life."

Commentators on the press argued about the extent of press influence and whether newspapers shaped or reflected public opinion. We are unlikely ever to reach a satisfactory conclusion about the nature of press influence in Victorian Britain; indeed, this issue is very much alive in our own contemporary debates on the media.[9] Given the pervasiveness of the press in Victorian society, however, it is not surprising that politicians regularly employed the press in an attempt to influence public opinion outside Westminster. For example, they often used newspapers to advocate positions that they were not ready to identify with in Parliament.[10] Government politicians had long held an advantage; in the eighteenth and early nineteenth century they had subsidized papers to receive favorable coverage. Yet less well-connected political actors could also find newspaper support. The Chartist leader Feargus O'Connor operated the *Northern Star* to promote Chartism as a national movement and cement its organization and unity. More broadly, Hannah Barker has argued that radical politics in the first half of the nineteenth century depended heavily on newspapers. Radicals employed newspapers to publicize their cause and crystallize support and even developed and disseminated their political ideology in and through their pages. By midcentury, direct government subsidies had largely disappeared, but less formal means of influence remained. Lord Palmerston cultivated relationships with several newspapers and individual journalists to improve his standing among the cabinet and eventually propel himself to the premiership. His methods included rescheduling meetings to accommodate reporters' deadlines and providing advance notice of the subjects he intended to discuss, methods that recent commentators have, in a different context, referred to as "below the line." By ensuring a favorable press, he was able to suggest his usefulness to his party through his popularity outside Parliament.[11]

These examples illustrate a phenomenon that became increasingly widespread in the second half of the nineteenth century, as politicians developed what Stephen Koss has called "labyrinthine" interconnections with the press. According to Koss, in the second half of the century, "it was deemed mandatory for any political movement to have its own organ, or preferably several that might boom its slogans in unison. It was equally a matter of self-respect, for, without adequate journalistic backing, a party neither seemed to take itself seriously nor could it expect to be taken seriously by its rivals." Lucy Brown goes so far as to argue that "party organizations were a main force in the expansion of the press."[12] In the second half of the nineteenth century newspapers were a pervasive and expanding presence, one that politicians took seriously.

* * *

The appearance of newspapers in fiction and the wide-ranging and ongoing discussion of the press that is the topic of this book should not surprise us, given the press's large and expanding body of readers. If newspaper reading had remained the province of a relatively small number, debates about the press would likely not have assumed such urgency. Such debates were as much about the democratization of British society as they were about newspapers per se.

The readership of the press changed and expanded during the nineteenth century, though not in the ways and to the extent often assumed. A consideration of the readership of the press in Victorian Britain must begin with the problem of literacy. Formerly, many historians (as well as late-Victorian observers) credited the Education Act of 1870 with a rather sudden creation of a literate mass public. David Vincent has shown, however, that improvements in literacy occurred gradually throughout the century. Moreover, when considered from the perspective of families rather than individuals, the picture is one of continuity rather than an abrupt social transformation. Literate and illiterate people lived together. For example, during the period between 1839 and 1854, when evidence gathered from marriage registers suggested a 52 percent literacy rate, this actually translated into roughly one marriage in three with two literate partners, while in nearly two families out of three at least one partner could sign his or her name.[13]

When including the witnesses to weddings, whom Vincent has taken to belong to the bride and groom's "immediate social group," the collective literacy rate rises from 52 percent to 85 percent. While this skill does not necessarily indicate an ability to read very widely, this evidence nevertheless lends support to Vincent's denial of the existence in the nineteenth century of "ghettoes of illiteracy, complete sections of the community cut off from those able to make use of the printed word." Nevertheless, literacy rates varied along class lines, with the middle classes having nearly succeeded by the end of the century in "expelling illiteracy from the basic social networks." By contrast, among the skilled working classes only a quarter of wedding ceremonies included *solely* literate participants, while among the unskilled working classes only one in thirteen did so.[14] That is, among the working classes literacy tended to be a collective rather than an individual possession.

This revised interpretation suggests that, at least at a collective level, most had access to the literacy required for enjoying newspapers, even in the nineteenth century. Accordingly, newspaper reading was often a communal rather than an individual activity. This communal readership could take the form of one person reading a newspaper aloud to a group of listeners, some of whom may have been illiterate. At the same time, reading the newspaper aloud may have helped to ease the transition from an oral popular political tradition to a literate working-class public.[15]

Yet even where reading is considered solely as a literate, individual activity, ownership of individual copies of newspapers often was communal, particularly before midcentury. This observation makes any attempt to relate early Victorian readership to circulation problematic. In large part, newspaper sharing resulted from their high prices, which derived both from the "taxes on knowledge" and from the existing technologies of production. In the 1830s and 1840s, for example, radical newspapers often had more than twenty readers per copy, compared to only two to three readers per copy of popular newspapers at the end of the twentieth century.[16] As James Curran notes, even if the more cautious estimate of ten readers per copy is taken for the early Victorian radical press, this still means that papers such as the *Northern Star* in the 1840s or *Reynolds's News* in the 1850s attained a total readership of over half a million at a time when the population in England and Wales over age fourteen was just over ten million. Alan Lee points to the reading of newspapers in clubs, pubs, coffee houses, institutes, public libraries, or the illegal practice of hiring out newspapers. He argues that before the repeal of the taxes on knowledge between 1853 and 1861, each copy of a newspaper was seen by probably half a dozen readers.[17] In his 1915 "autobiographical novel" *Of Human Bondage,* William Somerset Maugham invokes the following description of a daily routine in a vicarage of the 1880s: "soon after breakfast Mary Ann brought in *The Times.* Mr Carey shared it with two neighbours. He had it from ten till one, when the gardener took it over to Mr Ellis at the Limes, with whom it remained till seven; then it was taken to Miss Brooks at the Manor House, who, since she got it late, had the advantage of keeping it."[18]

Yet despite the inadequacy of circulation as a guide to readership, it is worth considering as a topic in its own right, particularly as its expansion sheds light on the commodification of the daily press. In 1860 London had nine morning and six evening dailies. As for the provincial press, there were sixteen provincial dailies, sixteen semiweeklies, and one paper published three times per week. By the 1880s and 1890s, 150 daily papers existed across England. Not only did a greater number of titles now exist, they also sold more copies than previously. In 1851 a total of eighty-five million newspapers were sold in England, compared to 5,604 million in 1920. In per-capita terms, Britons over age fourteen bought six copies in 1850 and 182 in 1920. Some of this magnitude can be seen in individual titles: the *Manchester Guardian* had a *weekly* circulation in 1835 of 4,412 and in 1848 of 9,404; by 1880 it reached a *daily* circulation of thirty thousand, by 1888 it reached thirty-eight thousand, and by 1897 it reached forty-three thousand. The expansion was more dramatic in the popular press. In 1836, the *Weekly Police Gazette* set records with a circulation above forty thousand, while both *Reynolds's News* and *Lloyds Weekly* became in 1856 the first papers to reach sales of a hundred thousand. In the 1880s the *Star* quickly attained a circulation of two hundred thousand. By 1900, the *Daily Mail* reached almost a million, and by 1911 the *Daily Mirror* became the first paper to reach a circulation of one million.[19] In light of these figures, it is difficult to resist the conclusion that even if the actual *readership* did not expand so dramatically, newspapers at least became increasingly a disposable consumer good that readers could consume in private, perhaps further severing their connection with oral traditions.

Of course, we must remember that newspapers took their place within a diverse group of media. Besides daily newspapers, there were monthly magazines and elite reviews as well as the working-class weeklies such as *Reynolds's* or *Lloyds.* As Stefan Collini has reminded us, many of what we regard as the most influential "books" of the mid-Victorian period first appeared as articles in periodicals: Mill's *Utilitarianism,* Bagehot's *English Constitution,* Arnold's *Culture and Anarchy,* Fitzjames Stephen's *Liberty, Equality, Fraternity,* and Maine's *Popular Government,* among others.[20] The same can be said for many of the period's novels.

This distinction can indicate the difference between the "weighty" and the "ephemeral"; the latter was characteristic of the news and opinion produced for the daily newspapers in a "speeded up" society.[21] Time and again, journalists emphasized that they wrote for the moment, not for posterity. Yet we should keep in mind the relationship between the two forms: daily newspapers could give immediate publicity to books and periodical articles that purported to deal with less ephemeral topics. At the same time, the "ephemeral" press frequently became the subject of extended discussion in books and reviews.

Moreover, as suggested above, these literate modes of cultural production also interacted with oral modes. This could occur in "escapist" literature. As David Vincent argues of the late eighteenth century, the "precious, dog-eared pages were read and reread, borrowed and reborrowed until imperceptibly they merged back into the communal oral tradition whence most had originally come." At the same, time, however, even in political reporting, the links between orality and the press were quite pronounced. For example, the early Victorian radical press often presented causes not in abstract, rationalist terms but in terms of personal identification with an individual, such as O'Connor or Cobbett.[22] Despite differences, even the later Victorian press continued to interact with an oral tradition, for example when questions about the press's role constituted the subject matter for discussions in debating societies.[23]

There can be little doubt, however, that after midcentury the press was becoming the dominant partner in its relationship with oral culture. James Vernon has argued that an increasing privileging of literacy over orality contributed to a closing down of access to the public sphere. This argument is compatible with H. C. G. Matthew's demonstration that, even where the tradition of mass meetings continued, the audience present at a meeting often took a back seat to the newspaper audience. For example, Gladstone might speak so softly as to be audible only to those seated in the first several rows; upon making a mistake, he would lean over to the reporters in the audience to tell them the "correct" version for the newspaper audience. In an even more obvious favoring of the literate publics, during his whistle-stop tours Gladstone occasionally ran so late as to have no time to deliver his address, yet by leaving it with the journalists, he could ensure that the newspaper audience was able to read the speech the following morning.[24]

Both quantitatively and qualitatively, the press in the nineteenth century enjoyed a predominant cultural position, especially in political culture. This observation forms a backdrop to the "long argument" about the press and helps to make intelligible the reason that the struggle for "liberty of the press" took such a prominent place in political culture throughout the century.

* * *

The liberalization of press law throughout the nineteenth century was highlighted by discrete moments of obvious victory for the advocates of press freedom or reform. These victories, reaching their climax in 1855 with the repeal of the stamp tax, convinced contemporaries that freedom of the press and consequently liberty in general were becoming increasingly secure.[25] Their interpretation subsequently dominated much of the historiography of the Victorian press.

Yet this Whiggish picture has come under increasing attack in the past three decades, and the fact of increasing press freedom can no longer be taken for granted. Scholars like Alan Lee and James Curran have demonstrated that the mid- to late Victorian press, freed from the constraints of the state, became subservient to a commercialized order dominated by large-scale media ownership and circulation wars fed by the advertising industry.[26] We will return to this theme after a brief overview of the changing laws of the press.

Those defending a Whiggish interpretation of press history typically begin with 1694 and the ending of press licensing, or prepublication censorship. In terms of the growth of the British press, it would be difficult to overestimate this moment. Bob Harris deliberately focuses his study of press history from 1620 through 1800 on the period after 1695, pointing out that "[t]he assumption that news did not circulate widely in Britain before 1695 has proved hard to undermine." This event paved the way for the early eighteenth-century flourishing of provincial as well as London newspapers.[27]

In the lore of press history, another significant moment occurred in 1764–65 with the abolition of general warrants. This celebrated case began with John Wilkes's publication on 23 April 1763 of issue forty-five of the *North Briton*. Wilkes and Charles Churchill began the paper in 1762 as an answer to Tobias Smollett's ministerialist *The Briton*. Rather than offering original proposals for government, the primary function of the *North Briton* was to "ridicule the new government's conduct of affairs." In issue forty-five, Wilkes's attack on the king's speech appeared to accuse the king of being a liar—despite Wilkes's disclaimers and assertions that the speech was the product of the minister, not the king. Lord Halifax, a secretary of state, responded by issuing a general warrant for the arrest of the author, printer, and publisher of the newspaper. After much controversy, general warrants were ruled illegal.[28] This episode is generally interpreted as an important moment in the liberalization of British political culture.

Yet, as Harris argues, a great deal of self-censorship continued to occur in the press in late eighteenth-century Britain. Although events such as the Wilkes episode underscored the ministries' increasing difficulties in controlling the press, it is important to remember that, given existing libel laws, printers and publishers were subject to the "inconvenience of searches of premises, seizure of papers, payment of bail or recognizances to appear before the King's bench."[29]

In this context, the next important liberalizing moment occurred in 1792 with Fox's Libel Act. Before the passage of this act, juries' roles in libel trials remained undefined. Most often they acted simply to establish the fact of publication, not to establish that a libel had indeed occurred, which was generally left to the judge's discretion. Despite the ending, a century earlier, of prepublication censorship, a powerful weapon of de facto censorship against the press remained in the hands of the state. That is, a publisher could not be legally prevented from publishing material unfavorable to the government but could be punished after the fact. Besides those actually punished in this manner, countless others must have exercised self-censorship to stave off such punishment. The 1792 act placed the decision of whether libel had occurred squarely in the hands of a jury. While this piece of legislation did not end harassment on libel charges, it significantly diminished the power of the state to regulate the press.

The question of libel was to remain important throughout the next century. In the early nineteenth century, the plight of radical publishers was made more difficult by the fact that "scurrilous libel," even as determined by a jury, was legally defined according to the perceived effects of publication: truthfulness was no defense against the charge of libel.[30] So long as a jury's decision remained guided by this rule, the government still enjoyed a potent weapon against its journalistic political opponents. This law was changed only in 1843, at which point truthfulness became a defense against the charge of libel.

At the same time that oppression by the state impeded the efforts at newspaper production, the laws also tightly regulated distribution. The first newspaper tax was imposed in 1712, at a nonprohibitive half-penny per newspaper. During the course of the century, the tax gradually increased; by 1797 it stood at three and a half pence and in 1815 at four pence. With this tax, a newspaper minimally cost the buyer six to seven pence per copy, beyond the reach of most Britons. Following the infamous Peterloo Massacre in 1819, one of the repressive Six Acts vastly extended the scope of this tax so that it was applied to every periodical appearing more frequently than every twenty-six days and selling for less than 6 pence that contained "any Public News, Intelligence or Occurrences, or any Remarks or Observations thereon, or upon any Matter in Church or State."[31] This definition ensured that the act would be aimed at the radical working-class press: *The Times,* selling for six pence, would be exempt, as would any monthly publication, which the government deemed as appearing too infrequently to maintain control over a coherent, radical movement. In addition to the newspaper tax, an advertisement tax had been raised to three shillings, six pence per advertisement by 1815, and a paper duty of three pence per pound was in place by 1803. The latter duty affected publication of books more than that of newspapers, but newspapers felt the burden of this duty as well, and it helped to account for the closely packed pages of early Victorian newspapers. Together, these three taxes priced the legitimate press beyond the reach of the less affluent members of society, a fact that helps to account for the prevalence of sharing newspapers, but also a fact that made the existence of the radical press more precarious.

These taxes on knowledge became a rallying point for middle- and working-class reformers. In the early 1830s, an illegal "unstamped" press emerged, avoiding the severe financial imposition of the taxes by simply refusing to pay them. For working-class radicals, this course of action served to protest the taxes and to seek "representation" in the absence of adequate representation in Parliament; this concern became more prominent following the perceived middle-class "betrayal" in the Great Reform of 1832, when the franchise was moderately extended and electoral districts somewhat rationalized. Opponents of abolition of the taxes on knowledge tacitly supported this interpretation through attacking it; like the radicals, they argued that the radical press would undermine the established state and social order, but they differed from their opponents in not seeing the desirability of this result. Middle-class proponents of the abolition of taxes argued, contrary to both conservatives and radicals, that the press was an educational agent that could actually promote working-class commitment to the existing order by teaching the working classes their true self interests; they argued that ignorance was the cause of revolution. Despite strident Tory opposition to reform, during the course of the 1830s the taxes were sharply reduced. In 1833, the advertising duty was reduced to one shilling, six pence per advertisement, a reduction of 57 percent; in 1836, the paper duty was halved to one and a half pence per pound. Most dramatically, in 1836 the newspaper duty was reduced from four pence to one penny per copy.[32]

Following the collapse of the Chartist movement after 1848, momentum built for a campaign to repeal the remaining taxes on knowledge. John Bright and Richard Cobden were among the most prominent leaders of this movement. The advertising duty vanished in 1853; the most onerous charge, the newspaper tax, was repealed in 1855; and the final tax, on paper, disappeared in 1861. At the heart of this campaign of the early 1850s was the "educational" ideal of the press, or what Alan Lee has called a "liberal theory." The People's Charter Union, consciously modeling their campaign on the example of the Anti-Corn Law League, argued in 1849 that while national education was delayed, at least the working classes should be allowed to educate themselves in order to become fit for the vote. Through a popular press, it argued, the working classes could learn the "natural laws" of political economy.[33]

The repeal of the taxes, especially the repeal in 1855 of the newspaper tax, entered into the mythology of press history as the birth of the (liberal, uncorrupt) popular press. For example, Fox Bourne regarded it as ensuring the general demise of the more sordid and "unwholesome journalism" as it was drowned in a sea of respectability. Nearly a century later, Lee asserted that 1855 created a "golden age" in newspaper history.[34] In one respect, he is surely right: after 1855, the provincial daily press expanded dramatically, both in circulation and in numbers of titles, and a large-scale penny press emerged. It was only later, in the 1880s and afterwards, that the tendency toward concentration of ownership became more pronounced.

As Curran has argued, however, the entire history of the repeal of the taxes on knowledge takes on an opposite meaning when looked at from the perspective of the radical press, which was unable to compete in the new commercial environment. Moreover, if one pays attention to the nineteenth-century history of newspaper financing and distribution, a Whiggish interpretation of the changing laws of the press becomes less plausible. In the early nineteenth century, leading ministerialist papers received subsidies from the government.[35] More importantly, during the early 1830s, despite all of the arrests and prosecutions, an unstamped press flourished, selling many more copies than the legitimate, stamped press. The drastic reduction in the 1830s of the taxes on knowledge was a Benthamite construction of a moral arithmetic. By sharply reducing the financial penalty of paying the taxes, those reformers who implemented the policy hoped to make avoiding the taxes less attractive, thus undermining the basis for an unstamped press.[36] This device succeeded, and the radical press receded dramatically in the decade after 1836.

Likewise, the abolition of the advertising duty created the possibility of a sound commercial basis for the press, freeing it from the necessity of state patronage. Far from having unambiguously liberating effects, however, this transformation entailed the press's dependence upon advertisers' interests, or at best a subservience to a "tyranny of the majority" filtered through advertisers. Advertisers' increase of power over the press resulted not simply from the abolition of taxes but also from changes in production techniques that vastly increased the cost of starting and maintaining a newspaper.[37] In Curran's words, the reforms around the middle of the nineteenth century "introduced a new system of press censorship more effective than anything that had gone before. Market forces succeeded where legal repression had failed in conscripting the press to the social order."[38]

A final reform contributed to the creation of the twentieth-century press: the further changes in the Libel Law in 1881 and 1887. Without detailing the entire history of libel in the nineteenth century,[39] we can note that these reforms sought to relieve newspapers and their proprietors from undue restrictions on their ability to report public speeches in the public interest. Proprietors found themselves liable for damages simply for reporting the libelous words contained in public speeches, even though the newspapers made no claims for the accuracy of the speeches' contents. This constraint on newspapers' freedoms was exacerbated by the emergence of a category of lawyers who purportedly made their living by encouraging "injured" parties to sue.

The act of 1881 sought to redress this constraint on press freedom and provided a privilege to newspapers to report public meetings "lawfully convened for a lawful purpose, and if such a report was fair and accurate, and published without malice, and if the publication of the matter complained of was for the public benefit."[40] This provision, however, left courts the task of deciding whether copy was libelous as well as whether the venue in which a speech had been made constituted a "public meeting." The 1888 act sought to rectify these lingering difficulties by freeing proprietors from the possibility of criminal prosecution, except by order of a judge in chambers, and by providing for a consolidation of libel, so that a plaintiff could not initiate separate actions against more than one newspaper for the same libel.[41] It is easy to see why these acts have been cited in support of a Whiggish interpretation of press history, as they enacted the liberal wisdom that the press's freedom to report public events was more important than the possibility of occasional injury to individuals.[42] Yet it is important to remember that this interpretation leaves unanswered the question of whether the newly freed press effectively spoke from the perspective or in the interests of either "the people" or the journalists who provided the copy.

* * *

As Curran has argued, legal freedom did not automatically translate into genuine freedom of the press; indeed, it could facilitate the emergence of censorship by the market by raising the costs of operating a press and raising the importance of advertising. Most radical unstamped papers in the 1830s were printed on hand presses, which cost as little as ten pounds to acquire. After 1836, the most important stamped radical papers were printed on steam presses, but costs remained relatively low. The *Northern Star*, for example, cost £690 in initial capital, most of which was raised by public subscription. With the low maintenance costs of the period, even after 1836, when radical papers began paying the one penny tax, a relatively low circulation could ensure success. At a selling price of three and a half pence, the *London Dispatch* could break even with a circulation of sixteen thousand. With a selling price of four and a half pence, the *Northern Star* could break even with a weekly circulation of sixty-two hundred. These papers and others could subsist on the income generated from sales alone.[43]

Beginning in the late 1830s and fed by the abolition of the taxes on knowledge between 1853 and 1861, the creation of a cheap press led to greatly increased consumer demand for newspapers. Curran credits this increased demand with stimulating the drive to develop more sophisticated production technologies.[44] Attempting to capture ever larger shares of the newspaper market, papers had to devote greater and greater resources to the collection of news and to printing technology that would service larger circulations. The use of web rotaries became possible after the repeal of paper duties, and they allowed fewer laborers to produce significantly more issues of a newspaper. The *Glasgow Herald* reduced its machine operatives from twenty-three to four unskilled workers. In 1870, *The Times* supposedly could produce the same output with seven men working two of the Walter presses developed two years earlier as forty-eight men had formerly produced on hand-fed hoe machines. The introduction of Linotype machines, beginning in 1889, did away with the need to redistribute type, thus cutting down further on labor costs.[45]

Yet these new machines were expensive and thus stimulated the increasing scale of the newspaper industry. In 1858 the *Manchester Guardian* spent ten thousand pounds on new machines, representing a year's profits. In some cases, the need to purchase new machines led to a decision to sell the newspaper, at which point a larger consortium of businessmen might step in. Such costs and others were paid for by advertising revenue. Between 1854 and 1858, *Reynolds's News* increased its advertising volume by more than 50 percent. In the second half of 1867, *The Times* brought in £94,463 from sales and £104,766 from advertising. In 1888 the *Manchester Guardian* made £35,866 from sales and £54,208 from advertisements. Such figures support Curran's claim that advertisers "thus acquired a de facto licensing authority since, without their support, newspapers ceased to be economically viable."[46]

The changing relative importance of sales and advertisements derived in large part from the decreasing cover prices per issue that accompanied—and fed—the circulation wars of the later nineteenth century. Broadly speaking, 1855 introduced the daily penny press, especially in the provinces. This included new titles and others, like the *Manchester Guardian,* that had existed since 1821 but became a daily in 1855 (with its price reduced from two pence to one penny in 1858). At the same time, a half-penny evening press began to flourish in the provinces. Eventually, following the success in the 1890s of the *Daily Mail* as a half-penny morning paper, other morning dailies dropped their price to compete.[47] These prices fed the vastly increased circulations, but they also meant that even a huge circulation could not bring in enough revenue to ensure profits. Rather, the function of large circulations was to attract support from advertisers.

Circulation alone, however, was not enough to ensure advertising revenues, particularly with the rising importance of large companies alongside individual advertisers. The socialist *Evening Echo,* after its launch in 1901, increased its circulation by 60 percent between 1902 and 1904, only to close in 1905 because its "growth of advertising had failed to keep pace with the growth of circulation." As early as 1857, the radical *People's Paper* had to close down with a circulation much larger than weeklies like *The Spectator* and *John Bull.* By contrast, *Reynolds's News* attracted advertising revenue only by sharply muting its original radicalism.[48]

A few more technological and economic developments deserve mention. The price of paper fell throughout the nineteenth century, making possible the vast expansion of circulation. The increased attention to news gathering, which helped to attract larger circulations, was itself facilitated by advances in telegraphy. A Dover-Calais cable was successfully laid in 1858, though it was not very functional before 1865; the trans-Atlantic cable was first laid successfully in 1866. An act in 1870 transferred the telegraph companies to the Post Office, fixing the price for charges. Taking advantage of these facilities proved costly for the largest newspapers such as *The Times,* which spent around forty thousand pounds per year on foreign news services in the 1870s; the *Manchester Guardian* spent a more modest two thousand pounds in 1888. For smaller provincial papers, the emergence of Reuters in 1851 and the Press Association in 1868 brought a cheap news service.[49]

* * *

Beginning in the 1880s, contemporaries began to observe changes in the structure and content of the press, changes that they sought to capture in the phrase "New Journalism." Among the features ascribed to the New Journalism were a lightness of tone, an emphasis on the personal and the "sensational," and reliance on gimmicks to sell newspapers in high-stakes circulation wars. These gimmicks included contests and publicity stunts as well as the more typical reliance on large headlines. A focus on the assertion of opinion gave way to the presentation of decontextualized news.[50] These traits all seemed to underscore the idea that the press was becoming more of a commodity than it had been in the mid-Victorian years, although newspapers had even then been seen as businesses. Historians as well as contemporaries have linked these changes with the increasing concentration of press ownership and, in some cases, with the 1870 Education Act.[51] Matthew Arnold coined the term "new journalism" in 1887, yet for many observers and subsequent historians the decisive event was Alfred Harmsworth's creation of the half-penny *Daily Mail* in 1896.[52]

Other scholars have asserted a more gradual transformation. Raymond Williams pointed out that if anything, what was "new" about the New Journalism was that qualities that had been featured in the midcentury popular Sunday papers and in other cheap literature now made their way into the new half-penny daily papers.[53] Joel H. Wiener similarly concludes that "the New Journalism had a more secure pedigree than [Matthew] Arnold and many of his contemporaries and subsequent writers were prepared to concede." He cites the earlier development of women's articles, gossip columns, sports coverage, and illustrations in the mid-Victorian popular press.[54]

Not only did the transformations attributed to the New Journalism seem to have developed more gradually than contemporaries recognized, but we should resist seeing these or any other developments in press history as unambiguously linear. One of the important changes often linked to the New Journalism was the shift in emphasis from "views" to "news." In the words of Anthony Smith, describing the early nineteenth-century *Times*, "The readers bought the paper for its opinions and the editorial writers were the lynchpins of the news organisation. The reporters and correspondents who supplied the news had the function of keeping the editor as well-informed as possible in order that his editorial line would be unassailable in later debate. . . . There was still, however, no firm doctrine of hard news, 'faits secs,' as the French call it, on which to build the profession of journalism."[55] Observers in the late nineteenth century would use similar language to describe the penny press that emerged after 1855. Yet such a description does not work for the popular Sunday papers even in the mid-nineteenth-century "golden age." In the eighteenth century, moreover, quite unsober practices often prevailed, practices that strongly resemble those of the New Journalism. According to Hannah Barker, the following quotation from a 1728 pamphlet describes "what was to prove one of the most long-standing practices" of eighteenth-century journalism: "Persons are employed (One or Two for each Paper) at so much a Week, to haunt Coffee-Houses, and thrust themselves into Companies where they are not known; or plant themselves at a convenient Distance, to overhear what is said, in order to pick up Matter for the Papers." In addition, some London news gatherers were accused of soliciting information from servants, making "matters sacred to Privacy and the fireside . . . the talk of the World." These quotations could just as easily describe the notorious "keyhole journalism" of a century and a half later—or even the behavior of the infamous paparazzi that fatally hounded Princess Diana in 1997. Moreover, even though eighteenth- and early nineteenth-century newspapers attracted political subsidies and were not yet mass-circulation organs, they were thoroughly commercial enterprises and thus tailored their copy to popular tastes.[56] That is to say, to the extent that mid-Victorian editors were able bravely to articulate their views, as the nostalgia would have it, this ability was the product of a fleeting commercial environment. In the mid-nineteenth century it was relatively profitable to take a strong political line, supported by lengthy leading articles, a condition that did not always hold in earlier and later periods.

Finally, as the quotations above illustrate, the mid-Victorian emphasis on "views" rather than "news" did not extend backwards into the eighteenth century. In part, this reflects the previously mentioned gradual ascendancy of newspapers over other media during the course of the nineteenth century. This ascendancy did not belong to the eighteenth century, and readers of that period looked to other media, such as pamphlets, for commentary. Newspapers of that earlier period attracted readers by providing news, including local news. Only with the growing importance of newspapers at the end of the eighteenth century did they begin to offer their own extended commentary.[57] The late-Victorian shift in emphasis from "views" to "news" was thus not a brand-new development but in some ways a return to older emphases.

Despite these continuities and antecedents, which should caution us against seeing the developments in the 1880s and after as cause for alarm, the New Journalism was real in the minds of its champions and opponents. While revisionist scholarship can point out how wrong contemporaries were in many of their assumptions and observations, this is not necessarily the most interesting approach. In trying to recover the ways in which contemporaries conceptualized their world, it is at least as important to pay close attention to their own claims and counterclaims.

Beyond the need to recognize perception, moreover, we must be wary of the danger in emphasizing continuity to the extent that we lose sight of the very real changes that did occur. Some slopes really are slippery, and the contemporaries who bemoaned Stead's crusading spirit or Harmsworth's commercialism may have been prescient rather than paranoid. Even if we take a gradualist rather than a cataclysmic view, it is clear that the newspaper of 1850 and that of 1950 differed in significant ways, not least in discursive style. Donald Matheson argues compellingly that between 1880 and 1930 a distinctly news discourse emerged, independent of external social conventions, in place of a Victorian style of collecting separate items, such as letters and speeches, and relying upon readers to interpret them. In his view, this transformation occurred gradually in the British press as a whole, but only because it took a generation for the "traditionalist *Times*" to adopt the discursive practices pioneered by the "American-style London halfpenny evening papers" in the early 1880s.[58] Undeniable transformations—real and imagined, sudden and gradual—formed the backdrop for a debate that became increasingly fierce as our period unfolded.

The Twentieth Century

In the twentieth century, the press continued to develop along the lines of the New Journalism. Newspaper ownership continued to become more concentrated, newspapers' tones became increasingly lighter, and papers were treated increasingly as commodities sold to readers (who would in turn be sold to advertisers). This development heightened the debates about the tensions between the commercial and public-service functions of the press. It is not my purpose to provide a comprehensive treatment of these developments; that story has been well told by other scholars.[59] The following pages will simply outline the structure of the newspaper industry in the first half of the twentieth century, particularly during the interwar years.

According to Graham Murdock and Peter Golding, the most salient characteristics of the years between 1914 and 1950 were "the rise of a mass-circulation daily press based on London, involving a vast increase in readership but a considerable reduction in the number of titles." Circulation expanded dramatically. The sales of national dailies grew from 3.1 million in 1918 to 4.7 million in 1926 and to 10.6 million in 1939. John Stevenson writes, "By the 1930s the newspapers were easily the most important form of mass communication in Britain.... [T]he era between 1920 and 1947 was a halcyon time for the press."[60]

This expansion resulted in part from newspapers' continuing to broaden their scope far beyond the purely political. Commentators observed this transformation in the last decades of the nineteenth century, but it truly accelerated in the twentieth century. Many scholars credit Lord Northcliffe for this transformation, which entailed a "general depoliticisation of contents, as newspapers covered 'life as a whole.'" According to Jean Chalaby, Northcliffe's *Daily Mail* contained deliberately less politics than any other daily paper at the turn of the century. Northcliffe believed that newspapers should captivate readers, amusing and entertaining rather than merely informing them. Most importantly, Northcliffe's success forced other newspapers to undergo similar changes—even newspapers whose proprietors had founded them for largely noncommercial reasons, such as George Cadbury's *Daily News*.[61]

With Northcliffe leading the way, newspapers became more diverse in their content, including many "human interest" items along with the now-abbreviated political news and opinion. Dorothy Sayers's 1933 portrayal of a fictitious London journalist, Hector Puncheon, illustrates the extent to which journalism had come to cover "life as a whole":

> He ate with leisurely zest, pleased with himself and his good fortune, and persuaded that not even the most distinguished of the senior men could have turned in a column more full of snap, pep and human interest than his own. The interview with the cat had been particularly full of appeal. The animal was, it seemed, an illustrious rat-catcher, with many famous deeds to her credit. Not only that, but she had been the first to notice the smell of fire and had, by her anguished and intelligent mewings, attracted the attention of night-watchman number one, who had been in the act of brewing himself a cup of tea when the outbreak took place. Thirdly, the cat, an ugly black-and-white creature with a spotted face, was about to become a mother for the tenth time, and Hector Puncheon by a brilliant inspiration had secured the reversion of the expected family for the *Morning Star*, so that half a dozen or so fortunate readers might, by applying to their favourite paper and enclosing a small donation for the Animals' Hospital, become the happy owners of kittens with a prenatal reputation and magnificent rat-catching pedigree. Hector Puncheon felt that he had done well.[62]

Nothing could be further from the mid-Victorian ideal, and often reality, of newspapers as organs of opinion. Journalists learned from experience that such subject matter attracted readers who simply were not interested in the minute workings of Parliament. Sayers's description might, of course, be taken as satire rather than realism. It does, however, complement Chalaby's description of the 13 October 1908 edition of Northcliffe's *Daily Mirror*. According to Chalaby, two representative pages of that issue contain thirty-three different news items, including the divorce of the Earl of Yarmouth, the story of a woman killed to save her dog from a motorcar, and the death of Ireland's "allegedly oldest inhabitant."[63] Writing in 1940, Robert Graves and Alan Hodge described the typical contents of the *Daily Mail* in the years immediately after the First World War: "It also followed attentively the progress of new inventions, such as aircraft, motorboats and wireless. Spiritualism, the question of what moral attitude to adopt toward bottle-parties, night-clubs, revues and chorus girls, and all problems involving women: those were its leading features."[64]

Such a broadening of newspaper content certainly helped to attract readers. Simply put, newspapers became more interesting to more people during this time. Newspaper content was not, however, the only factor in the expanding circulations. During the first part of the twentieth century, especially during the interwar period, advertising revenue increased its influence over newspaper fortunes. In this commercial environment, attracting advertisers became the key to success, and circulation was one key to attracting advertisers.[65] Readers thus became, in many cases, a means to an end, and, particularly during the "circulation wars" of the 1930s, newspapers expanded their use of stunts and gimmicks to attract not readers so much as purchasers. The *Daily Mail* and *Daily Express* had offered insurance to subscribers throughout the 1920s, spending a million pounds per year by 1928. By the early 1930s, even the relatively sober *Daily Herald* had entered the fray. The three papers employed door-to-door canvassers to entice subscribers with gifts; these canvassers accounted for 40 percent of all press employees by 1934. Gifts included "flannel trousers for husbands, mangles for wives, cameras, kettles, handbags, and tea-sets."[66] Such schemes neatly bypassed the difficult question of whether a paper's news values were compatible with commercial demands; rather, they treated newspapers as commodities to sell by any means possible.

In addition to expanding the definition of "news" and employing various gimmicks to close the sale, newspapers increasingly employed stunts to stimulate sales. A stunt might be usefully defined as an artificial, even contrived, news item manufactured to publicize and thus sell a particular newspaper. Like many aspects of the twentieth-century press, the stunt had Victorian antecedents, but the twentieth century witnessed an explosion in the use of this method. Chalaby credits Northcliffe with pioneering the stunt. He describes "social crusades" and "jingo crusades," both of which had nineteenth-century antecedents, most notably, perhaps, Stead's "Maiden Tribute of Modern Babylon." According to Chalaby, Northcliffe's stunts "were the most entertaining type and included calls for action on issues of minor importance." Some included a "social dimension," but others were pure stunts, including calls for a new hat shape, the "*Daily Mail* Hat." In 1920, the *Daily Mail* offered a thousand pounds in prizes for "whoever could make the best sand-design advertising the *Daily Mail,* on the seashore."[67] Newspaper managers had to ensure that such contests required a sufficient amount of skill to circumvent the gambling laws. Throughout the late 1920s and 1930s, the Home Office often analyzed these contests, looking to punish newspapers whose prizes rewarded pure chance. According to a Home Office memorandum from 1928, in avoiding the technical definition of gambling, newspapers "displayed ingenuity worthy of members of the legal profession, and no doubt with their aid."[68]

As indicated above, the increased circulation did not benefit all newspapers equally, and the number of titles decreased during this period. The decline was greatest in the provincial press, with morning titles decreasing from forty-one to twenty-eight between 1921 and 1937 and evening papers decreasing from eighty-nine to seventy-nine during these same years. In addition, newspaper conglomerates acquired multiple titles, so that by 1948 the top three press groups owned 43 percent of all circulation.[69] Lord Northcliffe exemplified this concentration as well as anyone, at one point owning the leading mass-market, midmarket, and up-market dailies, the *Mirror, Mail,* and *Times,* respectively.

Such concentrated ownership of the most important medium of mass communication gave the interwar Press Barons an unprecedented power.[70] Newspapers had long been able to make governments uncomfortable, and W. T. Stead had claimed credit for the passing of the Criminal Law Amendment Act in the 1880s. By the interwar era, however, the power of the newspaper owners had increased dramatically. During the First World War, Northcliffe had been widely credited with bringing down the Asquith government in favor of Lloyd George. According to Curran, during the interwar years the "enormous expansion of advertising weaned the national press from dependence on the political parties." This independence emboldened Press Barons such as Northcliffe, Rothermere, and Beaverbrook to attack the government with impunity. Contemporary critics were alarmed at this power, even though press theory had long demanded an "independent" press. As George Boyce argues, "the paradox of the Fourth Estate was that the only truly independent newspaperman of the day—Lord Northcliffe—was also regarded as the man most likely to damage the reputation of the British press."[71]

By the time the National Union of Journalists (NUJ) requested a Royal Commission on the Press in 1947, many journalists, critics, and Labour politicians regarded the tendency toward monopoly as the greatest threat to press freedom. It should be noted, however, that both world wars prompted significant state interference with the press. Because of the well-developed tradition of noninterference, combined with pressure from the NUJ, the governments during World War I preferred to rely on self-censorship where feasible. The governments censored some information, such as troop movements or casualty figures, that could have a deleterious effect on public morale; such information was protected by the 1911 Official Secrets Act. During World War II, the government exerted even greater control, most notoriously by closing the Communist paper, the *Daily Worker,* whose offense was not betraying official secrets but merely taking too critical a stance toward the government. This anticommunist censorship resumed during the Korean War in 1950, under the Attlee Labour government.[72] Self-censorship was common as well. Kingsley Martin, for example, made H. G. Wells omit from a 1939 *New Statesman* article a passage that might have offended Mussolini; Martin cited the difficulty of current diplomacy and the inevitability of the government's seizing the paper if the offending passage stood.[73]

In addition to such overt intervention in press content, the state also restricted paper supplies during both wars and for several years following World War II. Particularly during World War II and its aftermath, newspapers were forced to cut their size, reduce their subscription list, or both in order to accommodate the paper shortages. Depending on the context, this measure reflected either wartime scarcity or a desire to improve the nation's balance of trade and should be seen as a part of general austerity programs. Journalists were quick to argue for the distinctive role of the press in a functioning democracy and to point out that restrictions on paper supplies could amount to a de facto suppression of the press.[74] Censorship and paper restrictions reminded journalists and all those interested in the press that commercialization did not constitute the only threat to press freedom.

In sum, the first half of the twentieth century saw an increased commodification and concentration of the British press. By 1950, the press had moved beyond being part of the "normal furniture of life" and had become easily the most important medium of mass communication. This importance, combined with concentration of ownership, gave unprecedented power to a small handful of Press Barons.

* * *

During the course of the nineteenth century, the press underwent important transformations. From being a small, infrequently or even irregularly published collection of opinions, newspapers emerged as daily conveyors of a wide range of domestic and foreign news. From being shackled by laws and the authority of the state, the press developed into an enterprise almost entirely governed by market forces and mediated by advertisers. From one form of communication among many, the daily paper became the dominant form within print culture.[75] These transformations accelerated in the first half of the twentieth century. This chapter has sounded a cautionary note against seeing any of these developments in exclusively Whiggish terms. Despite continuities and antecedents, however, the press was transformed in obvious and visible ways, and these transformations formed the backdrop to the evolving debates on the press.

What were the meanings of these transformations? Did they entail the democratization of knowledge or the debasement of a serious mode of communication? Did they bring greater freedom of thought and expression or a stultifying commercial or mass society? Who would gain control over the production of language and meaning within the press, and on what basis? Such questions engaged nervous observers in an increasingly lively debate.

Notes

1. Brown, *Victorian News and Newspapers*, 273; Jones, *Powers of the Press*, xi.
2. Quoted in Brown, "Compelling but Not Controlling?" 44; Seacole, *Wonderful Adventures of Mrs. Seacole in Many Lands*, 147.
3. Bunce, "Church and Press," 388; Symon, *Press and Its Story*, 1.
4. Maugham, *Of Human Bondage*, 472.
5. Conrad, *Secret Agent*, 95, 101.
6. Thackeray, *Pendennis*, 107; Gaskell, *Mary Barton*, 80, 274–75.
7. Forster, *Howard's End*, 49.
8. Orwell, *Road to Wigan Pier*, 8–9, 89.
9. See Seaton, "Sociology of the Mass Media," and Corner, "'Influence.'"
10. Koss, *Rise and Fall of the Political Press in Britain*, vol. 1, 9.
11. Epstein, "Feargus O'Connor and the *Northern Star*"; Barker, *Newspapers, Politics, and English Society*, 223; Brown, "Compelling but Not Controlling?" Barnett and Gaber describe the "below the line" methods of Tony Blair's propaganda machine in *Westminster Tales*, 106–13.
12. Koss, *Rise and Fall of the Political Press in Britain*, vol. 1, 9; Brown, *Victorian News and Newspapers*, 54.
13. Vincent, *Literacy and Popular Culture*, 22.
14. Ibid., 23.
15. See, ibid., 243, Lee, *Origins of the Popular Press in England*, 35, and Conboy, *Press and Popular Culture*, 24–25.
16. Curran, "Press History," 14. Curran's statistics for the nineteenth century are derived from Hollis, *Pauper Press*, and Epstein, "Feargus O'Connor and the *Northern Star*."
17. Curran, "Press History," 16; Lee, *Origins of the Popular Press in England*, 35–36.
18. Maugham, *Of Human Bondage*, 23. Maugham calls this an "autobiographical novel" in his preface (7).

19. Brown, *Victorian News*, 4, 52–53; Read, *Press and People*, 211–12; Curran, "Press History," 13; Wiener, "How New Was the New Journalism?" 56.

20. Collini, *Public Moralists*, 51.

21. Jones, *Powers of the Press*, 4–5.

22. Vincent, *Literacy and Popular Culture*, 198, 244.

23. See Jones, *Powers of the Press*, 180–203.

24. Vernon, *Politics and the People*, 105–60; Matthew, "Rhetoric and Politics in Great Britain."

25. See, for example, Aberdeen Journal, *Our 150th Year*, 10.

26. Lee, *Origins of the Popular Press in England*, 76–93; Curran, "Press History," 28–41.

27. Harris, *Politics and the Rise of the Press*, 6. See also Cranfield, *Development of the Provincial Newspaper*, and Harris, *London Press in the Age of Walpole*.

28. Harris, *Politics and the Rise of the Press*, 36.

29. Ibid.

30. Gilmartin, *Print Politics*, 145–47.

31. This paragraph is drawn from Wiener, *War of the Unstamped*, 2–5.

32. The classic renderings of this campaign are Wiener, *War of the Unstamped*, and Hollis, *Pauper Press*.

33. See Lee, *Origins of the Popular Press in England*, 42–49.

34. Bourne, *English Newspapers*, vol. 2, 370; Lee, *Origins of the Popular Press in England*, 210–12. Lee generally imputes the ideal of a "golden age" to late-Victorian and Edwardian critics of the New Journalism, but his tone throughout suggests that he shares their view.

35. Aspinall, "Social Status of Journalists at the Beginning of the Nineteenth Century."

36. Curran, "Press History," 22–27.

37. Ibid., 28–41.

38. Ibid., 9.

39. A useful overview is provided in Lee, *Origins of the Popular Press in England*, 95–101.

40. Quoted in ibid., 99.

41. For the text of the 1881 and 1888 acts, see Fisher and Strahan, *Law of the Press*, 263–71. Other contemporary commentaries on the acts include Kelly, *Law of Newspaper Libel*, and Elliott, *Newspaper Libel and Registration Act 1881*.

42. Lee, *Origins of the Popular Press in England*, 98.

43. Curran, "Press History," 14–16.

44. Ibid., 31.

45. Brown, *Victorian News and Newspapers*, 8–9, 11; Lee, *Origins of the Popular Press in England*, 58.

46. Brown, *Victorian News and Newspapers*, 9–11, 16; Curran, "Press History," 34.

47. Lee, *Origins of the Popular Press in England*, 274 (table 1); Brown, *Victorian News and Newspapers*, 32–33.

48. Curran, "Press History, 35–37.

49. Brown, *Victorian News and Newspapers*, 4, 11–15. Reuters and the Press Association focused on foreign and domestic news, respectively.

50. Curran, "Press History," 18, 34.
51. Lee, *Origins of the Popular Press in England,* 73–130; Ensor, *England 1870–1914,* 310–16.
52. Thus the dating to 1896 of two recent books on the modern popular press. See Engel, *Tickle the Public,* and Catterall, Seymour-Ure, and Smith, eds., *Northcliffe's Legacy.*
53. Williams, *Long Revolution,* 218–19; Williams, "Press and Popular Culture." More evidence for this point is available in Berridge, "Popular Sunday Papers and Mid-Victorian Society."
54. Wiener, "How New Was the New Journalism?" 47–71, esp. 65.
55. Smith, *Politics of Information,* 149.
56. Barker, *Newspapers, Politics, and English Society,* 103–4.
57. Ibid., 126–27.
58. Matheson, "Birth of News Discourse."
59. See Engel, *Tickle the Public,* Catterall, Seymour-Ure, and Smith, eds., *Northcliffe's Legacy,* Murdock and Golding, "Structure, Ownership, and Control of the Press," and Richards, *Bloody Circus.*
60. Murdock and Golding, "Structure, Ownership and Control of the Press," 130; Stevenson, *British Society 1914–45,* 402, 405.
61. Seymour-Ure, "Northcliffe's Legacy," 17; Chalaby, "Northcliffe," 30, 32, 33.
62. Sayers, *Murder Must Advertise,* 197.
63. Chalaby, "Northcliffe," 32.
64. Graves and Hodge, *Long Week-End,* 59.
65. Not, however, the only key, for advertisers paid attention to audience demographics.
66. Murdock and Golding, "Structure, Ownership, and Control of the Press," 131; Graves and Hodge, *Long Week-End,* 291.
67. Chalaby, "Northcliffe," 36; Graves and Hodge, *Long Week-End,* 60.
68. "Memorandum on Newspaper Competitions," p. 4., Home Office 45/20015 (437083/96), Public Records Office, London.
69. Murdock and Golding, "Structure, Ownership, and Control of the Press," 132, 135.
70. On this theme, see Chalaby, "No Ordinary Press Owners." I am using the term "Press Baron" less precisely than Chalaby; he would, for example, exclude Rothermere on grounds that he did not possess exceptional journalistic skills.
71. McEwen, "Press and the Fall of Asquith"; Curran, "Press History," 50; Boyce, "Fourth Estate," 31.
72. On World War I, see Hiley, "Making War," Sanders and Taylor, *British Propaganda during the First World War,* Messinger, *British Propaganda and the State in the First World War,* Hopkin, "Domestic Censorship in the First World War," and Lovelace, "British Press Censorship during the First World War." On World War II, see Curran, "Press History," 59–70, and Williams, *Press, Parliament, and People,* 3–84. For the Official Secrets Act, see Vincent, *Culture of Secrecy,* 121–28. For the Korean War, see Jenks, "Enemy Within." For an example of the NUJ opposing censorship during World War I, see the minutes of the Emergency Committee from 20 May 1915, Mss. 86/1/NEC/5, National Union of Journalists' Archive, Modern Records Office, University of Warwick (hereafter NUJ Archive). For examples from World War II, see the minutes of the National Executive Committee meet-

ing of 1 March 1941, Mss. 86/1/NEC/15, and the minutes of the Administrative Committee meeting of 25 July 1942, Mss. 86/1/NEC/17, NUJ Archive. It also bears mentioning that the British media has often been censored in accordance with prevailing understandings of morality. See, for example, Savage, "Erotic Stories and Public Decency."

73. Martin to Wells, 13 October 1939, H. G. Wells Papers N-95, University of Illinois at Urbana-Champaign.

74. See, for example, "Deputation from Newspaper Proprietors," 9 January 1917, Treasury 172/485, Public Records Office, London; "Deputation of Newspaper Proprietors to the Prime Minister at 10 Downing Street, London, S.W.," 19 March 1918, Treasury 172/841, Public Records Office, London; *The Times,* 18 February 1947, 5B-C; *The Times,* 22 February 1947, 5D; *The Times,* 24 February 1947, 6B. In addition, see the November 1941 exchange between Kingsley Martin and John Maynard Keynes in the Kingsley Martin Papers, 13/3 and 13/5, University of Sussex.

75. Jones, *Powers of the Press,* 5.

2. Imagining the Press, 1850–80: The Educational Ideal Ascendant

Any discussion of modern theories of the press has to begin with the mid-nineteenth century. Not only did the twentieth century inherit much of its thinking about media from this period, but this period occupies an important position in the mythology of the press as a "golden age" foil with which to criticize subsequent developments. To be sure, some historians have questioned the sharp distinction between the journalism of that era and the New Journalism beginning in the 1880s.[1] Others, particularly James Curran, have presented that period as the end, not the beginning, of a golden age. In Curran's view, despite the repressive "taxes on knowledge," radical papers were nonetheless viable in the 1830s. By contrast, after the repeal of those taxes, most importantly the repeal of the stamp tax in 1855, newspaper ownership grew in scale, ultimately becoming industrialized. The 1855 repeal, writes Curran, "introduced a new system of press censorship more effective than anything that had gone before," not through overt legislative repression but through turning loose the forces of the market.[2]

Yet this revised view remains rare. More broadly, the midcentury retains its place as a golden age, a period when the press was serious and focused on the "important" questions of politics. Robert Ensor institutionalized this view in *England 1870–1914*, originally published in 1936 as part of the Oxford History of England. He treated the press in three brief sections, covering the years 1870–86, 1886–1900, and 1901–14, with the press embarking on a steadily downward spiral from one period to the next. Concerning the first period, Ensor had little but praise for the conduct of the press. During these years, wrote Ensor, the press "did not deviate" from the course set by the midcentury repeals of the taxes on knowledge.[3] Acknowledging that the press catered almost exclusively to the upper- and middle-class male, but by no means lamenting the fact, Ensor insisted that although these papers "as a rule . . . earned commercial profits, their ownership was not primarily commercial." Ensor continued: "the staple was politics, especially speeches; and proceedings in parliament were reported and read all over the country at full length. The way in which the news-matter was handled would to-day be thought incredibly dull and matter-of-fact. Headlines were few and paragraphs long. But the reader was at least fairly given the facts, on which he could form his own judgment. Editorial opinion was more or less confined to the leading articles. . . . Propaganda was made by open argument; not, as in the twentieth century, by the doctoring of news."[4]

Although much of what Ensor claims is unambiguously true, his emphases and some of his terminology seem aggressively polemical in such an important scholarly history. The general picture created by these words is of a serious medium, a serious and deeply reflective audience, and noncommercial newspapers that nevertheless earned profits almost as an afterthought. Ensor mentioned the monthly and quarterly reviews as well, which wielded a "great influence," which "everybody in the governing classes read, and to which all the best writers of the day contributed." Nowhere in these pages does Ensor mention the Sunday papers, such as *Reynolds's,* which presumably would not have met with the same praise. Rather, Ensor argued that "this dignified phase of English journalism reigned unchallenged till 1886 and indeed beyond." By 1886, only George Newnes's *Tit-Bits* offered even a "seed" of the ultimate "destruction" of this golden age.[5] The history of journalism plays only a small part in Ensor's large book. Yet it is significant in the present context because he forcibly articulated an interpretation that continues to attract many scholars and journalists.[6]

It is not the purpose of this chapter to call such a view into question. Rather, the argument here is that this celebratory view derives from the mid-Victorian period itself. That is, mid-Victorian champions of the press set the terms in which their own era's press would, with a few exceptions, be remembered. This perspective was not unanimous, of course. Yet an immersion in the sources reveals that in the years from about 1850 to 1880, commentators on the press generally attributed to it vast powers of education, moral uplift, "elevation," and influence.

Alan J. Lee has called our attention to this vision of the press, though in somewhat different terms. For Lee, this ideal of the press was unmistakably liberal—and no viable alternative ideal existed. To contemporaries, the emerging newspaper itself was of one piece with the "political power of emerging Liberalism." The press occupied a niche within a broader picture of "improvement," which was itself a prominent characteristic within the "classical liberal model of society." As Lee puts it: "The model operated upon several planes, the political, the ethical, the economic, the intellectual, each having its respective equilibrium, peace, freedom, wealth and truth. Temporary states of disequilibrium and conflict would be ended by the advance of reason, and the accumulation, dissemination, and absorption of knowledge. In the liberal pursuit of certainty it was as much the pursuit as the certainty which counted."[7]

As applied to the newspaper press, this liberal view reflects the intersection of journalists' attempts to champion their medium, on the one hand, with prevailing notions of self-help and improvement, on the other hand. This ideal seems to have been relatively new in the nineteenth century. In the seventeenth century, periodical news publications attracted criticism precisely because they were antieducational; that is, they were merely temporal, drawing attention away from timeless questions. Sommerville has demonstrated that the classic seventeenth-century defenses of the liberty of the press, particularly Milton's, emphatically did not pertain to periodical literature.[8] By the nineteenth century, however, what Sommerville calls the "news revolution" had been accomplished, and timeliness became a virtue rather than a detraction. The idea of progress was prevalent by midcentury, and periodicals, so recently seen as agents of sedition, became a viable arena for improvement.

The emphasis on the educational uses of the press had two distinct and potentially contradictory elements. The press was seen as a facilitator of politics by public discussion and an arena for conveying established wisdom to readers, particularly working-class readers. The apparent contradiction is between separate emphases on process and result. The contradiction was neatly resolved, however, by elite confidence that the "right" opinions—those dignified by the title of "truth"—would prevail in any open contest.[9]

This optimistic view of the press, this confidence that newspapers could serve an educational purpose, belongs to the broader context of what Asa Briggs has called "the age of improvement," which began in the late eighteenth century and reached its climax in the mid-nineteenth century. Middle-class social reformers devised countless schemes for reforming England's institutions; more importantly, however, they expected individuals to practice "self-help." Much institutional reform, and the ideology that underwrote it, aimed either at taking away impediments to individual improvement or at creating an environment in which individuals' "moral calculus" would produce socially desirable results. Reformers believed in social progress, but not through collective action. In the famous words of Samuel Smiles, "'No laws, however stringent, can make the idle industrious, the thriftless provident, or the drunken sober. Such reforms can only be effected by means of individual action.'"[10] According to the historian J. F. C. Harrison, "One of the social effects of evangelicalism was to internalise the puritan values of hard work and self-reliance, and inculcate a strong sense of duty. To spread these values beyond the middle classes and skilled artisans to the labouring population at large was the object of most schemes for mental and moral improvement in the 1830s and 1840s."[11] During the turbulent 1830s and 1840s, such "schemes" were proposed in a frightened tone; in the 1850s, they were proposed more confidently.

Most germane to the present discussion, mid-nineteenth-century reformers championed improvements in primary education. Such proposals demanded governmental action, including action by the central government, yet could be justified by arguing that individual improvement was impossible without adequate primary education.

Such an argument had a disingenuous side. Early nineteenth-century advocates of education reform were frankly preoccupied with the problem of social disorder and viewed education as more than a precondition of individual initiative. Education was, in addition, a tool for the conveyance of propaganda, not merely to prepare workers to be self-reliant but to convince them of the virtues of self-reliance. Following Peterloo, when fear of workers' revolutionary potential exploded, education was held out as the last best hope for containing the influence of demagogues and their dangerous ideas. In Altick's words, if "the millions could be herded into classrooms, if only for a brief time, they could be permanently immunized against Jacobinism, radicalism, subversion, blasphemy, atheism, and every other ill to which they were exposed by the east wind of social change. Their native reason, however crude and untutored, could be depended upon to accept the truths of religion and society as laid before them by the superior classes, and the storms that were roiling the waters of English life would end."[12] Altick's statement nicely captures the ambiguity of reformers' hopes for education. They had a definite doctrinal end in mind; certain ideas were acceptable, while others were beyond the pale. At the same time, they did not envision this "education" in a manipulative or heavy-handed sense, as captured in the twentieth-century concept of "indoctrination." Instead, they assumed the truth of their own ideals, such as political economy and constitutional monarchy, and assumed that only workers' ignorance could prevent them from reaching the same conclusions.[13]

Reformers made extravagant claims for the benefits to society of improved education, as well as the dangers of ignoring this need. Writing in 1846, Joseph Kay argued that England's celebrated commercial system was destined to increase dramatically the working-class population. But, he asked, "are we prepared to increase this population, without attempting to change its character? Is it safe, to say the least of it, to multiply indefinitely a population improvident, ignorant and irreligious?"[14] Answering his own questions in the negative, Kay claimed, "In assembling masses of workmen, there are always two special dangers; a low state of intellect, occasioning improvidence, and an absence of religious feeling, producing immorality and insubordination."[15] Education could redress both of these problems, teaching thrift and morality and thereby lessening the dangers of "insubordination." Philanthropy was all well and good, but education was the better part of philanthropy: "It is this which every true philanthropist should desire; to create virtue and providence among the poor, and to raise their character and increase their happiness by improving this foresight. By these means we may reasonably hope materially to diminish our number of criminals, to lessen the dangers of social convulsions, and to unite the different classes of society by bonds of common interests, mutual confidence, and affection."[16]

In some respects, this quotation calls to mind twentieth-century liberalism's search for "root causes" of poverty, particularly in linking crime and "social convulsions" to inadequate education. For Kay, however, the true root cause was individual moral failure, and it was this problem that education should address. Published during the height of the "Hungry Forties," this book not surprisingly revealed Kay's preoccupation with crime, disorder, and the need for social harmony. Nearly two decades later, in 1864, despite more than a decade of relative political stability, Kay remained attached to this theme. Crime statistics, he wrote, show "how fearfully crime is increasing among our poor, and how clear and undeniable it is, THAT THE GREATEST PART OF THEIR IMMORALITY IS THE DIRECT AND IMMEDIATE EFFECT OF THE UTTER NEGLECT OF THEIR EDUCATION."[17] Unfortunately, "About ONE HALF of our poor can neither read nor write, have never been in any school, and know little, or positively nothing, of the doctrines of the Christian religion, of moral duties, or of any higher pleasures, than beer or spirit drinking and the grossest sensual indulgence." This being the case, "If these poor creatures commit what the more intelligent classes call 'crimes against society,'—if they are improvident and immoral,—if they have no love for society which has left, if it has not made, them thus degraded,—and if they punish that society by burdening it with vice and pauperism, is it a matter of great surprise?" He continued, arguing that the poor had "no idea that it is possible to attain any higher condition," nor were they "even sentient enough to desire, with any strength of feeling, to change their condition." They were not even "intelligent enough to be perseveringly discontented."[18]

Education, wrote Kay and other reformers, could raise the poor from this morass of vice and pauperism, prepare them for self-reliance, and reconcile them to the dictates of English society. Kay's analysis exemplifies what twentieth-century sociologists would call the "individualization of social problems," although in a manner well-attuned to the prevailing evangelical and utilitarian spirits: it assumed that although governmental initiatives in education were necessary in order to eliminate pauperism, this intervention would work precisely because it would help individuals to address their own moral failings.

Although the phrase "social control" has fallen out of favor with historians, it is difficult to resist Richard Johnson's conclusion that early Victorian educational policy aimed at exactly that.[19] Yet the reality was both more complicated and more generous. As already indicated, education reformers believed in the correctness of their various views and saw education as a more progressive approach to pauperism and crime than the workhouse and prison. Not seeing education as coercive, these reformers saw coercion as inherently undesirable in a progressive nation such as England. Kay, for example, linked the need for education to England's glorious Protestantism, a religion commonly linked to English freedom in contrast to continental despotism. In Kay's words, "The Romish forms of worship exert an empire over the minds of the ignorant, by their imposing observances, but the cold exterior of Protestantism repels all but the intelligent worshipper."[20] In a Protestant country, relations between the poor and their betters should only be based on persuasion and consent, qualities that could only come with improved education.

This did not amount to democracy; there existed a definite hierarchy of people and values, and "education" entailed the transmission of beliefs and virtue from betters to inferiors. In the words of a Birmingham justice of the peace in the early 1840s, "'I have no other conception of any other means of forcing civilisation downwards in society, except by education.'"[21] Again, these discussions of educational reform presumed that workers could be coerced *into civilization,* not merely coerced. Altick's description of reformist agitation for public libraries is equally applicable here: "The inconsistency implicit in this view of the working population as being simultaneously a touchy rabble, ready for crime and revolution, and a respectable class desiring nothing more than intellectual improvement, went unchallenged then, as it usually did in Victorian discussions of reform."[22]

Enormous hope and an enormous burden was placed on education reform. Even in the best scenario, however, most workers could be given no more than a basic elementary education. This would extend literacy, making workers (it was argued) less vulnerable to demagogues. Yet despite the claims of Kay and others, the entire burden of "improvement" could not rest on the slender shoulders of education reform. According to J. F. C. Harrison, "Early industrial society, to a far greater extent than any previous age, was based on the written word. The socialising functions of print were fully realised, and the 'whip of the word' was a most powerful agent in shaping the new society."[23] Reformers thus focused considerable attention on working-class reading materials, particularly on the newspaper press.

In the years after 1819, in debates concerning the newspaper stamp and other taxes on knowledge, middle-class reformers tended to articulate educational uses of the press. Opposing the stamp tax, John Crawfurd insisted in his 1836 pamphlet that it was "inflicted upon the people with the avowed object of arresting the progress of information, and of confining knowledge, or at least political knowledge, to the ruling factions."[24] In his motion before the House of Commons in 1832, Edward Lytton Bulwer underscored the link between ignorance and crime as measured by the illiteracy of the criminal population. Arguing that crime was a social cost of ignorance, Bulwer urged the commons that "[i]t was, then, their duty to diffuse instruction in all its modes; yet he thought it would be scarcely necessary for him to contend that newspapers were among the readiest and most effectual instruments of diffusing that instruction." He went on to link the promotion of education through newspapers to the spread of political power through the expansion of the electorate, arguing that with the help of newspapers, "by degrees there would grow up that community of intelligence between the government and the people."[25]

Middle-class defenders of the greater freedom of the press emphasized its usefulness as a means of educating the people. During an era of political turbulence and fear of "the people," this claim could potentially serve as a powerful propaganda device on behalf of the press. Hence, in a pamphlet published in 1836 by Charles Knight, the proprietor of *Penny Magazine,* the link between education by means of the press and the development of good government was made more explicitly:

> The people of England, by the recent great changes in the constitution, have acquired the power not only of influencing the measures of government by the

force of public opinion, but of controlling and directing them more immediately than at any former period of our history. It is not only necessary that the people should feel their rights, but that they should exercise them wisely and temperately. They cannot do so without political knowledge. Without political knowledge it might be possible that the nation would suffer as much from the ignorance of the many, who will influence public affairs, as from the selfishness of the few, who have influenced them. The time, however, is now past . . . when it is possible to refuse the people political knowledge through the medium of cheap newspapers.[26]

While the linking of "the people" to the reforms of 1832 might suggest that Knight did not intend to include the working classes under that rubric, the context of the debates on the role of the press suggests that that is precisely what most commentators meant. Time and again, the taxes on knowledge were attacked on the grounds that they prevented the poor from affording the legal newspapers and that they forced the poor to read the cheaper illegal papers, whose lies subsequently could be refuted only by the prohibitively priced stamped papers.[27]

In this campaign against the taxes on knowledge, however, "education" and "knowledge" were contested concepts. Many among the working classes suspected, rightly, that these middle-class reformers merely wished to teach them to acquiesce to the existing political order. Journalists writing in the unstamped press argued that "useful knowledge is useless" and claimed that the legal press was not properly educational. They argued that what the people needed was not lessons in political economy or hydrostatics or any of the other topics featured in journals like *Penny Magazine* but explicit, factual knowledge about the ways in which the ruling classes were oppressing the poor. Many radical journalists argued that proper education would effectively "represent the people," a key issue in an era of Parliamentary "virtual representation." Later, in the 1880s, when boasts of the press's educational role were relatively scarce, champions of the press would draw on the language of these radical journalists.

During the mid-nineteenth century, defenders of the press's political and social role continued to emphasize its function in educating or "improving" readers. At this time, concepts of education and knowledge seem to have become much less contested within the many discussions of the press. The defense of the free trade in ideas, like that in the commercial or imperial realms, reflected as much as anything a confidence among the enfranchised classes that their vision of the world would win in any open contest. James Curran rightly points out that one person's education was another person's social control. This observation should by no means surprise us. During this period, popular liberalism flourished to an extent that allowed the educated and professional classes to remain optimistic about the disenfranchised working classes' commitment to the existing political and social order. In addition, in the context of an expanding franchise, universal education, academic and political, was seen as the only alternative to the "abyss."[28] Nevertheless, the ritualistic manner in which these phrases were used should not obscure the fact that behind them lay a meaningful belief in the power of discussion that, as H. C. G. Matthew states, was beginning to pervade one political party and to some extent to penetrate the other.[29]

An overemphasis on social control also undervalues the high premium placed on the ideal of disinterestedness during the nineteenth century. We may note ideological and social blinders that limited the imaginations of the political and educated classes, but this is a different matter from charging them with cynical manipulation. It was important for many to believe that their actions served the public good and not merely their self-interest. Anthony Trollope's *The Warden* richly captures this ideal. One of the novel's main conflicts concerns the elderly clergyman, Mr. Harding, as he contemplates whether or not his actions are really in the best interests of the church that employs him. He can accept his interests coinciding with those of the church; what he cannot accept is the thought that the church's supposed interests are merely a mask for his own. "If it were necessary for him to suffer, he felt that he could endure without complaint and without cowardice, providing that he was self-satisfied of the justice of his own cause. What he could not endure was that he should be accused by others, and not acquitted by himself."[30] Such qualms lead him to give up a lucrative post, even though it appears that he is legally entitled to hold it.

The point is not that Mr. Harding represents the typical member of the midcentury elites, nor that self-interested scheming did not exist. The believability of this character attests to the mainstream quality of his ideals, even if his fellow characters' shock at his carrying his principles so far cautions us that Mr. Harding would probably have been considered a fanatic. The point here is merely to illustrate that the principle of disinterestedness, or putting the public good ahead of private interest, exercised a significant hold over the nineteenth-century mind. This principle appeared in specific discussions of the press, both public and private. A leader in *The Times* in 1855, during the peak of the campaign against the taxes on knowledge, reflected on the qualities people expected of that newspaper: "Above all, they want absolute honesty and independence; they want a perfect conviction that *The Times* is inaccessible to corrupt influence in its coarsest and its subtlest forms; that it is subservient to no minister, devoted to no clique, and constantly on the watch against the thousand and one inroads of private interest or feeling."[31]

Around the turn of the twentieth century, this ideal would increasingly appear naïve, but it lingered in many contexts. At the height of the Boer War, with the *Manchester Guardian* under fire for opposing the war, a vacancy opened for special correspondent to South Africa. John Taylor, the proprietor, wrote to his editor, C. P. Scott, that they should take care not to "send a man too far committed to even our views. He should be a justice loving, high principled & strong man; but not a partisan."[32] Similarly, J. Passmore Edwards, an anti–Corn Law activist in his twenties and the owner of the leading half-penny evening London paper, *The Echo* in the 1880s, reflected on his long career in his 1906 memoirs: "I do not say I have not made mistakes, or, if at times I had been better informed, that I should not have written, spoken or acted differently; but I do say—and I take no credit for saying or doing it—that I have always treated public questions purely in the light of general and enduring interests."[33] Such a statement in a journalist's memoirs could obviously be self-serving. Whether or not he was sincere, or however successfully he may have avoided his self-interested biases during a long career, his words attest to the value he perceived that the principle of disinterestedness held in the minds of his readers. Moreover, belief in at least the possibility of the public good was a necessary component of the educational ideal.

The educational ideal of the press derived from a belief in the desirability of popular self-government through rational public discussion. Many among the elite classes professed a faith in the educability of the popular classes, and the press was one of the chief agents proposed. This is not to claim that the elites desired to turn Britain into a democracy, at least not any time soon. Indeed, opponents of franchise reform could still score political points by calling the reformers "democrats." The mission to "civilize" the popular classes resembles the imperial civilizing mission in at least one key respect: its defenders usually hesitated to specify when the masses would be truly prepared for self-government, but that date seemed safely in the distant future. Still, belief in a painfully gradual process of education is not the same as a belief in the hopeless ineducability of the masses.

The educational role of the press received theoretical justification in John Stuart Mill's forcible statement on the need for "liberty of thought and discussion" in the second chapter of his 1859 classic, *On Liberty*. Mill argued that the free expression of diverse opinions was necessary to ensure that the true opinion would have a chance to win ascendancy and that its advocates would believe it for a justifiable reason, not merely because of prejudice. For Mill, the desirable outcome of discussion was a consensus around a true opinion; until that state had been reached, discussion was necessary to arrive at the truth, and even then, it would remain necessary in order that the opinion would not be held complacently.[34]

A writer in *Blackwood's* during the same year applied Mill's logic more explicitly to newspapers. The truth would prevail in an open contest for the same reason that any good product would triumph over the bad. In the writer's words, opinion followed the rules of "any other item of merchandise; that it follows the known laws of supply and demand; that if a journal sends forth bad articles and unsound advice, it must suffer; that if it issues good articles and trustworthy opinions, it will reap the reward." More surprisingly, he claimed that Mill's ideal state of consensus had already been reached. Journalism had produced "harmony, of success, of the creating a public opinion in the main so true to reason, and therefore, in spite of differences and distortions innumerable, so unanimous in the end, that the authority of any individual journal is forgotten in the universal sentiment."[35] It is not for nothing that this period has been described as an "age of equipoise." Moreover, such confidence in the triumph of "better" news or opinions was quite common at this time. Mill himself wrote to William Dougal Christie in 1871 that the only method of newspaper reform that he knew of "would be to start a first rate newspaper."[36]

Not all defenders of the press's educational role would articulate such a thorough and consistent view as Mill's. Nor would they all have agreed with Mill on all particulars. Nevertheless, Mill's defense of public discussion broadly undergirded the predominant view of the press in this period. Such a view appeared in many different contexts. In 1846, in an article entitled "What Are the People Doing to Educate Themselves?" Samuel Smiles singled out the press as a tool "to teach working men that they must be their own elevators, educators, emancipators; and that if they help not themselves, assuredly they never will be helped." He went on to argue that the press "must inevitably, in a free country, be the great agent and instrument of Public Instruction. It is not only the Educator, but the Creator, of public opinion ... it is read about, talked about, discussed; and its lessons sink deep into the heart, materially influencing the conduct of after life." A generation later, in 1866, when Prime Minister Gladstone argued before the House of Commons on behalf of the extension of the franchise because of the increasing "fitness" of a segment of the working classes, he cited the educational character of the cheap press. For J. Boyd Kinnear, writing in 1867, the press exercised an important "influence in the formation of national character and the determination of national conduct." James Grant, in justifying his two-volume history of the press, published in 1871, wrote of "the great work of seeking to improve men's minds . . . and to transform their moral character." Citing Carlyle, he wrote of the great "power, for good or evil, which is produced by the Editor of one of our morning journals, influencing, as it does, every succeeding day, some hundreds of thousands of our fellow beings."[37] Despite his reference to "power, for good or evil," Grant exhibits an unswaying optimism about the press's good effects.

In the minds of many elite commentators, working-class audiences needed such guidance. No book or article conveyed this perception better than Wilkie Collins's anonymously published article, "The Unknown Public." Published in 1858 in Dickens's *Household Words,* this article conveyed shock that an entirely new reading public existed, unknown to Collins's peers: "My favorite Review is, as I firmly believe, at this very day, unconscious of their existence." Collins's article reads like imperial travel literature, discovering a primitive, even savage culture in need of elevating. "I went into a lovely county of South Wales; the modest railway had not penetrated to it, but the audacious picture quarto had found it out." The fruits of civilization had not reached this remote people, but objectionable periodicals had. Describing this public of an estimated three million as "right out of the pale of literary civilization" and as "lost literary tribes," Collins expressed amazement at the ignorance betrayed in the "Answers to Correspondents" section common to all the "penny-novel Journals": "Inconceivably dense ignorance, inconceivably petty malice, and inconceivably complacent vanity, all consult the editor, and all, wonderful to relate, get serious answers from him. . . . Now he is a father, now a mother, now a schoolmaster, now a confessor, now a doctor, now a lawyer, now a young lady's confidante, now a young gentleman's bosom friend, now a lecturer on morals, and now an authority on cookery."[38]

Collins presented an "unknown" reading public that seemingly lacked understanding of even the most basic social or cultural practices: "Two lady readers who require lovers, and wish the editor to provide them. . . . A soreheaded reader, who is editorially advised to use soap and warm water." Such readers were not only a surprise to Collins, but he acted as if he expected his own readers not to believe his report. Twice he protests his veracity, insisting that he neither portrayed these journals selectively, nor "exaggerated," "invented," or "misquoted." Admitting that these journals could do no "moral harm," he saw them as evidence of a "monster audience" awaiting the instruction of their betters. "An immense public has been discovered: the next thing to be done is, in a literary sense, to teach that public how to read."[39]

All of these examples concentrate on the "influential" aspect of education. To a modern observer, the idea of influencing an audience can seem sinister, smacking of propaganda, spin, and public relations. In the mid-Victorian years, however, nothing could appear more laudable; even the word "propaganda" generally possessed a favorable connotation. If some contemporaries noted the press's capacity for influencing its audience, others noted the ways that the press had altered the conditions of politics so that now it was necessary to influence the electorate. A writer in *Blackwood's* in 1874 asserted that the manner in which the 1867 Reform Bill was carried demonstrated these new rules of politics: "It certainly shows that in these days of a free press, diffused political knowledge, and published Parliamentary debates, a Prime Minister . . . must make it his business to educate public opinion before he can hope to carry his measures." The press had contributed to the diffusion of power. No longer could a politician simply direct; he had to take the trouble to persuade public opinion beforehand. The writer continued: "he [the prime minister] can neither precede nor lag behind public opinion; he can neither bully the people into what he calls 'progress,' nor, in the spirit of reaction, compel them to recede from a policy which they have finally decided upon."[40]

This language emphasized that influence was not a one-way process. The presence of a free press had created an environment in which the public could influence ministers as well: "There is an omnipresent and omniscient Parliament always sitting in the public press. Nothing escapes its vigilance; and although its decisions are by no means final, a Minister must take its opinions, which are almost always representative, into account, and be largely influenced by them."[41] Through a process of mutual influence, a politics by public discussion was created. The metaphor of the press as Parliament suggested that it was a forum for discussion and that it represented the people, both of which were putative functions of Parliament. Moreover, the cabinet was responsible to Parliament, although sometimes it would act contrary to the wishes of the parliamentary majority, if judgment demanded. At the same time, the idea of representing the people contained elements of what I have called the "representative ideal" of the press, which would become ascendant within the next decade.

At the same time that some commentators noted the press's contribution to politics by public discussion, others argued that the press had helped to create a critical public. A writer in *The Economist* in 1871 credited the 1855 repeal of the stamp tax with creating a "real independence of discussion and criticism all over the country" in place of an earlier dominance by London. This development had affected the pulpit in particular. Preachers now had to confront "congregations whom a popular press has fully informed beforehand of the merits and history of nearly every topic which the pulpit can take in hand." In this context, the "ordinary didactic and perfunctory preachers" had to adapt or they would become obsolete.[42]

Such observations underscored that the emergence of mass newspapers challenged prevailing cultural authorities. The problem of intellectual authority preoccupied many Victorians, and not only in the context of discussions of the press. Baldwin Brown, lecturing in 1870, argued that his era was characterized by "'the utter overthrow of ancient and venerated authority, the searching and to a large extent destructive criticism of ideas and institutions, on which, as on an immovable rock, the order of society was believed to rest; the submission of every thing and every method to the free judgment of reason.'"[43] Yet this "critical spirit" was accompanied, as Walter Houghton has pointed out, by the "will to believe" and the "recoil to authority."[44] Houghton refers most prominently to the same decline of religious authority seen in the quotation above from *The Economist,* but his point applies to the question of popular education more broadly.

It was for precisely this reason that the educational ideal of the press included emphases on both discussion and persuasion. According to George C. Brodrick, it was only through the mentoring function of the press that even the most liberal enthusiast could maintain the "generous confidence in popular intelligence" that during the debates of the 1850s had "fortified Liberals against the Conservative fear of a cheap newspaper press."[45]

Nor did the mentoring voice of authority constitute the only control in a messy process of discussion. For the truth or common good to emerge from a politics by public discussion, multiple voices had to contend. This concern remained in various guises throughout the nineteenth century and will resurface as a theme in the following chapter. The concern for multiple voices retains its attraction today, both in radical critiques of the press's institutional bias and in conservative attacks on a "liberal bias." During the first campaign for repealing taxes on knowledge in the 1830s, middle-class reformers pointed out that, ironically, the laws restricting radical, working-class papers ensured that the more respectable, middle-class voice was stifled. Not only did critics charge that the "lies" of the cheap press were answered only by prohibitively priced stamped papers. As S. Carter Hall argued in 1834, organizations such as the Society for the Diffusion of Useful Knowledge had helped to teach the "manufacturing classes" to read just well enough to understand "the journals which contain the poison, but not enough to give them the power of reflection which might serve them as an antidote."[46] In this context, the implied answer was less working-class literacy. A generation later, in the midcentury, similar logic would suggest aiming "respectable" papers a bit farther down the social scale.

One of the underlying assumptions of the midcentury educational ideal was that leisured readers would read more than one paper, thus encountering more than one opinion on "questions of the day." Aside from the obvious question of whether many people actually did this, what if the entire press, considered as a whole, were one-sided? While a general confidence prevailed concerning the (at least potential) rationality of the people, some observers noted that the apprehension of "truth" required a disinterested spirit that was not always abundant. As a writer in *Blackwood's* noted in 1851, "delusion and error" sometimes prevailed, causing the "most ruinous public delusions in an advanced and complicated state of society." This condition arose "from the strength and influence of the classes who become interested in the perpetuating of error because they profit by it, and the impossibility of getting the great bulk of men to see, among the numerous causes which are then acting upon their fortunes, the real ones to which their sufferings are owing." When this state prevailed, unfortunately, the press would become "the most powerful engine for the diffusion and continuance of error."[47]

This concern surfaced again a few years later in Samuel Warren's lectures on labor. Warren noted that as newspapers were "commercial ventures, they naturally seek, as their first object, to enunciate views acceptable to the class to whom they address themselves." This natural occurrence became ruinous to public discussion when one group within society achieved a predominance: "Whenever any party in the country happens to attain a great preponderance over its rivals, that preponderance is followed by an increase of newspapers in that interest, which in turn tends to augment the preponderance, it may be, even into a tyranny. And accordingly, at times when party-spirit runs high, the side which chances to possess a virtual monopoly of the newspaper press has it in its power, by bold assertion and frequent iteration, to make any misrepresentation or false charges against an antagonist pass generally current as truth, and at the same time keep from view the real principles by which the opposite party are animated." Warren welcomed the recent trend of "making public addresses" as the best counter to this dangerous but "natural one-sidedness of the newspaper press."[48]

This concern for multiple perspectives reveals one of the most salient points at which the educational ideal of the midcentury and the emerging representative ideal would intersect. At bottom, multiple perspectives meant merely that more than one section of society was "represented" by the newspaper press. In the 1880s, the emphasis on the press's representive qualities would predominate. At that point, representing readers would stand in place of influencing them; journalists would claim to speak on their behalf, thus attaining an authority for their newspapers. In the period considered here, by contrast, the concern for representing the readers was more a concern for ensuring that multiple perspectives on the same question were heard, so that the truth might be discovered and tested. For this reason, the anonymous *Blackwood's* writer of 1859, who believed that an ideal consensus had already been attained, credited this happy state of affairs in part to the fact that "[e]very class has its organ; every topic finds a journal; every interest has its friend in the press. And this system of classification is so complete that here we have a genuine system of popular representation."[49]

In addition to prevailing in general discussions on the press, the educational ideal can also be seen in the period's two most important press-related controversies: the repeal of taxes on knowledge between 1853 and 1861 and the question of anonymous journalism. We will examine these debates in turn.

* * *

The year 1855 has long been recognized as one of the most important in the history of the modern British press. The repeal of the newspaper stamp tax allowed the penny press to develop, especially in the provinces. This meant, among other results, that a new segment of British society was reached by the daily newspaper and that the *Daily Telegraph* surpassed *The Times* in circulation, breaking what had been a formidable predominance. That repeal was part of a congeries of press reforms, yet it is generally regarded as the most important individual reform.

The reasons for the agitation were many and varied. In part, it was simply a continuation of the long British tradition of campaigning for press freedom. Some of the agitators were working-class radicals who had been dissatisfied by the stamp tax reduction in 1836 but who had considered the Chartist demands a more important cause in the 1840s, and had thus put press-reform agitation on hold. For middle-class reformers, part of the rationale for repeal was a broader commitment to abolishing all forms of protectionism. Like the anti–Corn Law movement, on which this later movement was consciously patterned, opponents of the stamp tax were able to point to an artificial monopoly. Specifically, many critics believed that *The Times* owed its overwhelming ascendancy to the partial reform of 1836 and an unfair advantage bequeathed by the remaining taxes. As *The Times*'s influence became clear during the Crimean War, an anti-*Times* backlash contributed to the antitax campaign. Another factor, as the Hungry Forties ended, was the general calming of politics. In this quieter environment, campaigners possessed the confidence to extend the newspaper press's availability.[50]

The campaign's rhetoric emphasized two main themes: first, that the taxes were not fiscally necessary, and second, that they hindered the improving work of education. The second line of argument took clear precedence, as seen in the phrase "taxes on knowledge."[51] As Richard Cobden would tell the House of Commons in 1853, while attacking the paper duty in particular, "You talk of promoting education, and yet here is a tax on the material by which knowledge is conveyed."[52] Two years later, in advocating the repeal of the stamp tax while preserving the right of "retransmission," John Bright asserted that members of Parliament "had a deep interest in the diffusion of political intelligence and useful information by means of newspapers."[53] Several weeks earlier, he had argued that following repeal, "the existing papers will retain all their powers of usefulness," and the "advantage of having laid before us each morning a map of the events of the world" would filter down to "classes at present shut out from it."[54] Lord Palmerston weighed in as well, also calling for the extension of educational newspapers to the poorer classes: "I believe there will arise cheap publications for the use of those unable to buy dear ones, which will convey instruction, enlarge their understandings, improve their morals, and at the same time make them good and useful members of society."[55]

While advocates of repeal emphasized the impediment to education caused by the taxes, they also had to reassure those who feared that cheap newspapers would have all the worst qualities of the American papers. The 1851 Select Committee on Newspaper Stamps concluded that such a fear did "not rest on any good foundation": "No deterioration of the newspaper press, but, on the contrary, an improvement followed the reduction of the stamp which took place in 1836; and doubtless the character of newspapers would continue to improve in proportion to the advance in public taste and morals, although the stamp should be entirely abolished."[56]

On 24 May 1855, Viscount Canning defended the working-class press in the House of Lords, claiming that the "most demoralising" newspapers had never been the unstamped ones but had been stamped papers purchased by the higher classes.[57] Bulwer Lytton, one of the chief architects of the tax reduction in 1836, claimed in 1855 that "any danger to be apprehended from the sudden diffusion of cheap newspapers is . . . considerably less now than it was then." He claimed that popular intelligence had increased as a result of cheap publications, particularly because "the public have had the wisdom to choose the best and reject the worst." Several minutes later, he claimed that the bad qualities of the American press need not concern Parliament because they derived not from taxes but from the quality of the American people: "if our press is superior to the Americans, it does not depend upon fiscal laws, but upon the general standard of civilisation."[58]

This distancing from the American press was already in circulation a few months earlier. *The Economist* had argued earlier in 1855 that a cheap press but not an immoral one would emerge: "There is no demand for the vile trash which people profess to apprehend, or such as is published in the United States. But the absence of demand is not caused by the penny stamp, but by the moral character of the great mass of the population. It is not that the people will be moulded to the character of the press, but that a press will be supplied consistent with the demands, the tone of mind, and the moral perceptions of the people."[59]

Whether genuine sentiment or mere posturing, the claim that the goodness of the British people would defend them against the American excesses was frequently echoed and constituted a statement of confidence in popular intelligence. We have seen that exponents of the educational ideal exhibited confidence that "respectable" ideas would prevail in any open contest. This linking of the free trade in ideas to free trade more broadly was made even more explicit in other arguments in *The Economist*. On 27 January 1855, *The Economist* claimed that "of this we feel confident, that neither this nor any other change will enable low priced and inferior papers to interfere with the best portion of the press as it now exists."[60] Two months later, that journal linked opposition to repeal to those farmers who had defended the discredited Corn Laws: "it is the same want of self-reliance."[61] A month later, and in a slightly different context, it affirmed that "the journals which are the most diligent, most careful, and the best informed . . . get the largest circulation."[62] Not cheapness but quality would prevail.

Nor was such confidence limited to *The Economist*. Speaking in the House of Commons, Chancellor William Gladstone attacked those worried that the repeal would "open the floodgates of sedition and blasphemy, and . . . inundate the country with licentious and immoral productions which will undermine the very foundations of society, and scatter the seeds of revolution broadcast all over the land." Such results depended not merely on press laws but on the character of the nation. The government could entertain repeal because "[t]hey have the greatest confidence in the stability of our political institutions, in the soundness of our political institutions, in the loyalty and good disposition of the great body of the people; and they do not believe that increased facilities for public discussion through the press will lead to any such consequences as some have apprehended."[63] Throughout the successful agitation to repeal the taxes on knowledge, the press's educational role was repeatedly proclaimed.

* * *

The educational ideal was seen in a second debate, concerning whether journalistic contributions should be signed or anonymous. The tradition of anonymity proved one of the most enduring and one of the most contentious journalistic practices of the mid-Victorian period. This is not the place for a comprehensive treatment of anonymous journalism.[64] Yet it bears mentioning that, although the present concern is for the light that can be shed on the educational ideal, this was not the only question at stake. The defense of anonymity stemmed in part from a belief in the degrading quality of writing for pay. Anonymity would protect a gentleman's social status; by contrast, revealing the authorship of periodical articles would expose the gentleman's status as a mere trader in words and could be socially ruinous. Of course, such a defense was better suited to journalists at the upper end of the social and salary scales, those elite "public moralists" who could command twenty, twenty-five, or sometimes even fifty pounds for a single contribution, those whose earnings allowed them the luxury of worrying about status. As the century progressed, however, and as the social stigma attached to authorship receded, these contributors increasingly saw their names attached to their contributions and their intellectual property thus protected.[65]

For those journalists at the lower end of the scales, anonymity had a darker side: in the absence of a signature, it was impossible for journalists to ensure adequate compensation for their intellectual labor, particularly since the papers for which they wrote could sell the contributions to other papers and keep the earnings. These less prominent journalists tended, as a group, to remain anonymous to the latest date, in part because without bringing to the newspaper an already established name, they could provide no incentive to their employers to allow their signatures. The result was that a journalist whose columns were read daily by thousands or even millions could nonetheless remain obscure, receiving neither credit nor adequate remuneration for his or her efforts.[66] By contrast, contributions from the better known, such as a John Morley or a Leslie Stephen, let alone a William Gladstone, were valuable to the periodicals more for the contributors' names than for their writings' content. During the mid-Victorian period, the perception of anonymous journalism changed. From constituting a shelter for a gentleman's reputation, allowing him to protect his name from association with a trader's status, it became more obviously an impediment to reporters' and penny-a-liners' receiving adequate recognition and the accompanying professional standing.

The debate on anonymous journalism focused in part on concerns for occupational reward. The debate was not always couched in these terms, however; the prevailing educationalist rhetoric was employed as well. Defenders of anonymous journalism insisted on the benefits of anonymity to public discussion, while proponents of signatures took pains to demonstrate that anonymity obscured rather than facilitated public discussion.

Proponents of anonymous journalism emphasized that anonymity forced the readers to consider the opinions offered on their own merits rather than on the reputation of their authors. This position derived from a belief that truth transcended context, and thus that the identity, social position, partisanship, or other narrowing factors of the authorship need not be considered in evaluating the validity of a particular claim. These factors were seen as irrelevant in a culture in which a disinterested writer was expected to speak from the "point of view of the universe."[67]

Closely related to this question was the question of authority. Proponents of anonymity defended the concept of an "editorial 'we'"—a stable, unified, editorial identity to a particular paper, one that ensured continuity in logic from one day to the next.[68] *The Standard* lead writer Thomas Escott, among others, insisted that the "editorial we" was real, not merely a device; it secured continuity in "that nebulous, but most potent entity, 'the policy of the paper.'"[69] Signatures would undermine this unity of voice and, as a result, undermine the authority of opinions offered within the newspaper. An opinion thus would be seen as merely the opinion of a particular individual rather than, for example, the opinion of *The Times*. William Rathbone Greg wrote in 1855 in the *Edinburgh Review* that the "high tone and character of Journalism" in part derived from anonymous journalism. It contributed to the weight of the ideas expressed in an article, for "[a]n article signed by a name, however able its reasoning, however vigorous its style, however well established and widely circulated the journal in which it appeared, would carry with it scarcely greater weight than that name could bestow upon it. It would be reduced to its personal dimensions." Yet for Greg the question of authority worked both ways: if a well-argued essay lost weight when linked to a mere person, a less rigorous argument might be carried by a prominent name. "Already in England we are too much disposed to be swayed rather by authority than by argument—to consider not the thing said but the man who says it. Were all articles signed, the public would devour with eagerness and curiosity the feeble and unsound reasoning of a celebrated name, but pass lightly over, or perhaps not read at all, the unanswerable logic of a signature 'unknown to fame.'"[70]

John Oldcastle boiled the issue down to a debate between recognition for the journalists versus weight with public opinion, concluding that the latter was more valuable. As late as 1900, Brodrick noted that anonymity brought seclusion but bigger audiences, transforming the journalist into a sort of unrecognized statesman.[71]

Opposition to anonymous journalism sometimes came with an admission that its abolition would privilege the individual over the idea. John Stuart Mill admitted in his *Autobiography* that personal reasons led him to insist that while he was editor of the *London Review,* "every article should bear an initial, or some other signature, and be held to express the opinions solely of the individual writer." By this device, Mill could register his personal dissent from the Benthamite radicalism of that journal, taking the opportunity to exhibit that he had moved beyond certain of his colleagues' orthodoxies.[72] The novelist Anthony Trollope, in an article on anonymous literature, paused to consider the consequences of anonymity in journalism. Arguing that a newspaper was "chiefly used as an instructor and informant in politics," Trollope defended anonymity on the grounds that a newspaper "is not a lamp lighted by a single hand, but a sun placed in the heaven by an invisible creator." Although anonymity was "useful and salutary" for the public, he acknowledged that it was less beneficial to the journalist. Moreover, he was quick to insist that his persuasive arguments on behalf of anonymity did not apply to reviews and magazines.[73]

Similar arguments could become intertwined with politics. A new radical penny journal, *The Anarchist,* announced in March 1885 that it would print signatures so as to encourage "individual and independent expression of opinion." The editorial continued: "Each writer must be alone morally responsible for his or her own views, and can only be expected to necessarily endorse such statements as may appear over his or her own signature."[74] Yet in a notable twist, a year later the journal announced a change of policy, which it attributed to its "Communistic" leanings; henceforth, articles would be "purely impersonal, thereby allowing the true force of an argument to stand entirely upon its intrinsic merit, and not carry undue preponderance with it because this or that particular individual has contended for it."[75]

In addition, anonymous journalism could be seen as a means of protecting the field from the wrong sort of journalist, the seeker of literary fame, who would not put the public interest first. In an 1861 article condemning newspapers that catered to the "momentary passions" of the public, the *Saturday Review* denied that signed articles in *The Times* would ensure more scrupulous writers but insisted that it would render journalism "a profession for an ambitious man."[76]

This position could be attacked in at least two different ways. Some proponents of signatures denied that the revelation of authorship in any way precluded a fair consideration of the opinions offered; to the contrary, it could actually facilitate an open-minded reading. Writing in 1867, J. Boyd Kinnear argued that the ways in which leaders were written and read undermined arguments on behalf of anonymous journalism. Writers did not openly offer their opinions as such but purported to speak the truth. "They argue not with the air of pleading, but with that of deciding.... Their conclusions are couched in the form and language of impartial but authoritative judgments." For their part, readers blindly accepted the positions of their chosen newspapers rather than carefully weighing them. As evidence, Kinnear insisted "that scarcely any one reads a paper on the other side, which he certainly would feel bound to do if he felt his own to be merely a partisan advocate, and not a fair arbiter."[77]

Not simply the pretensions of writers and inadequacy of readers but the very implications of anonymity and an "editorial we" could prove deluding. Tighe Hopkins, writing in 1889, argued, "If the leading article be the sincere expression of a competent mind it will lose nothing in 'weight' or in 'effectiveness,' amongst the thinking portion of the public, by being signed with its author's name. If it be the insincere expression of a mind, whether competent or incompetent, it may indeed, by being unsigned, impose upon the mass; but its power is then a hopelessly immoral one."[78] Hopkins continued his emphasis on the deluding effect of anonymous journalism, insisting that writers of anonymous articles, bearing only the name of the paper, "assume such an authority because they know that there is a large section of the public which is willing to impose on itself, and which does impose on itself, a belief that the use of the 'We' in place of the 'I' endows the writer with a semi-miraculous wisdom. The power of anonymity is derived, in a word, from the willingness of the most credulous and ill-informed portion of society to accept and bow down to a huge and imposing symbol without consideration as to whether there be any reality with which the symbol corresponds."[79]

In an interesting putting into practice of his own views on anonymous journalism, Hopkins did not simply state his case and allow reason to carry the day but admitted, "I could advance but a very feeble claim to be heard out of my own mouth alone." Instead, he presented quotations from Gladstone, Morley, Joseph Cowen, and other famous journalists; that is, he deliberately presented not merely his own views but "a collection of utterances from persons whose right to be heard all journalists would acknowledge."[80]

* * *

The idea of the press as an educational agent was broadly predominant during the period between 1850 and 1880. This theory of the press reflected a wide elite optimism in England's institutions, in the potential for "progress," in the possibilities for integrating the people into a politics by public discussion. More fundamentally, this theory of the press reflected a confidence in the possibilities of rational communication and persuasion.

This optimistic theory was based on blind spots. Observers disregarded

PUNCH, OR THE LONDON CHARIVARI.

PUNCH'S FANCY PORTRAITS.—NO. 179.
[AUTHENTIC.]

THE WRITER WHO SIGNS HIMSELF "G." IN THE *FORTNIGHTLY*.

"Punch's Fancy Portraits" typically caricatured prominent public servants. Here, the practice of anonymous journalism is lampooned. From *Punch*, 21 June 1884.

the less "serious" Sunday papers and assumed that the worst cheap literature would eventually be crowded out by the more wholesome daily newspapers. They falsely universalized the midcentury conditions of production; in that commercial environment, the ascendancy of "views" and parliamentary reports made sound economic sense, but it would not necessarily always do so. Perhaps most importantly, they glossed over the fundamental conflict between the two aspects of the educational ideal: the creation of a public discussion and the transmission of the "right" ideas. In an era of seeming consensus, in which England dominated the world's economy and sea lanes and appeared immune to continental-style revolutions, it was easy to take for granted the rectitude of prevailing institutions and virtues, such as the limited monarchy, political economy, and self-reliance, and to assume that they would triumph in any genuinely open contest of ideas.

These conditions would not hold sway indefinitely. With the economic turbulence after 1873, the radical expansion of the electorate and the transformation of political parties in the 1880s and later, and the growth of militant unionism and feminism in the 1880s, optimistic theories appeared less realistic; they were less of a "fit" than previously. In addition, the idea of rational communication appeared increasingly naïve in the era of the Oxford idealists, to say nothing of Freud, Le Bon, and Bergson. Finally, the increasing industrialization and commodification of the press made the educational ideal less convincing as an explanation of what actually happened when newspapers were bought and sold. What would become of the educational ideal in this changed environment?

Notes

1. See the essays in Wiener, ed., *Papers for the Millions*.
2. Curran, "Press History," 9. More recently, Jean Chalaby has presented the 1855 stamp tax repeal as the beginning of a specifically journalistic field of discourse. While Chalaby's emphasis differs from Curran's, they are not strictly incompatible. Chalaby, *Invention of Journalism*.
3. Ensor, *England 1870–1914*, 143.
4. Ibid., 144.
5. Ibid., 145.
6. In the case of Alan Lee's pathbreaking book, *Origins of the Popular Press in England*, the press had always been commercial to the core, but high ideals were able to coexist with commercialism until the 1880s. A similar picture of mid-Victorian sobriety steadily deteriorating over the next century prevails in Engel, *Tickle the Public*.
7. Lee, *Origins of the Popular Press in England*, 22.
8. Sommerville, *News Revolution in England*, 28–32, 44–45, 122–23. Other discussions of "liberty of the press" have not acknowledged this point. See Lee, *Origins of the Popular Press in England*, 23; Negrine, *Politics and the Mass Media in Britain*, 21–31. A suspicion of ephemeral literature can be seen among some cultural conservatives in the nineteenth century. See, for example, Jonathan Edmondson's exhortations to read "with *moderation.* Some devour whole libraries, and scarcely learn anything; and no wonder,—for one thing drives another out. We know some who are book-mad; and yet they scarcely ever read a

work with careful attention. This mania should be cured with all speed; for, like every other excess, it only impedes and weakens the active energies of the mind." See "Autobiography of the Rev. Jonathan Edmondson," 115 n.

9. See Lee, *Origins of the Popular Press in England*, 22–23. Dallas Liddle makes a distinction between a more orderly "mentoring" role of the press and the messier visions of the journalist as sportsman or salesman. While the idea of journalist as mentor closely corresponds to the educational ideal, I am not convinced that the other two metaphors constituted full-blown "theories of journalism." In the case of sportsmen, Liddle's examples can be interpreted not so much as discussions of fair play but of the danger that unfair advantages would distort the truth. In the case of salesmen, all of the examples narrowly concern critics and specialists, not political journalism. In any event, Liddle takes all three metaphors exclusively from contemporary debates about the merits of anonymous versus signed journalism. Liddle, "Salesmen, Sportsmen, Mentors."

10. Quoted in Briggs, *Victorian People*, 123–24.
11. Harrison, *Early Victorians*, 163.
12. Altick, *English Common Reader*, 141–42.
13. For the Victorian ideal of education, broadly defined, see the essays in Scott and Fletcher, eds., *Culture and Education in Victorian England*.
14. Kay, *Education of the Poor in England and Europe*, x.
15. Ibid., xi.
16. Ibid., xix.
17. Kay, *Social Condition and Education of the People in England*, 32–33.
18. Ibid., 215–16.
19. Johnson, "Educational Policy and Social Control in Early Victorian England."
20. Kay, *Education of the Poor in England and Europe*, xii.
21. Quoted in Johnson, "Educational Policy and Social Control in Early Victorian England," 201.
22. Altick, *English Common Reader*, 225.
23. Harrison, *Early Victorians*, 163.
24. Crawfurd, *Taxes on Knowledge*, 3.
25. National Political Union, *Taxes on Knowledge*, 4–5, 10.
26. *Newspaper Stamp and the Duty on Paper*, 8. For a discussion of Charles Knight's attempts to elevate working-class readers through *Penny Magazine* and other publications, see Anderson, *Printed Image and the Transformation of Popular Culture*.
27. See, for example, National Political Union, *Taxes on Knowledge*, 7.
28. Biagini, *Liberty, Retrenchment, and Reform*; Lee, *Origins of the Popular Press in England*, 25.
29. Matthew, "Rhetoric and Politics in Great Britian." See also Jones, *Powers of the Press*, 140–79, on the contrasting levels of enthusiasm with which the Liberal and Conservative parties greeted the emerging mass newspaper.
30. Trollope, *The Warden*, 80.
31. *The Times*, 14 May 1855, 8.
32. Taylor to Scott, 12 January 1901, *Manchester Guardian* Archives 130/153, John Rylands Library, University of Manchester.
33. Edwards, *Few Footprints*, 38.

34. Mill, *On Liberty*, 15–52. For a contemporary lecturer linking the liberal ideal of politics by public discussion (including through newspapers) to the Reform Bill of 1867, see Dale, *Politics of the Future*.

35. "Popular Literature," 192, 194–95. The author does not mention Mill by name.

36. Mill to Christie, 2 January 1871, in Mill, *Later Letters of John Stuart Mill*, 1793. Naturally, Mill saw securing finances as the chief obstacle to this plan of action.

37. Smiles, "What Are the People Doing to Educate Themselves?" 230; Gladstone, *Speeches on the Great Questions of the Day*, 26–27; Kinnear, "Anonymous Journalism," 324–25; Grant, *Newspaper Press*, vol. 2, 456, 458.

38. [Collins], "Unknown Public," 217–19.

39. Ibid., 219–22.

40. "Founders of Modern Liberalism," 503.

41. Ibid., 503–4.

42. *The Economist*, 30 September 1871, 1175–76.

43. Quoted in Houghton, *Victorian Frame of Mind*, 93.

44. Ibid., 96–106.

45. Brodrick, "What Are Liberal Principles?" 184.

46. Hall, "Penny Press," 178.

47. "Dangers of the Country," 201–2.

48. Warren, "Public Lectures," 170–71.

49. "Popular Literature," 181.

50. This account derives from Lee, *Origins of the Popular Press in England*, 42–49. See Trollope, *The Warden*, 118–20, for a satirical 1855 portrayal of the influence of *The Times* (as the fictitious *Jupiter*).

51. The Select Committee on Newspaper Stamps avoided discussing the question of revenue, "But, apart from fiscal considerations, they do not consider that news is of itself a desirable subject of taxation" (*Report from the Select Committee on Newspaper Stamps*, xii). See also Francis Place, James Watson, and C. Dobson Collet, "The Memorial of the Newspaper Stamp Abolition Committee," 13 November 1850, Inland Revenue 56/9, Public Records Office, London.

52. He delivered this speech on 28 April 1853. Cobden, *Speeches on Questions of Public Policy*, 292.

53. *Hansard's Parliamentary Debates*, 7 May 1855, cols. 189–90.

54. *Hansard's Parliamentary Debates*, 19 March 1855, col. 811.

55. *Hansard's Parliamentary Debates*, 26 March 1855, col. 1163.

56. *Report from the Select Committee on Newspaper Stamps*, x.

57. *Hansard's Parliamentary Debates*, 24 May 1855, col. 959.

58. *Hansard's Parliamentary Debates*, 26 March 1855, cols. 1117–18, 1120.

59. *The Economist*, 17 February 1855, 169.

60. *The Economist*, 27 January 1855, 83.

61. *The Economist*, 24 March 1855, 305–6.

62. *The Economist*, 28 April 1855, 448.

63. *Hansard's Parliamentary Debates*, 19 March 1855, col. 782.

64. See Liddle, "Salesmen, Sportsmen, Mentors"; Salmon, "'Simulacrum of Power.'"

65. This and the following paragraph are derived from Collini, *Public Moralists*, 39–42,

and Leahy, "Conditions of British Journalism," 5–47. For a statement of the low social status of journalists in the middle of the nineteenth century, see Aspinall, "Social Status of Journalists at the Beginning of the Nineteenth Century."

66. See, for example, "Lament of a Leader Writer," 663.

67. The term "point of view of the universe" is taken from Collini, *Public Moralists*, 57. Similarly, Seligman suggests that in the classical eighteenth- and early nineteenth-century notion of "civil society," "there was the progressive articulation of Reason as embodying universal principles valid for all people at all times." Seligman, *Idea of Civil Society*, 60.

68. This concept was not mere posturing. For a discussion of editorial unity on the late nineteenth-century *Manchester Guardian*, see Hampton, "Press, Patriotism, and Public Discussion," 181.

69. Escott, "John Delane and Modern Journalism," 531.

70. [Greg], "Newspaper Press," 487–89.

71. Oldcastle, *Journals and Journalism*, 71–72; Brodrick, *Memories and Impressions*, 131, 141.

72. Mill, *Autobiography*, 120.

73. Trollope, "On Anonymous Literature," 493–94.

74. *The Anarchist* (March 1885): 2.

75. *The Anarchist: Communist and Revolutionary*, 20 April 1886, 1. For the context in which this change occurred, see Bevir, "Rise of Ethical Anarchism in Britain."

76. "Public Opinion and Journalists," 163.

77. Kinnear, "Anonymous Journalism," 330–31.

78. Hopkins, "Anonymity," 522.

79. Ibid., 524.

80. Ibid., 513.

3. The Educational Ideal of the Press in the Era of the New Journalism, 1880–1914

The mid-Victorian educational ideal of the press came under material challenges in the era of the New Journalism. Alan Lee has thoroughly documented these pressures in what he calls his "broadly Marxist" account, and they contributed to what Habermas has termed the "structural transformation of the public sphere."[1] The object here is not to rehash these arguments but to suggest that we need to consider another dimension in our explanation of what became of the educational ideal. The waning of this ideal did not merely signal the triumph of a crass commercialism over idealism. Rather, another ideal asserted itself, one that for many seemed better suited to the "structure of feeling" of the 1880s and after: the press as a "representative" agency. In addition to strictly material pressures, the educational ideal faced various intellectual and other (nonmaterial) cultural pressures that contributed to its receding. Where the educational ideal persisted, it had to adapt to a changing cultural and intellectual climate.

The educational ideal of the press did not vanish quickly or quietly. Not only did its vestiges persist in formulaic, unexplained references, but there also existed a number of journalists and other commentators on the press who continued throughout this period to argue more substantially for the idea of the press as an educational agent. This chapter will first consider some of the more interesting of these arguments. It will conclude with an examination of a few of the challenges that helped to break the hold of this ideal of the press.

In Lee's account, the educational—or what he terms the "liberal"—ideal of the press predominated at midcentury and gradually became obsolete during the era of the New Journalism largely because the independent, principled owner of a mid-Victorian paper could not compete with the large-scale newspaper empires built by speculators like Lord Northcliffe.[2] This interpretation mirrors arguments from the period. Yet despite lamentations about the changing newspaper environment, the educational ideal persisted throughout the era of the New Journalism. It will become clear that those who held to this ideal comprised an eclectic group and that their ideal was adaptive rather than static; they were hardly the anachronistic bunch that tends to appear in Lee's account.

It is worth noting more generally that while the 1880s did not belong to the "age of improvement" captured in the title of Asa Briggs's classic textbook, and although the decade can be seen as a period of acute social tensions or even a crisis of modernity,[3] the optimistic discourses of improvement and education endured throughout this period in many contexts. Logie Barrow and Chris Waters have shown, for example, the extent to which preoccupations with education and rational recreation guided the leaders of the socialist movement. At the same time, many social "improvers," such as the Fabians, were frankly statist and elitist, looking to "experts" to marshall the resources of the state for the social betterment of the majority. Nevertheless, those who continued to hold that the press should educate readers and contribute to their self-improvement, not merely their social and economic betterment, should be seen in relation to the enduring attraction of an educational ideal more broadly to late Victorians and post-Victorians.[4]

Not only did those holding to an educational ideal of the press share the concerns of many of their contemporaries, they also adapted their ideals to changing conditions. One of the major changes in the journalism of the 1880s to which they had to adjust was its growing professionalization. Although this change had implications for working conditions, the significance of professionalization in the present context is that it entailed a growing commitment to impartially gathering the "facts." Critics of the New Journalism often pointed to its glorification of facts or "news" at the expense of "opinion." A writer in the *Westminster Review,* for example, complained that the "public does not want opinions and arguments, it wants facts, or, what is better, *facetioe.*"[5] Even W. T. Stead, not a critic but a pioneer and defender of the New Journalism, insisted that opinion still had its proper function.[6]

Despite such complaints and hesitations, the striking characteristic of the discourse on the press in the late nineteenth and early twentieth centuries was the growing emphasis on the desirability of presenting facts. This emphasis needs to be seen in the context of the rise of the social sciences and the claims of many journalists that their occupation constituted a profession; in this context, professional credibility derived in large part from a command of facts. At the same time, this emphasis drew on a long-standing association of facts with social reform.[7] I do not mean to suggest that a greater appreciation of facts or news was inherently uneducational. Rather, this development in journalism meant that the persistent holders of the educational ideal had to accommodate to new professional practices that had scarcely troubled those of an earlier generation.

The clash of opinions thus had to take a back seat to accurate reporting. Commentators on the press constantly emphasized the primary importance of news gathering. In his 1908 *History of English Journalism,* J. B. Williams asserted that "the desire to know the events of the day, to be told what distant friends are doing, and to hear of occurrences in far-off countries is an instinct implanted in human nature."[8] Accordingly, he presented his work as a study of "letters of news" or "intelligence," descriptors that served as the basis for the word "newsletter" and its successor, "newspaper."[9] Robert Blatchford, the editor of the socialist weekly *The Clarion,* emphasized the importance of precise figures. Writing to A. M. Thompson, he insisted, "Figures are sacred emblems. They are the skeleton of thought. Lack of precision in figures, lack of reverence for the exactitudes in estimates, are intellectual immoralities of the deadliest kind." He went on to suggest a shampoo and turpentine punishment for the person who botched estimates, who should afterwards be "soundly basted as to his posterior seat of intelligence with bunches of nettles."[10] The foreign correspondent Henri de Blowitz so emphasized accurate reporting that he thought journalism would be well served if a newspaper existed called *The Judge,* whose function was to point out to the public "every morning the errors of allusion—historical, political, geographical, or what not—committed in the other newspapers, and put them in the pillory. It would call attention as well to the wilful errors which are lies, the mistakes of ignorance, and even of expression."[11] This idea betrayed a naïve expectation that if only the truth were published, readers would gratefully disregard the errors, rather than allowing the distinction to become swamped by an increasingly media-saturated environment.

In 1905, Sir Alfred Harmsworth, the founding proprietor of the *Daily Mail* and the future proprietor of *The Times* (and the future Lord Northcliffe), gave as his ideal of the perfect newspaper "the quick, accurate presentation of the world's news in the form of a careful digest." As a newspaper reader, Harmsworth expected journalists, rather than offering opinions, to "ascertain for me that which is requisite I should know in order that I may be able to form a judgment on the ways of the world."[12] Similarly, John Davidson's poem "Fleet Street" does not emphasize opinion but rather the "miracle" of news gathering:

> Within your wholesome and convenient field
> The truest miracle is daily done.
> Never forget that men have tamed and taught
> The lightning; clad it in a livery known
> As news; and that without your constant aid
> Our modern, actual magic, black and white,
> Momentous mystery of telegraphy,
> Resounding press, accomplished intellects
> And pens expert would be impossible.[13]

With so many writers emphasizing news gathering and presentation of facts, it is not surprising that H. W. Massingham could write in 1892 that news had come to dwarf opinion in the London daily press.[14] The emphasis on facts over opinion, moreover, rendered newspapers the record of public life. As early as 1881, during the discussion in the House of Commons leading to the Newspaper Libel Act, a Mr. Hutchinson based his call for easing the legal plight of proprietors on the grounds that "[a] newspaper was the record and expression of what took place in public, of all political life, and of all municipal and social activity—in short it was the record of everything outside the domain of strictly domestic intercourse." According to the editor of the *Yorkshire Post*, J. S. R. Phillips, a newspaper provided subsequent generations with an ideal historical source. In the words of the Liberal journalist Sir Hugh Gilzean-Reid, "rightly conducted, it is a history and reflex of its time in daily or weekly chapters."[15]

Not that the emphasis on facts was unprecedented. In 1850, the editor of the *Daily News*, F. Knight Hunt, even while affirming the newspaper as a "great teacher, and an all-powerful instrument of modern civilization," also saw it as a "mental camera" that conveyed, "day by day, week by week, the experience of the whole world's doings for the amusement and guidance of each individual living man." As observers in the late nineteenth and early twentieth centuries repeatedly noted, however, midcentury journalists had been less committed to impartial news gathering. Writing in 1907, for example, S. T. Sheppard dated the "beginning of the rush to get news first and to be ahead of other papers" to the Franco-Prussian War.[16] In addition, earlier journalists lacked the means available to their later counterparts. Reuters was founded in 1851 and the Press Association in 1868; the Transatlantic telegraph cable was laid in 1866. Collectively, these developments facilitated the gathering and presentation of news.[17]

Such developments also forced editors and advocates of an educational ideal of the press to adapt to new conditions. As Aled Jones has pointed out, greater reliance on news agencies reduced editorial control over much of the content of newspapers.[18] Many aspects of the newspaper could thus become standardized. An 1897 article in *Chambers's Journal* praising the Press Association pointed out its efficiency: "One efficient report of a speech, for instance, would obviously serve for any number of papers, and in a great many cases, at least, one good descriptive account of any occurrence of interest would be as good as fifty." The author argued that this method of news gathering could serve all newspapers, regardless of their political ideals.[19] From the perspective of an educational ideal, however, this transition relegated the space available for education and influence, as previously conceived, largely to the leading articles and correspondence columns.

Nor was this development merely negative; those who still held out for an educational, rationally persuasive function for the press generally insisted on papers' duty to present the facts first. This emphasis can be seen in C. E. Montague's 1907 tribute to his *Manchester Guardian* colleague, and Matthew Arnold's nephew, W. T. Arnold. According to Montague, Arnold believed that the newspaper was "an instrument of civilisation." He rejected the prevailing representative model of the press as "attempts by journalists to 'govern the country,' as he put it—meaning, to formulate positive policies on their own responsibility and try to force them on Ministries." At the same time, he rejected the notion of "reflecting public opinion." In Montague's words, "there must be no uncritical assents, in politics, morals, or criticism, to fashionable second-bests, no vending to foolish people of expression for their foolish thoughts.... [H]e must say, not what his clients might like, but what he believes." Nevertheless, Montague insisted on subordinating advocacy to professional responsibility. He asserted that a journalist who "cares for his craft," although intent on promoting his preferred cause, would come to appreciate the "intrinsic value in other, ancillary things—modes or by-products of advocacy; to be fair, to keep to the point, to treat as a trust the use of words—more and more do these seem to him to be no mere means to win a case, but ends."[20]

George Binney Dibblee's 1913 book *The Newspaper* illustrates how far this emphasis on facts or news had penetrated even the educationalists by the end of this period. Dibblee, who became manager of the *Manchester Guardian* in 1892, attempted in 1905, on the death of the proprietor, John Edward Taylor, to purchase that paper. In the event, the editor, C. P. Scott, succeeded in becoming proprietor.[21] Following his failure to acquire the *Guardian,* Dibblee spent a few years as a fellow of All Soul's College, Oxford. Dibblee's account follows the pattern, increasingly common among educationalists in this period, of affirming the ideal negatively by arguing that contemporary developments tended to corrupt the ideal. Dibblee saw the last half of the nineteenth century as the "Augustan age of the press," a "golden period" in which the penny press "really raised British journalism to a height of dignity and power, which has never been equalled and most probably never will be again." According to Dibblee, however, this golden age had vanished largely because, following the Boer War, virtually all of the quality papers presented the views only of the Conservative party. Unlike the interpretation many of his contemporaries would have given to such a scenario, Dibblee did not argue primarily that the Liberals' views or interests were not represented but that the presentation of only "one aspect of society" led to a distortion of truth. By contrast, during the golden age, "impartiality was more strictly maintained in our press as a whole by the adequate representation of both sides."[22] Dibblee's use of the word "representation" should not confuse the issue; in the representative theory of the press, the two sides tended to equal Right and Wrong, "corruption" and "the people." For Dibblee, the two sides comprised legitimately opposing positions whose struggle against each other, if permitted, would produce the truth.

Yet Dibblee did not merely reproduce a mid-Victorian commitment to conveying opinions. He argued that newspapers had three major functions: providing news, serving as an organ of opinion, and serving as the "great introducer of business from one trader to another." Of these functions, Dibblee argued that "by far the most important task" was the presentation of "all the news." He did not, however, regard facts or news merely as the "raw material" of opinion.[23] Rather, almost uniquely among those in this period who theorized about the press, Dibblee questioned the distinction between fact and opinion:

> As far as the public is concerned, there is very little distinction made between the function of newspapers as newsgatherers and their duties as purveyors of opinion. This arises from a very simple case. While news is nominally an impersonal thing, as a matter of practice it is far from being so. In obtaining it the faculty of selection is required in the highest degree by the newsgatherer or "story-writer." Selection again is strenuously required in determining the competition between one item of news and another. Finally the presentation of news in words and paragraphs leaves a wide opening for individual preferences and inclinations. Thus it comes about, naturally enough, that the same series of habits, which govern the conduct of avowed opinion in a newspaper, habits summed up briefly in the term, the policy of the paper, express themselves, not so consciously but even more effectively, in its news columns.[24]

This view of news implies a distinct understanding of communication, and we will return to Dibblee below. At this point, however, it is worth remembering that in a period of large-scale reliance on news agencies, the selection and presentation of facts did not always emanate from the same mind that directed the "policy of the paper." Additionally, Dibblee noted a categorical difference in the attention that different types of newspapers devoted to facts and opinion. The "more popular and cheaper papers" emphasized "giving the largest number of items of ordinary news, which it is their aim to transform as far as possible into matters of exceptional interest." By contrast, he wrote, the "old-established organs of social and political weight are content to state their news impartially, if not boldly, and rely on their powers of interesting the reader by able discussions on political, artistic or literary topics."[25] As in much criticism of the New Journalism, Dibblee noted the emergence of news as the driving concern of the popular press; even the quality press, however, was constrained (or altered) in its presentation of opinions by the emerging cult of facts and "impartiality."

Dibblee was unusual among commentators on the press during this period in noting the tenuous line between news and opinion. For most educationalists, the two departments stood autonomously in an uneasy relation to each other. Francis Hirst, editor of *The Economist,* offered a typical solution: news and opinion must be separate, with opinion relegated to the leading articles and in no way supported by the presentation of the news. This represented a danger to the educational ideal, however, for the leading articles, to which discussion of opinion was relegated, were dwarfed by the news content. In an era of sensationalistic divorce and murder stories, this balance between news and opinion was fatal, for, as the radical editor H. W. Massingham pointed out in 1892, the newspapers "feed on page three the appetites that breed the sins deplored upon its other side." Moreover, as Fox Bourne had noted in 1887, few people any longer read the leaders.[26]

The educational ideal was therefore forced to come to terms with the conditions of the New Journalism, in which facts or news took precedence over opinion. Nevertheless, the ideal persisted, maintaining its hold particularly among the "forward" section of the Liberal party and among the leaders of the socialist movement, two groups that remained close to each other on an ideological continuum between the Liberal and Labour parties.[27] The educational ideal continued to resurface on occasion deep into the twentieth century, for example in the views of Kingsley Martin, the editor of the *New Statesman,* and John Reith, the director of the British Broadcasting Corporation (BBC). The late nineteenth century, however, marked the onset of the relative decline of this ideal. The remainder of this chapter will consider the major challenges that helped to render it untenable and paved the way for the widespread acceptance of a representative ideal or theory.

A major factor in undermining the educational ideal was, not surprisingly, the commercialization of the press. Yet it is important to understand the ways in which contemporaries made sense of this new media phenomenon. For proponents of the representative ideal, commercialization could take on a positive guise. For now, however, we will consider contemporary discussions of the commercial threat to the educational or liberal ideal of the press.

In one way or the other, laments of commercialization usually took on a class dimension. On the one hand, commercialization could be seen to liberate the working-class consumer, who in a less commercial scenario would not receive adequate representation. On the other hand, it could appear as the driving force behind the production of "feather-brained" journalism that subverted the educational or liberal ideal by concentrating ownership in the hands of fewer and fewer capitalist proprietors, whose commercial interests led them to give the hopeless "quarter-educated" members of the working class what they wanted.[28]

Few disputed that the willingness of proprietors to tap into new, generally working-class markets was undermining the rational or educational content of newspapers. That is, the hopes of optimists like Wilkie Collins that the "unknown public" could be elevated gave way to jeremiads that this new readership had debased the press. In 1893 Oliver Fry defended the paragraph but lambasted the "snippet," such as those found in *Tit-Bits*, "for the promotion of which, I suppose, the school board mainly is responsible." His defense of the paragraph included pointing out that its origins were respectable, deriving not from cheap journalism but from "Society Journalism" in the pages of the *Owl*, under Algernon Borthwick's guidance.[29] The Liberal H. R. Fox Bourne, despite arguing in his two-volume *History* that "enlightened public opinion" had established a "censorship" after 1855 that staved off the worst sensationalistic excesses, also pointed out that complaints about the content of contemporary journalism failed to take into account that "things are only as they are because so many newspaper readers require journalism of the obnoxious sort."[30] This argument was echoed constantly by writers of many ideological stripes. J. S. R. Phillips noted in 1916 that the "enormous" circulations of his day "result, largely, from an endeavour to cater for classes whose education has been restricted to the elementary school, or who, of a more advanced schooling, always run with the crowd—possibly a tendency natural to democratic times."[31] In a 1906 antiwar polemic, Walter Walsh blamed the press's "moral and, at times, intellectual poverty" on the fact that "its members are chosen less for their attachment to principles, or their proved ability to become teachers in the realms of art and literature, philosophy and science, religion and politics, than for their knack of hitting

| 122 | PUNCH, OR THE LONDON CHARIVARI. | [MARCH 18, 1882 |

THE TURF.

Elderly Clergyman (who was passing). "I'M VERY GLAD, CABMAN, TO SEE YOU IMPROVING YOUR MIND BY READING DURING YOUR SPARE TIME."
Cabby (with a Sporting Paper). "IMPROVIN' MY MIND! I DUNNO. I BACKED THIS 'ERE 'OSS ALL THROUGH LAST SEASON, AND HE NEVER LANDED ME ONCE!—AND I'VE FOLLERED 'IM UP, AND NOW HE'S DROPPED ME ANOTHER DOLLAR ON THE 'GRAND INT'NA-TIONAL 'URDLE!'" *(Gloomily.)* "IF YER CALL THAT IMP——" [*The Parson retires!*

In the 1880s, the idea of the press as an educational agent did not always reflect newspapers' actual content. From *Punch*, 18 March 1882.

the popular taste in style and opinion."[32] Massingham pointed out that "the newspapers only give the public what they ask for and insist on having."[33]

This emergence of working-class readers and a commercialized press to serve them was often blamed on the 1870 Education Act, which had authorized the election of local school boards that were empowered to levy taxes, build schools, and hire teachers whenever the number of private schools was insufficient. Edward Dicey, a former leader writer on the *Daily Telegraph* and editor of *The Observer*, in 1905 linked the "changes in the character and tastes of the newspaper reader" to the 1870 act.[34] A writer in the *Westminster Review*, complaining of the declining importance of leader writing, blamed the school board for producing readers unable to follow more complex writing: "The mental condition of the masses is such that they cannot sustain any process of thought which extends beyond a short paragraph, and for this large, indeed the largest, class of readers, long leaders are of no avail."[35] The autodidact and former Chartist W. E. Adams provided a typical assessment of the link between 1870 and the debasement of the popular press:

> When few people could read, the matter provided was mostly of an elevating character—rarely of a debasing character: for the few in all ages have invariably been more refined than the many. But since our children have been taught to read without being taught to think, and since everybody can read, whether able to think or not, the general quality of popular reading has distinctly deteriorated. Newspapers find it necessary to play to the groundlings and the gallery, pandering to the lowest tastes because the lowest tastes pervade the biggest multitudes. And so vulgar sensationalism has taken the place of sober earnestness. Instead of being the instructors of the people, many of our newspapers have become mere ministers to the passions of the people.[36]

Other contemporaries, of course, would interpret "ministers to the passions" differently, as representing the people.

The anonymous writer of *Bohemian Days in Fleet Street*, published in 1913, echoed the link between 1870 and a commercialized press. First, in language friendly to the representative ideal although without any pretense to political importance, the author asserted that "if there be anything at all in the law of supply and demand, we are bound to infer that the proprietors of newspapers must be supplying that which the public demands. Public taste is not created or directed by newspapers. The clever editor is he who shrewdly anticipates the direction of the public taste, and caters for it. 'Find out what the public wants, and give it to 'em!' was the advice given me once by the managing director of a syndicate of newspapers in the North of England. And it was sound advice."[37] The author then immediately linked this condition of publication and the birth of the half-penny daily press to the act of 1870: "The new conditions under which the newspaper exists, and the new methods introduced by its conductors, were foreordained, though not foreseen, when Mr. Forster's Education Bill became law, and the School Board education was offered to the youth of merry England. . . . The generations that developed under Forster's Act demanded newspapers of their own, but they were not prepared to pay a penny for them."[38]

A. Kinnear, in an article replete with language of commercialism, noted the effects of changing reading audiences in cheapening public discourse. Specifically, he blamed the new readers for the demise of the verbatim report of parliamentary proceedings. Referring to journalism as a "Stock Exchange," he insisted that "the demand of the public regulates the supply in this as in any other form of merchandise." He continued, "The public now demand lucidity, which is interpreted as brevity. The papers wisely supply what their readers prefer."[39] At the same time, however, he tacitly acknowledged that such commercialism was not new but had merely taken on a new and insidious form with the expansion of the reading nation. As a result, the character of circulation wars had altered importantly:

> For years it was the proud "boast" of the great London dailies in competition to give the longest, which meant the fullest reports of the debates in Parliament. They maintained large staffs for the purpose. It was also a triumph of beauty to set the report in close type, so that the delighted reader looked upon a broad page of dead black lead, broken only by the spaces required for the names of the successive speakers. That is now all changed. Where we sat down to six or seven columns of political rhetoric, we now sit down to two, and the story, moreover, is broken into paragraphs, headlines, and notes of exclamation. John Bull's stern solidity was then marked in his Parliamentary reports; apparently his mood now is for lightness, vivacity, and variety.[40]

Kinnear concluded that "[r]eaders of the business class or of the lozenge intelligence prefer to take their legislation and politics first in the homeopathic doses of a ten line summary."[41] The supposedly poor reading behavior of these new readers, it seemed to John Garrett Leigh in 1904, "almost makes us wish that the masses could not read."[42]

Such recognition of the intellectual limitations of the new readership did not only occur in critical contexts. The tensions between the educational ideal and the intellectual limitations of the "unknown public" came into particularly strong focus during a 1911 governmental inquiry into prisoners' reading material. Launched by Winston Churchill in response to W. T. Stead's displeasure that a chaplain who was a "veritable child of Satan" would not allow prisoners of Dartmoor to read the *Review of Reviews,* this inquiry invoked the same links between criminal behavior and reading that Joseph Kay had pointed to more than half a century earlier. The final report expressed concern over the popularity of "bound magazines": "But to a large extent we fear the preference for the bound magazine arises from a desultory habit of mind which finds difficulty in keeping attention sustained on a single story of any length. Irrespective of the matter of the bound magazine, the manner in which it is often read is not likely to promote any sort of intellectual progress." The report refrained from recommending their banning but cautioned that some articles and illustrations were particularly unsuitable either because of their "undesirable moral tone" or because they presented crime in an attractive light. Recognizing that there was more than one kind of education, the report noted that "there have even been articles which were actual guides to the commission of crime, containing minute descriptions of the apparatus necessary for coining or burglary."[43]

Political reviews were more promising from an educational standpoint, but there were additional practical concerns: "Were weekly or monthly periodicals to be supplied in the shape of current numbers, every inmate of a prison would have an equally good claim to have the current number, and that claim would not fail to make itself heard." Although we may smile at the idea of a prison riot breaking out over insufficient provision of the *Fortnightly Review*, the report rightly concluded that supplying all of the inmates a personal subscription would be financially prohibitive.[44]

This report does not fit neatly into the broader debate on the function of the press in the era of the New Journalism. Although most prisoners belonged to the working classes and in the minds of many elite observers would exist on a continuum with the noncriminal working classes, they were a distinct population that was hardly representative of the working classes. In addition, the report did not frame this discussion of reading materials in the context of a "new" readership. The report belongs to the broader debate, however, because it reflects prevailing assumptions about the possibilities of elevating readers. In addition, it indirectly echoes Joseph Kay's optimism about the positive influence of the right sort of reading material: Kay expected education to prevent workers from becoming criminals, and the authors of this report clearly believed that the proper reading materials could have a rehabilitating effect.

To return to Stead's original concern, how did newspapers fit into this picture? Immediately after discussing the impracticality of providing inmates with new copies of political journals, the report argued against trying to provide daily newspapers, concluding that "for the mass of prisoners, the daily newspaper is neither possible nor desirable."[45] The reason for the impossibility of supplying daily newspapers seems clear by analogy with political journals, but why were they undesirable? The reason is never stated, but we can posit that the authors thought of the newspapers in similar terms to magazines; after all, the critique of the New Journalism included the importing of "features" and a supposedly episodic quality from magazines.

Other examples more directly linked contemporary newspapers' inadequacies to the new readership. T. P. O'Connor, the founder of *The Star*, noted that the new public read newspapers in a hurry; therefore, he urged a greater clarity of style: "to get your ideas through the hurried eyes into the whirling brains that are employed in the reading of a newspaper there must be no mistake about your meaning: to use a somewhat familiar phrase, you must strike your reader right between the eyes."[46] Henry Leach wrote enthusiastically of "great journalists" who had "their fingers on the public pulse. They count the beats, and they provide in the matter of articles and news all that is just wanted at the moment."[47] Even a serious "movement" paper like *The*

Clarion could not avoid the pressures of the public demand for less serious fare. During the course of the 1890s, editor Robert Blatchford's *Clarion* letterhead underwent a change, from "Edited by 'Nunquam.' An Illustrated Weekly Journal of Literature, Politics, Fiction, Philosophy, Poetry, Theatricals, Criticisms, &c." to "An Illustrated Weekly Magazine of Progressive Literature, Whimsical Fiction, Poetry, Theatricals, Cycling, Cricket, and Everything Else."[48]

An exchange in the conservative *National Review* in 1893 centered on the need to take the new public's demands into account. Fitzroy Gardner, encouraging the Conservative party to make better use of the press to sell its message, compared journalism to any other business, pointing out the necessity of giving the public what it wanted.[49] In replying, Henry Cust actually advocated what we might call the "dumbing down" of newspaper content to appeal to the "new public," "a public that can be no more expected to work through the solid, periodic structure of a column of *The Times* than to digest the philosophy of Hegel." According to Cust, for Tory editors to imitate *The Star* would "not be vulgarizing the press" but would simply mean "acquiescing in the present conditions of existence, and pursuing a practical end by practical means."[50]

Although such an adoption of the style of the New Journalism threatened the type of communication required by the educational or liberal ideal, writers like Cust at least did not despair of the compatibility of an educational use of the press and the sort of journalism demanded by the new public. Since Conservatives did not embrace the educational ideal as enthusiastically as Liberals did, it is reasonable to suspect the discussants in the Tory *National Review* of mere lip service to an ideal in which they did not genuinely believe in order to put the best face on a rather naked desire to use the press for propagandistic purposes.[51] However, while the new public could be accommodated, the new type of proprietors struck many as a threat to the educational ideal.

J. A. Hobson's *Psychology of Jingoism* provides an apt illustration of this liberal wariness of the New Journalism and its proprietors. Most significantly, in Hobson's argument, the new proprietors at the end of the nineteenth century took advantage of the inadequacies of the new readers produced by the 1870 Education Act. Written against the background of the Boer War and the predominance of the "Jingo press," Hobson bemoaned the unanimity of the press, pulpits, and platforms, linking it with the ownership of much of the press by financial capitalist interests with strong ties to the South African mining interests.[52] Noting the dominance of a single voice in the British press, which, moreover, appealed to subrational mental processes, Hobson concluded that "for practical purposes there no longer exists a free press in England, affording full security for adequate discussion of the vital issues of politics."[53] Francis Hirst concurred. Citing Hobson as his source, he claimed that the "press monopoly" that helped to bring about war in 1899 was "created by extraneous financial influences"—in other words, that the Fourth Estate had been bought and had "produce[d] the popular feeling requisite to the designs of Mr. Rhodes, Mr. Chamberlain, and Sir Alfred Milner."[54] Arguing that the British press could now be purchased to serve the proprietors' narrow interests, Hirst stated, "By the quiet purchase of half a dozen honest papers with a large circulation, and by a gentle, gradual reversal of their policy, something that looks remarkably like public opinion can be fabricated. When that is done, a free people cannot be said to enjoy freedom of the press."[55]

The deliberate political manipulation of the press by various external commercial interests did not, however, strike Liberals as the greatest evidence of a commercial threat to an educational press. If this were the greatest concern, it could be combated through the admittedly costly yet simple expedient of purchasing or founding "liberal" newspapers to offer the other side of the various issues. If the greatest complaint was the undue representation of various illiberal interests, such as the Rand miners, then this challenge could be aptly incorporated within the educational tradition by supplying opposing viewpoints elsewhere in the press so that the "best" ideas could win the ascendancy of a rational, "liberal" public. Indeed, the preface to the first edition of Hobson's *Imperialism: A Study* reaffirmed this tradition by openly warning its readers that the book would provide only one side of the issue; even in attacking the imperialists Hobson recognized that an alternative position existed that other writers could articulate.[56] This possibility was undermined, however, according to various critics of the press, by the treating of newspapers themselves as mere commodities with which to maximize profits. This commercialization of newspapers' production, by offering sensationalistic copy in order to attract the new public of the New Journalism, threatened to undermine the "reading and reflective habits of their customers."[57]

No one attracted the ire of educationalists more than Alfred Harmsworth, later Lord Northcliffe. Founding the *Daily Mail* in 1896 as a newspaper for busy men, or "written by office boys for office boys," as the Conservative Prime Minister Lord Salisbury derisively commented,[58] Harmsworth became the symbol of the new generation of proprietors, to whom all notions of public service or political commitment took a back seat to the goal of circulation. Walter George Bell, a longtime staffer on the *Daily Telegraph,* noted that the journalistic practices introduced by the *Daily Mail* and imitated by others acted "to the unquestionable advantage of the hurried reader, and to the despair of those who have looked upon the newspaper as a means of forming and directing public opinion."[59] Many critics, most notably A. G. Gardiner, thought Northcliffe's politics inconstant, changing with the whims of readers; rather than leading public opinion with a firm direction, he slavishly followed it in pursuit of his commercial interest.[60]

The "new proprietors" did not simply allow their pursuit of sales to affect the content of the newspapers. Under pressure to raise circulation to attract advertisers, newspapers began to adopt sales techniques that some saw as undermining the serious tone of journalism, such as promoting contests or offering insurance. Northcliffe, for example, sponsored a one pound per week for life competition, which later was ruled illegal. Keir Hardie's *Labour Leader* somewhat unfortunately sponsored a contest during the Boer War whose second prize was a holiday in South Africa. Edward Dicey, the longtime editor of *The Observer*, gave his "indiscriminating disapproval" to this practice, asserting its inconsistency with claims that the "main object of cheap journalism is to elevate the moral tone of the masses and to promote the spread of sound political views."[61]

A final aspect of the commercialization of the press that observers saw as a threat to the mid-Victorian style of journalism was the speed of production. We have already seen that efforts to cater to readers who were "busy" or "in a hurry" justified the use of headlines and shorter paragraphs in place of longer columns. Similarly, providing this public with the earliest news required speedy production that threatened accuracy. Edward Dicey saw as an "almost invariable rule that the papers read must be in the hands of their ordinary readers by breakfast time."[62]

This condition threatened the accuracy of news, a threat that undermined an educational ideal whose exponents increasingly insisted that facts had to form the foundation of any opinion. As John Pendleton wrote, "Newspaper competition these days is very keen, and in some instances there is barely time to procure the news, much less carefully verify it." Alfred Baker, in a book that otherwise sang the praises of contemporary journalism, acknowledged, "Crude ideas, resting on a very slender foundation, are too often presented to the public where the writer has to supply daily a certain quantity of comment on the political, social, or intellectual problems of the hour." Such recognition need not imply criticism of journalists' laxity but could simply constitute a purportedly factual observation. In advocating greater protection of journalists against reckless libel suits, Fisher and Strahan, authors of a popular guide to press law, glibly asserted, "The verification of the news that pours into the office from all quarters of the globe in the small hours of the morning is of course impossible." Emphasizing the speed at which journalism had to be conducted, they contrasted it with the "abundant leisure" during which "a certain class of discreditable hangers-on of the legal profession" looked for these "inevitable slips" so that they could pursue damages.[63] J. B. Atkins, the onetime foreign correspondent for the *Manchester Guardian*, similarly blamed the pressure for sales for the inaccuracy of war news. This pressure derived in part from attempts to give as news what the journalist thought readers wanted to believe, and in part it derived from exaggeration bred by attempts to make descriptions more dramatic. In large part, however, it followed from the desire to present a scoop, a journalistic desire founded upon readers' increased expectation of seeing news, including faraway war news, instantly "at his breakfast-table." Atkins elaborated: "in order to be ahead of his fellows with important news the correspondent is often willing to risk accuracy. He sends off a description of something which he has seen only through another's eyes, knowing that if his news arrive early and turn out to be substantially true he will win more praise than he would ever earn reprobation if the news should turn out to be false. 'Substantial truth' is a new standard of sufficiency in British journalism, and it deserves to be discouraged."[64]

No single event did more to illustrate the tensions between accuracy and the imperative to secure a "scoop" than the Pigott incident. *The Times* ran a series of articles in 1887 on "Parnellism and Crime," discrediting the Irish nationalist leader Charles Stuart Parnell by implicating him in the Phoenix Park murders. During the subsequent parliamentary investigation, however, it emerged that the documents on which the story was based were forgeries by Richard Pigott, an Irish nationalist who had spent time in prison in the early 1870s for publishing seditious literature and contempt of court. Although the revelation that *The Times* had been taken in caused a minor journalistic scandal, perhaps exacerbated by Pigott's flight and suicide in Spain, what is striking is how quickly the paper was forgiven. Rather than producing a crisis of journalistic epistemology, this episode became merely a fleeting episode with which opponents could embarrass *The Times* and subsequently a case study by worldly wise journalists demonstrating the difficulty of maintaining accuracy under modern conditions of journalism.[65]

The speed-driven epistemology of commercialism touched leading articles and illustrated journalism as well. A pseudonymous "Leader Writer" complained in the *Westminster Review* in 1899 that leader writers regularly saw that telegrams on which they had based the previous night's leader had been "emphatically contradicted" by the next day. For example, a leader writer might be forced to recognize that "Li Hung Chang has not been beheaded, as was stated yesterday evening 'on the best authority'; he is still, until the next wire at least, a factor in the situation."[66] This writer complained, however, not of having to print an inaccurate leading article but of constantly

Any illusion of *The Times*'s infallibility disappeared with the Pigott forgery. *Punch* is delighted. From *Punch*, 9 March 1889.

having to incur the wrath of the printers by attempting to change the article at the last possible moment. One illustrator, Harvey Thomas, complained that contributors of photographs tended to send in "instantaneous photographs two days late. They spend the interval in developing them carefully." His colleague at the *Daily Graphic,* William Thomas, added, "The most blurred photograph, the roughest sketch, in time . . . is naturally far more useful than an elaborate representation of an event when the forgetful public has ceased to be interested in it."[67] Elsewhere, advocates of illustrated journalism and particularly the newly emerging photojournalism heralded the possibilities this development opened up for improving the presentation of facts in place of opinions. Yet as with printed facts, so with pictures: a distorted or "blurred" fact was preferable to a late one, however accurate.

Many observers thus perceived that the New Journalism, and particularly its commercial basis, produced what amounted to a new epistemology. This epistemology, which might be called an epistemology of speed and sensationalism, contrasted with a mid-Victorian epistemology founded upon deliberation and discussion. In the period after 1880, concerns for instantaneous news and lively presentation often superseded previous concerns for depth and accuracy.[68]

In many cases, late Victorians making many of the observations noted above attributed these new developments to the influence of American methods. As we will see, however, these perceived imports often invited imitation rather than revulsion. To Victorians, the idea of America conjured ambivalent sentiments. For many Europeans, America represented a "privileged site where Europe's future, for better or worse, [was] constantly being previewed." Among those perceived American traits that could prove contentious for British observers were populism, crude informality, commerce, and "anticulture."[69] These contests over an imagined America were played out on occasion in discussions of the American press and its British imitators, in which, for example, American importations could be seen as democratizing or as subversive of the distinction between the public and private spheres.

Attacks on the commercialization of the British press often cited the American example as the dangerous destination to which Britain was headed.[70] Time and again, commentators on the press made a distinction between borrowing from American methods and a blind imitation of all the worst qualities of American journalism. For example, Michael MacDonagh asserted in 1900 that the newspaper interview was an "American importation" introduced in Britain by W. T. Stead and the *Pall Mall Gazette* in the 1880s. Stead had "proved that interviewing, conducted with good taste and good sense, could be made a most useful, instructive, and attractive feature of a newspaper, and it as quickly sprang into popular favour here as in the United States." But MacDonagh contrasted Stead's judicious use of the interview with that in the United States, where it had developed an "objectionable, an evil, side." To the American practice "was due such outrages on good taste and decency as the inexcusable invasion of the privacy of the home life of distinguished personages; the exposure of the skeletons of many eminent families; the raking up of the long-forgotten youthful indiscretions of public men; the savage caricaturing of their personal appearances and manners; the wilful invention of scandalous or ridiculous stories, or the imputation of unpopular views, in order to discredit a political opponent."[71]

Writing in the conservative *National Review,* Frank Fox echoed this concern about the American invasion of privacy. Apparently defending American "yellow journalism," Fox insisted that while it might offend against good taste regularly, it did not offend against either "decency or morality." The American press did not take the trouble to verify the accuracy of its news, "reckoning that what is wrong may always be corrected the next day—or not corrected, as convenience may serve." Far from being wrong, however, Fox asserted that the American practice was simply unusual to British and Australian observers—but "then it has to serve an unusual population." Fox admitted that the "human interest" story tended, in American yellow journals, to "degenerate" into "'keyhole journalism'—into grossly offensive spyings on domestic privacy."[72]

Along with their emphasis on the personal or private, American papers sold by pitching their wares to the "largest and least cultured public."[73] In part, they attracted this audience by providing them with big, grotesque headlines. Frank Fox insisted that "there is no moral wrong in putting red-ink headlines on your big news if your public likes things that way," but others were not so sure. Edward Delille, noting the American belief that the biggest was always the best, questioned America's level of civilization: "A fondness for crude pictorial presentments is understood to be one of the marks of an undeveloped civilisation. Are the Americans of the *fin de siècle* sinking to the level of the Bogesmen or Maoris?"[74]

It has already been noted that critics of the New Journalism pointed to its obsession with news or facts. Delille and George Binney Dibblee both observed that the American press emphasized news gathering to an extent unmatched in Britain, but to the detriment of editorials or "comment."[75] Of the *New York Herald,* one of the papers that he considered a "type" of American newspapers, Delille wrote that "as a sensational newsmonger it was unrivalled. It would pay any price for 'news': if true, so much the better; if not true, then at least plausible and startling." Again, the cause for alarm was that this sort of degenerate journalism might spread to Europe, particularly England. Delille warned that its "example is not only bad, but contagious," and noted that in recent years European papers had followed their example.[76] R. A. Scott-James, the author of one of the most important books on the press in the prewar period, lamented that the American press had become the model for the British half-penny press.[77] At one point or another, there were few perceived negative developments in British journalism that could not be traced to the pernicious American influence.

By 1914, the educational ideal had receded to a considerable extent; even where it persisted, it underwent important transformations that arguably rendered it different in kind from the midcentury ideal. Thus far we have considered the effect on the educational ideal of an increased emphasis on gathering news or facts and the effect of the perception of greater commercialization of the press. The educational ideal faced perhaps its greatest challenge, however, in the waning of the belief in rational communication or persuasion. Unlike commercialization or the development of professional news-gathering journalism, a loss of belief in the rational could not be readily accommodated within an ideal that actually presupposed rationality. If an advocate of the power of the press emphasized the subrational or extrarational possibilities for communication, he or she was already calling for something qualitatively different from the ideal outlined thus far.

Again, a note of caution is in order. In suggesting these transformations in theories of the press it is important not to overstate the novelty of the developments of the late nineteenth century or to suggest too sharp a discontinuity with what had gone before. Aled Jones has shown that throughout the Victorian era, much discussion of the possibility of press influence focused on phrenology, hypnotism, and other elements of psychology.[78] The articulation of an educational ideal was in part a rhetorical tactic for staving off fears created by this awareness of the extrarational uses of the press. As Jones has argued, defenders of the press's role asserted that the power of the press was increasing as the information it provided grew ever more comprehensive and, by contrast, that its power also diminished as newspapers "nurtured the analytical skills of the readers that enabled them to make their own sense of the fragmented world portrayed in the news-sheets." As Jones points out, "This delicately balanced argument allowed newspapers to claim that their power was being prodigiously increased, as they became essential instruments for the conduct of modern life, but that this augmentation need not cause alarm since the increase was taking place under conditions that effectively prevented them from arbitrarily exercising that power by exerting a dominant influence over society."[79]

Jones concludes that by the late-Victorian period, observers and critics had largely rejected the view of readers as "helpless victims" and had come to believe in the "relative autonomy of the reader, who was capable of remaining critical of the new medium while engaging with it."[80] My argument parts from Jones's in suggesting that at least at the level of rhetoric, the "relative autonomy" of the reader, as early as the midcentury, was more pronounced and positive. It did not simply entail a rejection of the image of readers as victims but a positive articulation of the ideal of rational public discussion. By the end of the century, by contrast, this autonomy was coming under challenge, as fewer observers and thinkers believed in the possibility of the rational communication of ideas.

This late Victorian pessimism about rational communication has roots in the midcentury writing of John Stuart Mill, who, influenced by Alexis de Tocqueville, was an early critic of the potential tyranny of a mass public. In *On Liberty* Mill provided one of the most powerful justifications for the educational influence of rational public discussion, yet in the same work he revealed a pessimism concerning the proclivity of the masses for the type of intellectual rigor demanded by this ideal of discussion. As Elizabeth Rapaport has stated, although Mill "hoped with all his progressive heart that education and cultural improvement would be made available speedily to all, he feared the ignorance, the intolerance, and the leveling instinct of the common people."[81] Mill complained of "the mass," the "collective mediocrity," that "*their thinking is done for them* by men much like themselves, addressing them or speaking in their name, on the spur of the moment, through the newspapers."[82] Here we see a significant gap between the powerful logic of his earlier defense of the virtues of free discussion and his understanding of how people actually employed the institutions available for free discussion.

In positioning himself in *The Subjection of Women,* Mill employed a shrewd argumentative tactic in asserting that his opponents' opinions were based on feeling rather than reason and that his task as persuader was thus all the more formidable. In doing so, he offered a sweeping depiction of the intellectual temper of his day: "It is one of the characteristic prejudices of the reaction of the nineteenth century against the eighteenth, to accord to the unreasoning elements in human nature the infallibility which the eighteenth century is supposed to have ascribed to the reasoning elements. For the apotheosis of Reason we have substituted that of Instinct; and we call everything instinct which we find in ourselves and for which we cannot trace any rational foundation."[83]

At the same time that this quotation portrays an awareness of the legitimization of the nonrational, however, it also significantly reaffirms the validity of Mill's characteristic reliance on argument or discussion. Like much of the literature considered here, this piece is self-consciously polemical in purpose, and Mill showed an awareness in 1869 of the powerful resonance of the dichotomy between reason and nonreason and the attraction that the former would have for his readers.

As the century progressed, such a characterization and understanding of the formation of opinions became increasingly the rule. These understandings were not necessarily linked to ideas of the irrational but at least tended to exclude the notion of rational communication between autonomous, rational individuals. In the final decades of the century, social theorists increasingly emphasized individuals' position as "constituent parts of a wider social whole." As Jose Harris writes, "family life, education, industrial relations, private morals, and the distribution of wealth were all increasingly seen not as independent variables but as part and parcel of overall social structure." Even theology was not exempt from a shift toward collectivism, with a communitarian soteriology receiving increased prominence.[84] The collective emphasis was especially prominent in the writings of the Oxford-based idealists, such as T. H. Green and F. H. Bradley. Bradley, for example, insisted that the "individual" was an abstraction, or a "delusion of theory." In his Hegelian language, "In the realized idea which, superior to me and yet here and now in and by me, affirms itself in a continuous process, we have found the end, we have found self-realization, duty, happiness in one—yes, we have found ourselves when we have found our station and its duties, our function as an organ in the social organism."[85] Similarly, Green insisted that even the sacred cow of individual property ownership could be justified only by its contribution to the good of society.[86]

For many, the formation of opinion similarly belonged to the domain of the "organic," reflecting social and historical factors more than individual persuasion by rational argument. Thus Bradley saw "inherited habits" and early childhood influences as decisive. "Who can resist it?" he asked. "Nay, who but a 'thinker' could wish to have resisted it?"[87] Similarly, A. V. Dicey, the jurist, insisted first of all on the gradual and communitarian nature of changes of opinion, comparing them to the "gradual rising of the tide." He asserted that "an alteration in the condition of opinion more often than not, begins at the very time when the predominant beliefs of a particular age seem to exert their utmost power. The height of the tide immediately precedes its ebb." Citing Mill's recognition that most change of opinion originates in an individual's mind, he insisted that success in converting others to a new opinion "depends but slightly" on reasoning. Rather, Dicey wrote, "A change of belief arises, in the main, from the occurrence of circumstances which incline the majority of the world to hear with favour theories which, at one time, men of common sense derided as absurdities, or distrusted as paradoxes."[88] Even this severely limited appreciation of reason parted from Bradley. Discounting the value of theorists in moral guidance, as in other realms of life, Bradley insisted, "That which tells us what in particular is right and wrong is not reflection but intuition."[89]

For Dicey, this view led directly to a denunciation of what he regarded as Mill's optimism that "absolute freedom would stimulate originality and individuality."[90] Rather, he demanded, "What ground is there, then, for holding that human beings, simply because they are left free to think and act as they like, will in fact like to labour in the search for truth, or to strike out new paths for themselves rather than pursue the pleasant and easy course of imitating their neighbors?"[91] For Dicey and others, it appeared naïve to attribute rationality to most people's process of acquiring opinions; instead, one had to look to historical and social context to understand why a person believed as he or she did.[92]

H. G. Wells depicted this shift away from belief in the rational, educable individual in his 1911 novel, *The New Machiavelli*. His first-person narrator, a seasoned (but now disgraced) former reformist politician named Richard Remington, writes in a disapproving tone of his school days in 1895: "we believed men were swayed by purely intellectual convictions and were either right or wrong, honest or dishonest (in which case they deserved to be shot), good or bad. We knew nothing of mental inertia, and could imagine the opinion of a whole nation changed by one lucid and convincing exposition. . . . We were then fully fifteen and we were serious about it." A few pages later, he adds, "We perceived that great things were to be done through newspapers. We talked of swaying opinion and moving great classes to massive action." By his late twenties, though, Remington has lost his educationalist illusions. Running for Parliament in 1906, he begins to realize the limitations of his audiences. In his speeches he simplifies his ideas and imports "crudifications." He would then "lie awake at nights . . . wondering how far it was possible to educate a whole people to great political ideals" and lamenting the importance of personality in his campaign. Following a successful election early in his parliamentary career, he offers his friends, Crampton and Lewis, an assessment of the changing conditions of Liberal politics: "We haven't the same belief we used to have in the will of the people. It's no good, Crampton, trying to keep that up. We Liberals know as a matter of fact—nowadays everyone knows—that the monster that brought us into power has, among other deficiencies, no head. We've got to give it one—if possible with brains and a will."[93]

Such understandings of communication undergirded much discussion of the press in the decades considered here. In the following chapter, we will see the translation of this theme into a greater emphasis on a representative idiom of the press at the expense of the educational theory. In concluding the present chapter, it bears emphasizing that a waning belief in the rational characterized many observers even among those who still held to an educational ideal. Dibblee, as we have already noted, saw in the Edwardian press a greater emphasis on news than on opinion. Rather than interpreting this development as a move away from attempting to influence readers, however, Dibblee saw it as a recognition that less forthright means of influencing readers stood to be more effective. Fewer readers paid attention to leading articles than a few decades previously, and shrewd journalists recognized that greater influence could be exerted through the "presentation of news." Dibblee asserted of many newspapers that officially rejected the attempt to exert influence that "in reality they attempt to exercise influence by every indirect method." We have already seen that Dibblee attempted to break down the distinction between news and opinion. Significantly, he noted that the distinction often masked a duplicitous attempt to influence readers who, "on their guard against the intention of the editor in that part of the paper, which is avowedly the vehicle of opinion, retaining a certain critical faculty, wherever they have reason to believe that their favourite newspaper is not what they call 'sound,' [were] quite unsuspicious of the news columns and accept as plain facts statements, which have perhaps undergone three unconscious garblings."[94] In analyzing this phenomenon at greater length, he concentrated on the American press, which often stood in rhetorically for and was often regarded as a direct influence on the British popular press.[95] Dibblee suggested a hypothetical article in the American press about a man committing suicide, which the writer would then link to immigration laws, or Wall Street, or a beef trust, or some other political issue. He asserted that this type of article derived from a recognition that "on all serious questions the American public can be appealed to ten times more strongly through emotional sympathy than by reasoned discussion." Writing on American elections, Dibblee asserted that "persuasion is not a weapon adopted by the American press, because during a political campaign no reader has time or inclination to read the other side. Sheer battering force or biting ridicule are the common weapons." He continued, noting that influence was exerted by personal attacks on candidates' private character or by giving a policy a nickname with unpopular connotations.[96]

R. A. Scott-James similarly emphasized the irrational formation of popular opinion through the press. Quoting Seeley on the emergence of the "organic state," Scott-James wrote that in the realm of ideas, "the revolution of the world is taking place gradually, not suddenly and dramatically." Rather than using the press to try to persuade readers, "The knowing ones of the world have learnt that the Press is a manifold engine for moulding, controlling, reforming, degrading, cajoling, or coercing the public, while the great public reads its paper as it eats its bread, without a thought of the mighty trick that is being played on it." Scott-James wrote that "politicians are aware that the incessant pattering of ideas upon the heads of the public is like the pattering of rain which wears down rocks."[97]

Frank Taylor had anticipated this line of thinking with an important pamphlet published in 1898, *The Newspaper Press as a Power Both in the Expression and the Formation of Public Opinion*. Despite attributing in his title both creative and representative functions to the press, Taylor denied that the press could influence readers at the level of rational persuasion. Rather, he insisted that writing "really forms opinion because it gives shape to masses of half-articulate feeling, and because it stimulates the inert well-wisher into activity." Taylor emphasized a prevailing interpretation of public opinion as communitarian and organic. In his words, "insofar as the clever writer expresses to perfection what men are darkly groping after, he veritably forms opinion and often appears to create it." Significantly, while denying that the press often achieved conversions, he claimed that the most fruitful times for conversions by means of the printed word occurred between the First and Third Reform Bills (1832 and 1884). Interestingly, he appeared ready to attribute rational communication to the papers and readers of the period before the New Journalism—that is, before the emergence of the "mass reader." He concluded with the same metaphor of the dripping of water on a rock that Scott-James would use fifteen years later.[98]

Dibblee, Scott-James, and Taylor produced three of the most sophisticated treatments of the press in this period. Yet even less rigorous observers noted some of the same qualities in communication through the press. Arthur Shadwell, responding to H. W. Massingham's article on "The Ethics of Editing," asserted that "the mass of the people regard [the newspaper] with almost superstitious reverence. It is the modern Bible."[99] Earlier in the article he had asserted of the "less educated" that print "fairly hypnotizes them, and that is the secret of advertising quack medicines and the like."[100] Shadwell's observations constitute for us an ironic contrast to more recent insistences that print imposes a rationality and linearity that is absent in oral (or postliterate) cultures.[101] Far from assenting to such thinking, Shadwell attributed to print an almost talismanic charm that possessed its own, extrarational, epistemology: "A man may tell a roomful of people something, and they will pay no attention or disbelieve him; but if, instead of telling them, the same man goes down to an office and writes the same thing on paper, and it appears in the dignity of print the next morning, not only those people, but all their kind, as many as read the paper, will accept it with implicit confidence, adopt it as their own, force it upon their friends, and stoutly maintain its validity against all comers. 'O, but it is in the papers,' they say, and that settles the matter."[102]

With such writers expressing their disbelief in the possibility of rational communication through the press, it is not surprising that many writers wished to downplay the expression of opinions in a paper's pages. As early as 1887, Fox Bourne had expressed skepticism toward the idea of rational persuasion through leading articles, the blame for which he appeared to place on readers' shoulders. Contrasting readers of his day unfavorably with the readers of a generation earlier, he asserted, "When these articles coincide with the readers' opinions, they are approved. When the readers disagree with them, they resent them."[103] Whatever the motivations of a "new" proprietor like Northcliffe, this type of skepticism toward the possibilities for rational communication produced an intellectual climate in which his insistence on giving readers the facts they needed to form their own opinions could make sense. Indeed, Northcliffe's only apparent blind spot was his implication that facts somehow contributed to his readers' creation of opinions. Cecil Headlam satirically quipped that if the British were to "abolish the Press," then "we shall each of us have to form our own opinions on every subject, instead of finding them ready-made, like and with the toast. It is evident how great would be the waste of time and energy that this would involve. Nor can anyone who is proud of his country as it is, and of its past history, view with equanimity any change which threatens to convert the nation into a mere mass of rational, independent and thinking men."[104] In Reginald Lucas's words, "For the multitude the leading article is the obvious short-cut to convictions. And this must be so. It is not given to every man to draw conclusions from definite events; rarer still is the instinct for weighing evidence and distinguishing between rumour and reality."[105]

Throughout the end of the nineteenth century and through the outbreak of the First World War, many observers of the press continued to employ such words as "influence" and "educate," at least in passing. Yet, given the developments suggested here, the meanings of even these words shifted for many of these observers. The educational or liberal ideal of the press that predominated at midcentury postulated a public sphere that was both rational (or potentially rational) and inclusive (or potentially inclusive). In the era of the New Journalism, while marketing strategies and expanded circulation suggested that the press could become ever more inclusive, many writers expressed doubt that most readers could live up to the criteria of rationality demanded by the earlier ideal. In this sense, even as the educational ideal retained a strong appeal in some circles, for many it was undermined from within by an increasing reluctance to attribute rationality to readers of the press.

The educational ideal of the press retained a great deal of resonance throughout this period, and indeed it remains today one of the more common tropes in the Anglo-American tradition. During the era of the New Journalism, however, this ideal came under increased pressures from several quarters, including, importantly, from the concentration of ownership among fewer and larger-scale owners. A model of challenge, response, and decline is, however, too simple a way of understanding the pressures on the journalism of this period. The educational ideal itself was not static, but instead it became transformed by some of the emphases of contemporary journalism, particularly an increased emphasis on the facts or news gathering.

At the same time, commercialization did not merely impede the possibilities of realizing an educational use of the press, it also contributed to *perceptions* that such an ideal no longer adequately summed up the political role of the press, however admirable such an ideal might seem. It is worth reiterating that this perception of commercialization could not be separated from uneasiness about an emerging mass readership and mass electorate that Thomas Wright, as early as 1873, had famously (and sympathetically) called "our new masters."[106] Finally, the educational ideal came under additional threat from the domain of social theory, as the notion of individual rationality came under attack, a development that was not lost on observers of the press. All of these transformations meant that increasingly, many (not all) who spoke of the "influence of the press" intended something quite different from the Gladstonian ideal of rational persuasion. Although each has been considered separately here in the context of debates about the press's role and attempts to understand this mysterious creature, these categories (and others) merged and blended easily into each other. Americanization might mean commercialization; American society might mean mass society. Commercialization might mean appealing to the irrational new readers; one suspects that perceptions of irrational new readers contributed to late Victorian beliefs that communication was an inherently irrational undertaking. In their interaction, the developments considered here in isolation contributed to the relative waning of the educational ideal and thus to an important shift in the type of public sphere that observers of the press attempted to construct.

How could champions of the press reconfigure the press's role? In a period in which journalists were seeking a professional identity of some sort, those who lost their faith in the educational ideal could not retreat into a simple nihilistic pursuit of profits. One alternative was to reconfigure the press's role so that it was seen less as an educational agency than as representative of "the people."

Notes

1. Lee, *Origins of the Popular Press in England*, 18.
2. Ibid., 79–93.
3. Briggs, *Age of Improvement*; Jones, *Outcast London*; Walkowitz, *City of Dreadful Delight*.
4. Barrow, "Socialism of Robert Blatchford and the 'Clarion'"; Waters, *British Socialists and the Politics of Popular Culture*; Clarke, *Liberals and Social Democrats*; Perkin, *Rise of Professional Society*, 116–70; Searle, *Quest for National Efficiency*. See also the essays by Chris Waters and D. L. LeMahieu in Pedersen and Mandler, eds., *After the Victorians*.
5. "Lament of a Leader-Writer," 662.
6. Stead, *Journalist on Journalism*, 85–86.
7. See Collini, *Liberalism and Sociology*, 171–208; Goldman, *Science, Reform, and Politics in Victorian Britain*; Yeo, *Contest for Social Science*; Joyce, *Democratic Subjects*, 15.
8. Williams, *History of English Journalism to the Foundation of the Gazette*, 1. See also Gitlin, *Media Unlimited*, 50–51.
9. Williams, *History of English Journalism to the Foundation of the Gazette*, 1–2.
10. Blatchford to A. M. Thompson, n.d. [ca. 1903–4], Robert Blatchford Papers, 1/85, Central Library, Manchester.
11. Blowitz, "Journalism as a Profession," 45.
12. Harmsworth, "Daily Newspapers of Today."
13. Davidson, "Fleet Street," 17.
14. Massingham, *London Daily Press*, 156–57.
15. *Hansard's Parliamentary Debates,* 11 May 1881, cols. 261, 218–20; Phillips, "Growth of Journalism," 175; Reid and MacDonnell, "The Press," 291.
16. Hunt, *Fourth Estate*, vol. 1, 1–2; Sheppard, "In Memoriam," 573.
17. Brown, *Victorian News and Newspapers*, 4. See also Read, *Power of the News*; "Press Association."
18. Jones, *Powers of the Press*, 141.
19. "Press Association," 516–17.
20. Ward and Montague, *William Thomas Arnold*, 60, 76, 86.
21. For a discussion of this struggle between Scott and Dibblee, see Ayerst, *Manchester Guardian*, 303–19.
22. Dibblee, *The Newspaper*, 96–99.
23. Ibid., 12–13. By contrast, such was the suggestion of Henry Cust. See Gardner et al., "Tory Press and the Tory Party," 363.
24. Dibblee, *The Newspaper*, 20–21.
25. Ibid., 26.
26. Hirst, "English Newspapers and Their Authority," 157–58; Massingham, *London Daily Press*, 14; Bourne, *English Newspapers*, vol. 2, 387. Page four, the "other side" of page three, was typically the site of leading articles.

The Era of New Journalism

27. On this theme see Clarke, *Liberals and Social Democrats*. In his earlier book, *Lancashire and the New Liberalism*, Clarke addressed similar continuities between the two parties at the level of political organization and electoral sociology. For a critique of that argument and an alternate view, see Bernstein, *Liberalism and Liberal Politics in Edwardian England*.

28. "Feather-brained" was Matthew Arnold's description of the New Journalism. See Arnold, "Up to Easter," 638. "Quarter-educated" was Mr. Whelpdale's phrase in Gissing's *New Grub Street*. It was intended as a description of the class of newly literate readers that had arisen following the Education Act of 1870 but who remained "incapable of sustained attention." Mr. Whelpdale states: "Everything must be very short, two inches at the utmost; their attention can't sustain itself beyond two inches. Even chat is too solid for them; they want chit-chat." Gissing, *New Grub Street*, 379–80. Gissing's apparently autobiographical Henry Ryecroft is more charitable, calling this class "half-educated." Like Gissing's other character, Henry Ryecroft sees this class of readers as a new development and scorns them further: "the glib many, the perky mispronouncers of titles and of authors' names, the twanging murderers of rhythm, the maulers of the uncut edge at sixpence extra, the ready-reckoners of a bibliopolic discount" (Gissing, *Private Papers of Henry Ryecroft*, 48).

29. Fry, "In Defence of the Paragraph," 38–40.

30. Bourne, *English Newspapers*, vol. 2, 370–71.

31. Phillips, "Growth of Journalism," 169–70.

32. Walsh, *Moral Damage of War*, 206.

33. Massingham, *London Daily Press*, 14.

34. Dicey, "Journalism Old and New," 904, 915.

35. "Lament of a Leader-Writer," 660.

36. Adams, *Memoirs of a Social Atom*, vol. 2, 584.

37. *Bohemian Days in Fleet Street*, 293.

38. Ibid., 294.

39. Kinnear asserted that "Mr. Winston Churchill has at present no quotable value on the Stock Exchange of journalism." Kinnear, "Parliamentary Reporting," 370.

40. Ibid., 372.

41. Ibid., 374.

42. Leigh, "What Do the Masses Read?" 177.

43. W. T. Stead to Winston Churchill, 8 April 1910, Home Office 45/22702, Doc. 168032/3, Public Records Office, London; "Report of the Departmental Committee on the Supply of Books to the Prisoners in H.M. Prisons and to the Inmates of H.M. Borstal Institutions," 9, Home Office 45/22702, Doc. 168032/6, Public Records Office, London.

44. "Report of the Departmental Committee on the Supply of Books to the Prisoners in H.M. Prisons and to the Inmates of H.M. Borstal Institutions," 10, Home Office 45/22702, Doc. 168032/6, Public Records Office, London.

45. Ibid., 10–11.

46. O'Connor, "New Journalism," 434.

47. Leach, *Fleet Street from Within*, 170.

48. See, for example, Robert Blatchford to John Burns, 11 June 1894, Robert Blatchford Papers, British Library Manuscript Collection 46287/200; Blatchford to Burns, 9 May 1898, Robert Blatchford Papers, British Library Manuscript Collection 46287/202.

49. Gardner et al., "Tory Press and the Tory Party," 358.

50. Ibid., 363–64.
51. On the Conservative party's ambivalent response to the press, see Jones, *Powers of the Press,* 155–79.
52. Hobson, *Psychology of Jingoism,* 22, 108–9.
53. Ibid., 119.
54. Hirst, "Imperialism and Finance," 12–13.
55. Ibid., 63.
56. Hobson, *Imperialism,* v–vi.
57. Walsh, *Moral Damage of War,* 206.
58. Quoted in Koss, *Rise and Fall of the Political Press in Britain,* vol. 1, 369.
59. Bell, *Fleet Street in Seven Centuries,* 573.
60. See chapter 5.
61. Williams, *Long Revolution,* 225–26; Hopkin, "Left-Wing Press and the New Journalism," 234; Dicey, "Journalism Old and New," 917.
62. Dicey, "Journalism Old and New," 913.
63. Pendleton, *Newspaper Reporting,* 184; Baker, *Newspaper World,* 12; Fisher and Strahan, *Law of the Press,* xviii, xx–xxi.
64. Atkins, "Work and Future of War Correspondents," 82–84.
65. See John Macdonald, ed., *Diary of the Parnell Commission.*
66. "Lament of a Leader-Writer," 658.
67. Grew, "Journals and Journalists of To-Day," 637.
68. For a stimulating discussion of the ongoing "speeding up" of modern mediated societies, see Gitlin's chapter on "Speed and Sensibility" in *Media Unlimited,* 71–117.
69. Epstein, "'America' in the Victorian Imagination," esp. 107.
70. Recent scholarship has supported the Victorian British perception of an earlier American commercialization. Baldasty dates in midcentury the transformation of the American press from political party–based to commerce-based. See Baldasty, *Commercialization of the News in the Nineteenth Century.* This dating is earlier than that conventionally assigned to a similar British transformation. Richard Kaplan argues, however, that the commercialization of the American press did not end its partisan character, which would persist until the late nineteenth century. Kaplan, *Politics and the American Press.* See also Wiener, "Americanization of the British Press."
71. MacDonagh, "Newspaper Interview," 12.
72. Fox, "New York Journalism," 258–59.
73. Scott-James, *Influence of the Press,* 155.
74. Fox, "New York Journalism," 258; Delille, "American Newspaper Press," 15, 20.
75. Delille, "American Newspaper Press," 23–24; Dibblee, *The Newspaper,* 26–27.
76. Delille, "American Newspaper Press," 16, 23, 28.
77. Scott-James, *Influence of the Press,* 157.
78. Jones, *Powers of the Press,* 73–97. See also Winter, *Mesmerized,* to remove any illusions that the midcentury was hostile to the irrational.
79. Jones, *Powers of the Press,* 91–92.
80. Ibid., 97.
81. Mill, *On Liberty,* xiv.
82. Ibid., 63.

83. Mill, *Subjection of Women*, 3–4.

84. Harris, *Private Lives, Public Spirit*, 246; Walsh, "Incarnation and the Christian Socialist Conscience in the Victorian Church of England."

85. Bradley, *Ethical Studies*, 101, 103,

86. Green, *Works of Thomas Hill Green*, vol. 2, 517–35. See also Green, *Ideologies of Conservatism*, 42–71.

87. Bradley, *Ethical Studies*, 108.

88. Dicey, *Lectures on the Relation between Law and Opinion in England during the Nineteenth Century*, 21–23.

89. Bradley, *Ethical Studies*, 129. Such a focus on irrationality was not restricted to Britain. One sees a similar emphasis in much continental thought of the period, including Bergson's notion of intuition and the *élan vitale* and Freud's mapping of the unconscious terrain of the mind. See Hughes, *Consciousness and Society*, and Hobsbawm, *Age of Empire*, 262–75.

90. In my own reading of Mill's *On Liberty*, Mill appears much less optimistic than Dicey seems to have believed.

91. Dicey, *Lectures on the Relation between Law and Opinion in England during the Nineteenth Century*, 436.

92. Such powerlessness against the forces of circumstance is one of the major themes of Maugham's *Of Human Bondage*. Philip Carey concludes that his entire affair with Mildred stems from causes beyond his rational control. Elsewhere, the narrator reflects that Philip "could not be positive that reason was much help in the conduct of life. It seemed to him that life lived itself." Maugham, *Of Human Bondage*, 323. Again, "It looked as though you did not act in a certain way because you thought in a certain way, but rather that you thought in a certain way because you were made in a certain way. Truth had nothing to do with it. There was no such thing as truth" (258).

93. Wells, *New Machiavelli*, 82–83, 102, 189, 214.

94. Dibblee, *The Newspaper*, 20–21, 87, 108–9.

95. Dibblee associated the popular press with news and the quality press with opinion; he also associated the American press with news and the British press with opinion. See ibid., 26–27.

96. Ibid., 33-35, 90-91.

97. Scott-James, *Influence of the Press*, 12–14.

98. Taylor, *Newspaper Press as a Power Both in the Expression and the Formation of Public Opinion*, 12, 15.

99. Shadwell, "Proprietors and Editors," 593. Massingham's article appeared as "The Ethics of Editing."

100. Ibid., 592.

101. See, for example, McLuhan, *Understanding Media*, Postman, *Amusing Ourselves to Death*, and Mitroff and Bennis, *Unreality Industry*.

102. Shadwell, "Proprietors and Editors," 592.

103. Bourne, *English Newspapers*, vol. 2, 387.

104. Headlam, *Argument against the Abolition of the Daily Press*, 4–5.

105. Lucas, *Lord Glenesk and the Morning Post*, 155.

106. Wright, *Our New Masters*.

4. "Representing the People": The Press as a "Fourth Estate," 1880–1914

Beginning in the 1880s, journalists and their advocates tended to retreat from attributing an educational function to the press. While words such as "educate," "influence," and "elevate" appear in passing in numerous texts from the period, by and large they are engulfed by more numerous and more sustained claims on behalf of the press's role in "representing the people," in conveying rather than influencing public opinion. In part this shift reflected a loss of confidence in the educational capacity of the press in the commercial era of the New Journalism: sensational stories would not sit well with claims of rational persuasion, and proprietors who would shun the practices of the New Journalism could not do so and remain commercially viable. Even *The Times,* that bastion of mid-Victorian sobriety, did not "dare to be dull" in this new environment.[1]

In part this retreat from an educational ideal of the press signaled a pessimism about the possibilities of public rational discussion and political persuasion. Unlike the educational ideal, the representative theory—or, in another contemporary usage, the idea of the press as a "Fourth Estate"—did not presuppose rationality on the part of newspaper readers. Moreover, it did not cast newspapers as a tool to *prepare* readers for self-government; rather, it posited newspapers as *constituting* the readers' exercise in self-government. In other words, it can be argued that the representative concept did not require as much faith in the ability of individuals to govern themselves as the educational theory did. My argument is that the greater ascendancy of the representative model in the late nineteenth and early twentieth centuries reflects not merely the increasing implausibility of an educational theory in the context of changing press-ownership patterns but also an increasing pessimism about the possibilities of integrating the "masses" into a cohesive politics by public discussion.

* * *

Behind the Fourth Estate or representative model—sometimes only implicitly—stood the image of the press as representing the people either more directly or more completely than did Parliament itself. This theme was not entirely new in the 1880s but derived in part from long-standing arguments for "liberty of the press."[2] For example, an anonymous article in 1811, generally attributed to James Mill, referred to the press as "this best bulwark of our liberties." The press constituted "that sort of security for our liberties, without which all other securities would prove vain and ineffectual." Recognizing that the government ruled, at least to an extent, only with the acquiescence of public opinion, the author pointed out that "[b]y the free circulation of opinions, the government is always fully apprised, which, by no other means it ever can be, of the sentiments of the people, and feels a decided interest in conforming to them." In practice, writers "in the pay of the government, or who aspire[d] to share in the wages of servility" abstained from criticizing the government, praising it instead. The author argued that if these spiritless writers were given "full scope" to present their opinions, while "independent and virtuous" writers were "either prevented altogether from laying the mischief open to view, and creating a proper sense of its magnitude, or even to any considerable degree intimidated from doing so," then the government could more easily enslave the people. Such enslavement could only end unhappily in rebellion; the author went so far as to speculate that a free press could have prevented the French Revolution by allowing the government to know the actual views of the population it ruled.[3]

Similarly, Thomas Macaulay, in a panegyric for John Milton written in 1825, credited Milton with helping to bring about the demise of oppressive government. As a Whig, Macaulay spoke the language of education. Milton's "noble aim" had been to "reverse the rod, to spell the charm backward, to break the ties which bound a stupefied people to the seat of enchantment." Yet Macaulay affirmed the goal of overthrowing tyranny. He cast ignorance as slavery, as the "dominion of prejudice" from which the people needed "emancipation" as surely as from Charles's own tyranny. Moreover, he linked education with the aim of removing corruption or "abuses," arguing that Milton's "attacks were, in general, directed less against particular abuses than against those deeply seated errors on which almost all abuses were founded, the servile worship of imminent men and the irrational dread of innovation."[4] Here we see, not for the last time, an assertion of the link between knowledge and power. This link reappeared throughout the century, cautioning us against understanding the distinction between educational and representative idioms in an overly rigid way.

Beyond its roots in long-standing concerns for liberty of the press, the prevailing idiom at the end of the nineteenth century had an antecedent in the radical "war of the unstamped" of the 1830s.[5] Unlike their middle-class counterparts, whose educational ideal of the press extended to such "useful knowledge" as that found in *Penny Magazine,* plebeian defenders of the press often insisted that "useful knowledge" was useless. Instead they called for a more truly "educational" press that would "teach" the working classes that they were exploited, thus affording "representation" to a political class that had no representation in Parliament.[6] In contesting the meaning of "education," therefore, these plebeian radicals moved away from notions of discussion, consensus, and universal knowledge as ultimate ends, instead emphasizing an education that consisted of learning to attain representation.

Despite these roots and antecedents, the emergence of a representative idiom in the 1880s is significant for several reasons. First, during the third quarter of the nineteenth century this idiom had been notable for its relative absence.[7] During the period considered here, by contrast, the educational idiom was very much on the defensive, as the idea of a representative press gained increasing currency. Second, unlike in the period between the seventeenth century and the early nineteenth century, when the classical defenses of the liberty of the press found expression, few people can have believed that the press was any longer in serious danger of sustained governmental censorship. Finally, the language of "representative of the people" resurfaced ironically in an era in which vastly increasing numbers of people gained more directly political representation by gaining the franchise.

* * *

The idea of rational persuasion of individuals became increasingly difficult to accept at the century's end, yet for an activity such as journalism, whose practitioners sought greater public esteem, it was clear that some relationship must exist with public opinion. The obvious answer was that if the press could not "influence" or "educate" public opinion, then it could "reflect," "express," or "mirror" it. Observers in the late nineteenth and early twentieth centuries, even those who held to an educational ideal, made much of this distinction.

This distinction can be seen in the rhetoric of leading Liberal politicians at the Imperial Press Conference in 1908. Lord Roseberry, whose liberalism perhaps made him reluctant to disavow the possibility of influencing public opinion, said of the conference that it "summoned to London the men who permanently reflect and influence the opinion of this Commonwealth." At the conference's government banquet, Asquith, then prime minister, argued that "the Press is the daily interpreter and mouthpiece of the tastes, the interests, the ideas—one might go further and say the passions and the caprices" of the electorate.[8] Grey claimed that "as public men, if we have a proper conception of our duty, we labour to mould and form and strengthen public opinion according to what we believe to be right." He told the journalists that their duty consisted of the same. Yet even this frankly educationalist sentiment was qualified by deference to the prevailing "organic" conception of the formation of opinion: "I admit there are limits. It is not good for us, whether we speak or write, to atttempt to be too much wiser than our own generation. If we attempt that we had better write for posterity—(hear, hear)—and not for the newspaper of to-morrow or for the debate of tomorrow. And public life is not an opportunity for indulging oneself, in expressing one's own opinions in the way most gratifying to oneself. It is an opportunity for expressing one's opinions in a way most likely to make them acceptable to others, and in all we write and in all we say we have carefully to keep in view what the point of view is of the public opinion of the country in which we live."[9]

For New Journalism and its observers, this task of reflecting public opinion was paramount. Hugh Gilzean Reid, the charter president of the Institute of Journalists, wrote in 1896 that "[w]hatever may have been the position of the Press in former times, there is little doubt that at present it is the follower rather than the leader of public opinion."[10] Harmsworth (the future Lord Northcliffe) noted in 1905 that the two weaknesses that could lead to journalistic failure included reporting news a day late and having an editor who failed to "keep his finger on the public pulse." More than a decade later, during the war, Northcliffe claimed in a letter to H. G. Wells that through *The Times*, "we constantly make [our readers] think and do things that surprise themselves." Yet this influence was accomplished only by "tact": "we cannot shock all our readers all the time, or we should lose all influence."[11] Less ambiguously, J. D. Symon wrote in 1914 that the popular conception that the press could "guide" or even "form" public opinion was wrong; the views of a paper were really a "reflection" of opinion.[12]

If newspapers reflected rather than guided or influenced public opinion, then they were well positioned to represent the people to an extent unmatched by Parliament. A short book commemorating *The Scotsman* in 1886 asserted that newspapers "perform a function without which popular self-government would, in any real sense, be impossible, and they constitute a medium through which an immense proportion of the every-day wants and requirements of the community are announced and satisfied." Chronicling *The Scotsman*'s role in this process, the author boasted of that paper's early history of opposing the government. When *The Scotsman* was founded in 1817, "Between the people and those who ruled over them there was a great gulf fixed; and the result was oppression and corruption on the part of the possessors of power, and widespread suffering and discontent among the masses." Obviously the situation demanded a journalistic response, but the *Edinburgh Review*, with its infrequent publication and high price, "could not be made the medium for the ventilation of every-day grievances or the discussion of every-day controversies." Because of *The Scotsman*'s "independence" and combination of "moderation with zeal," it challenged corruption before 1830, promoting Liberalism *avant la lettre*. In those days, the commemorator boasted, "to be a reader of the *Scotsman* was to be an 'enemy of the Government.'"[13] Significantly, such unrespectable antigovernment origins had yielded by 1886 to a thoroughly domesticated claim to facilitate "popular self-government."

The hypothesized relationship between the press and Parliament can perhaps best be seen by looking in greater detail at a few prominent and often quoted texts. Charles Pebody, writing in 1882, the year he became editor of the *Yorkshire Post*, asserted that the newspaper press was "arrogating to itself some of the chief functions of Parliament—most of its chief functions of public criticism, most of its functions of debate, and many of its functions as a constitutional check upon the conduct of Ministers." The function of checking the conduct of the government evokes the idea of corrupt politicians attempting to pursue their own interests rather than those of the people they purport to represent. For Pebody, the press stood as the defender of the people's interests.

The function of the press, according to Pebody, was not to supersede or replace Parliament; rather, the newspapers should ensure that Parliament, along with other English institutions, served the people. In justifying his book, Pebody claimed that

> the history of the English Press is the history, if not of English liberty, of all those popular forces and political franchises which have given strength and solidity to English institutions; renewed the youth of the State; made England, with its ancient monarchical institutions, with its feudal relics, with its aristocracy, and with its Established Church, the freest State in the world; purified the public

service; raised the tone of our public life; made bribery and corruption, in the old sense of the term, impossible; and welded together the whole of the British Empire, with all its races, all its religions, into a compact and powerful mass, which moves, when it moves at all, with a force, a unanimity, and a decision that constitute Public Opinion one of the marvels of our time.[14]

How had the press succeeded in checking the power of hereditary privilege? The final clause of the quotation above suggests the potential of the press for organizing the people. The press could counter a government's "divide and conquer" principle; rather than emphasizing the differences among the nation's people, the press could emphasize their common interests, thereby creating a unified "mass" that the government could not treat oppressively.

Besides organizing the people to defend their interests, moreover, the press filled a second role: that of explaining to the people what their interests were. This emphasis reflects the continued resonance of ideas linked to education, even as the emphasis on public discussion receded. For Pebody, the press had exposed the truth, and the majority of the English had seen that their self-interest did not lie in being subjected to a privileged order. Pebody's understanding of the function of a reporter exemplifies this emphasis on the explanatory nature of the press. He believed that a reporter should write impartially; in fact, an "often partisan" quality was one of the few faults that Pebody found with English journalism. Yet at the same time he did not believe that a reporter's job was to provide "just the facts"; rather, he called telegrams, reports, and price lists mere "raw material" that needed to be "explained," "illustrated," and "criticised" and "to be set out in their true bearings upon the course of events, to be weighed, to be measured, to be tested and scrutinised in a hundred ways" by a reporter.[15] If a reporter could perform such a task well, and impartially, then a reader should certainly gain a rational understanding of how contemporary events affected his or her interests. Unlike the educational ideal, however, this interpretation did not emphasize including readers in a discussion of the common good. Rather, the crucial aim was that readers who were informed of their interests could not be so easily exploited by corrupt ministers.

The metaphor "Fourth Estate" posited the newspaper as the true representative of the people, not necessarily because the people used the paper to express their interests or opinions but because the paper itself spoke on their behalf. In either case, however, the important point was that the newspaper could shape policy through the function of publicity. That is, the press could reveal corruption and, because of the power of words, thereby bring it to a halt.

Pebody's book is a useful introduction to the Fourth Estate model of the press. The classic expression of the press as Parliament, however, belongs to W. T. Stead. For those contemporary critics of the style and tone of the New Journalism, Stead was among the worst of offenders.[16] Most famous for his "Maiden Tribute" attack on the "white slave" trade (and for sinking with the *Titanic*), Stead purportedly said during his tenure at the *Pall Mall Gazette* that "he was engaged in 'running the British Empire from Northumberland Street.'" Something of his self-image as a righteous champion of the popular cause can be gauged from his display of Cromwell's portrait in his editorial office.[17] Temporarily freed from his routine by a stint in prison, Stead published two articles in 1886, both in the *Contemporary Review*, advocating "government by journalism."[18] In the first of these articles, Stead made even more ambitious claims on behalf of the press's governing role than Pebody had made four years earlier. Rather than seeing the press as merely acting as a check on Parliament, Stead believed that it had become the "Chamber of Initiative": "No measure ever gets itself into shape, as a rule, before being debated many times as a project in the columns of the newspapers."[19] For Stead, the press was usurping the role of the House of Commons, and properly so: "Government by kings went out of fashion in this country when Charles Stuart lost his head. Government by the House of Lords perished with Gatton and Old Sarum. Is it possible that government by the House of Commons may equally become out of date? Without venturing into the dim and hazardous region of prophecy, it is enough to note that the trend of events is in that direction. Government tends ever downward. Nations become more and more impatient of intermediaries between themselves and the exercise of power."[20]

In Stead's opinion, newspapers had several advantages over the House of Commons as the source of effective and legitimate political power. Most importantly, the editor was closer to the general population than was the member of Parliament. In light of the Septennial Act, argued Stead, the House of Commons was "a usurpation based on fraud." Because the House of Commons was elected only every seven years, it was easy for its members to "cease to be in touch with the people." In Stead's words, the "member immediately after his election leaves his constituency, and plunges into a new world with different atmosphere, moral, social, and political. But an editor, on the other hand, must live among the people whose opinions he essays to express." Stead presented an alternative to the prevailing commercial criticism of the press; understood positively, the editor *had* to express the interests of his readers, even if it meant writing "sorely against his will" on topics that did not interest him, or else the public would desert him.[21]

> [FEBRUARY 28, 1880.] PUNCH, OR THE LONDON CHARIVARI.
>
> **AN ASSAULT OF ARMS**
> BETWEEN GENERAL SWORD AND CAPTAIN PEN—(*À PROPOS OF THE ZULU CAMPAIGN*).

The representative ideal of the press required newspapers to take on the government. Here the *Daily Telegraph* challenges the conduct of the Zulu War. From *Punch*, 28 February 1880.

For Stead, factors that enabled the editor more effectively to represent the people's interests included the fact that the newspaper was published daily. Far from receiving a mandate every several years, the editor received his mandate daily, for readers would not continue to purchase a paper whose editor was "out of touch." Moreover, the newspaper-as-representative did not feature the limitations of Parliament, for anybody who wished to pay a penny (or a half-penny) could cast a "vote" for a particular paper; there were no property or registration or age or gender qualifications.[22] Stead equates democracy with consumerism. Far from tainting the press, the demands of the market led directly to journalism's political and social legitimacy.

The editor's qualification as representative of the people rested on his proximity to them. But how did the editor actually exercise effective power? Stead described two distinct methods. First, he emphasized the role of publicity, or exposure of social evils that needed correcting. Echoing the radical critique of corruption of power, Stead asserted that abuses thrived in conditions of secrecy: "Whenever you shut off any department from the supervision of the Press, there you find abuses which would speedily perish in the light of day." He continued, arguing that the press was "the great inspector, with a myriad eyes, who never sleeps, and whose daily reports are submitted, not to a functionary or a department, but to the whole people." Here Stead seems to assume that public ignorance constituted the chief reason that official policies and practices that were contrary to the public interest were allowed to continue. Stead credited the "sensationalism" of the press with the passing of the Criminal Law Amendment Act and the appointment of the Royal Commission on the Housing of the Poor.[23] For Stead, the press could exercise power simply by exposing wrongs and then leaving to the elected government the task of rectifying them. Significantly, this line of thinking implicitly cast the journalist not simply as the conveyor of public opinion but as its interpreter as well. For the journalist decided which wrongs would be publicized or exposed and thus which wrongs most flagrantly flouted the interests of the people. This constituted an early statement of the press's "agenda-setting" function; unlike today's critics, however, Stead saw this as a democratizing exercise.

The editor's other means of exercising political power involved the communication of public opinion to ministers through the medium of the newspaper. Stead recalled an episode in which a permanent official, who was his friend, asked him to publish a "rouser" to give his chief the resolve to support a certain act "against which some interested clamour was being raised." Stead published the requested piece, and his friend's chief found the courage to defend the act.[24] Once again, Stead's argument on behalf of the editor's exercise of political power depended upon the editor's ability to speak for the people; his story does not suggest how to ensure that an unscrupulous editor would not provide an official with the resolve to support simply a different "interested" act. Rather, it seems to require of the editor a great measure of virtue and perception.[25]

Stead's rhetoric found expression in his practice. In his campaign against the Bulgarian atrocities and in his "Maiden Tribute," he drew on melodramatic tropes, presenting to his readers a world of good versus evil. In this world, Stead found no worthy political opponents to engage in debate, only the morally reprobate who must at all costs be thwarted.[26] While Stead's defenders could claim that he was "educating" his readers, it is significant that his articles did not present the readers with, say, a persuasive argument on behalf of his ideas on British foreign policy.[27] Rather, by presenting or publicizing facts that he knew would awake his readers' moral outrage, he sought to demonstrate that he spoke for the people, that he represented their interests or ideals.

Stead's claims and positioning in this article contained a share of irony. First, this democratic champion or "representative of the people" wrote as the editor of a newspaper with a tiny, elite readership. Second, this article appeared not in the daily press but in a monthly review, and it presented itself not as an exposé of wrongheaded journalism but as a rational argument that should be discussed. Moreover, the scathing criticism that Stead's articles provoked cautions us against seeing his ideas as broadly representative of those of late Victorian journalists.[28] Nevertheless, what is striking is not Stead's iconoclasm but the ways in which his bombastic rhetoric drew on a theme that was quickly becoming conventional.

Not all observers demonstrated Stead's confidence regarding the capacity of the press for controlling the government. Frederick Greenwood, one of Stead's predecessors as editor of the *Pall Mall Gazette,* suggested in 1890 that this model of journalism was more applicable to the press of Palmerston's era than to the contemporary press. Since midcentury, he argued, the government had become more complicated and complex and less compact. Hence, during the earlier period, the government was "more capable of being influenced by any single powerful agency than in these days of diffused and confused authority." Greenwood continued: "The 'questions of the day' were much less confused, presenting themselves to all concerned—public, press, and ministers alike—with fewer complexities of consideration than have since been introduced into the whole range of public affairs." On the one hand, a newspaper's potential influence was blocked by a general inability to discern exactly who controlled the government. On the other hand, the growth of the press meant that because so many good papers now existed, no one paper could have the degree of authority that *The Times* had possessed during Palmerston's administration. It should be noted, however, that Greenwood's analysis merely assessed the possibilities for a *single* editor to shape policy. Greenwood largely ignored an important aspect of the question of the press's political influence: to what extent did *all* newspapers, taken comprehensively, influence the government's actions? On this issue, Greenwood was silent; he did, however, acknowledge that "if ministers are less often disturbed by a press-created public opinion, they are frequently moved by a press-revealed public opinion," an observation that would have pleased Stead.[29]

Similarly, H. W. Massingham confirmed the Fourth Estate as an ideal by underscoring the press's failure to perform its proper political functions. Massingham, who would later become the editor of the radical *Daily Chronicle* and then, after its buyout during the South African War by a Conservative trust, a contributor to C. P. Scott's pro-Boer *Manchester Guardian*, published a survey of the London daily press in 1892.[30] Like Greenwood, Massingham affirmed representative goals for the press in asserting ways in which this function was impeded in practice. In addition to immorality and commercialism, which we have already seen Massingham condemning, he asserted that partisanship, or a lack of "independence," prevented the press from fully realizing its "mission": "Journalism, new and old, is, after all, too dependent on the party machine and the abiding interest in the right side of life to become a Prospero to the democratic Ariel. The average journalist is still too slight, too unbelieving, too conventional a citizen to rule his country."[31] This partisanship and narrowness was revealed, for example, in the *Daily News*'s failure to "distribute its enthusiasm more equally between the East End docker and the Bulgarian peasant."[32] This commitment to "independence" coexisted with Massingham's own left-wing political views and could be seen in other equally partisan journalists. Well into the twentieth century, as many prominent journalists accepted knighthoods or even elevation to the nobility, C. P. Scott and Kingsley Martin both rejected knighthood.[33] For these stalwart defenders of the educational ideal, overt political ideals were permissible and even admirable, but too close an identification with a government of the day compromised a journalist's independence.

It is worth reiterating that in discussing the role of the press in politics, observers did not always carefully hold to only one model or the other. Although the educational and representative or Fourth Estate ideals can be distinguished for analytical purposes, for contemporaries assessing the importance of the press in society and politics, both discourses could be drawn from for rhetorical purposes. If the representative theory was voiced more frequently, this reflected its greater hold over contemporary thought, but the educational ideal could still find its proponents. One could sometimes find these discourses interwoven within the same text. For example, in his 1906 pacifist book *The Moral Damage of War*, Walter Walsh used the phrase "Fourth Estate" but implied that the press could act as a Fourth Estate only by "educating" its readers. Walsh's book was not primarily a study of the press but a strategic antiwar polemic. His central argument was that neither reason nor pity for human suffering could prevent future outbreaks of war; rather, people had to be convinced that all war was immoral or sinful.[34] In chapter 6, "The Moral Damage of War to the Journalist," he referred to mid-Victorian journalists as "democrats praying for the extension of popular liberty; not members of the Three Estates creating a Fourth to be their tool, but citizens working for the broad ends of government." In the same context, he described journalists as knights-errant whose task it is "to ride abroad redressing human wrong." Both of these quotations vaguely reflected the concept of the press as a Fourth Estate as it has been developed above. The first quotation expresses the ideal of journalists as independent of rather than subservient to the government; the second implicitly echoes the radical critique of corrupt uses of power (for what other "human wrongs" could a journalist redress?). When Walsh described more specifically the mid-Victorian journalist's function, however, he borrowed directly from the educational theory. These knights-errant were "idealists desiring the spread of knowledge," and they used the press as "an instrument wherewith to make men free,—free from their own ignorance, prejudices, and superstitions, from degrading conditions of labor and life." Moreover, his criticism of the contemporary British press centered on its failure to employ journalists "for their attachment to principles, or their proved ability to become teachers in the realms of art and literature, philosophy and science, religion and politics."[35]

This interweaving of ideals could find expression in local contexts as well. In 1896, on the occasion of the *Falkirk Herald*'s fiftieth anniversary, an anonymous writer highlighted the paper's role in leading local government reforms. First, the writer presented a view of Falkirk's own brand of "old corruption": "The condition of Falkirk half a century ago, and for a good many years thereafter, can only be described as discreditable and scandalous in the extreme." No proper municipal government existed; the officials held positions that amounted to sinecures, with "hardly a vestige of genuine authority." In this scenario, the town suffered from bad drainage, poor sanitation, and primitive lighting. In 1859, however, the local government passed a Police and Improvement Act, which was "the result of years of debate, agitation, and conflict, in which it was the lot of the *Herald* to be hotly and incessantly engaged as the champion of local municipal and social reform and progress."[36] So far, the writer had not committed to either model; "years of debate" are invoked in which the *Herald* took a position, but the opponents in this debate cannot be seen as mere political adversaries but as melodramatic villains defending a situation "discreditable and scandalous in the extreme." In the next passage, however, the writer made the ambiguity more explicit. First, he or she portrayed opponents of the reform in terms familiar from a radical critique of "old corruption": "The opposition, led by men some of whom ought to have known better, but who allowed prejudice and an absurd regard for narrow views and paltry interests to overweigh their judgment, was exceedingly bitter and stubborn." In the following sentence, however, the writer conveyed a "liberal" closure that would have pleased John Stuart Mill: "Yet many who aided this hostility lived to see and to admit their mistake, and some of them to lend a meritorious hand in removing the reproach from our backward and neglected burgh and in giving it a fair chance of prosperous development."[37] In this sentence, opponents no longer appear as hopelessly corrupt; the "debate" appears to have born fruit, and former opponents, convinced of the common good, are welcomed back into the community.

These twin themes are presented yet again in a poem that can only be regarded as campy, read by its author, W. Maxwell, at a meeting celebrating the Jubilee of the *Falkirk Herald*. The representative theory found expression in these lines:

> For fifty years thy voice has been a power
> To guide the local rulers of the hour ...
> Parish and County Councils find in thee
> A truthful mirror in which all may see
> How hardly earned public money's spent
> And where the last increased assessment went.

Likewise, although the poem makes no mention of the newspaper's contributing to education or discussion directly through its columns, it nevertheless shows a continued appreciation for the newspaper's duty to promote education:

> To education thou wert e'er a friend,
> And thou hast never scrupled to defend
> Changes for good, and we must all acknowledge
> Thy friendly gift to Peter Wright's new college.[38]

Although elements of the educational ideal persisted, the general picture that emerges is that of its gradual retreat and supersession by claims to represent the people, that is, readers. This conclusion already qualifies Lee's argument: the commercialization and industrialization of the press in the era of the New Journalism did not unproblematically lead to the demise of a "public service" ideal of the press. Rather, one ideal was exchanged for another. Drawing on older, heroic images of the press as popular champions, this representative idiom could prove more congruous with the commercial conditions of journalism and the awakening fears of mass society.

Representing the people did not, however, consist solely of keeping Parliament in check. In addition, contemporaries noted that the press increasingly recognized that life was bigger than Westminster. If "the people" or "public opinion" were to be represented, then journalists needed to recognize that these readers cared less about Home Rule or Bulgarian attrocities than about football scores, divorce cases, murder trials, and fashionable dresses.

This concern for presenting the commonplace in the press can be read in two contrasting ways. On the one hand, it appears as a more inclusive approach to journalism: readers were invited to participate in a public (journalistic) conversation about topics that actually interested them. Richard Hoggart observed in 1957 that "to wish that a majority of the population will ever read *The Times* is to wish that human beings were fundamentally different, and is to fall into an intellectual snobbery."[39] Similarly, in the 1880s observers came to recognize that readers of the popular press simply would not plough through a dull mid-Victorian paper. On the other hand, this opening of the press to the commonplace meant an acceptance of the notion of multiple publics that were not equal participants in political power relations. Gareth Stedman Jones has noted that the remade working class of the late nineteenth century became depoliticized through focusing on a consumer and entertainment culture.[40] The New Journalism contributed to this depoliticized culture by advertising wares and simply by its presence as an alternative to politics. Readers of the New Journalism were increasingly included in a public conversation but effectively excluded from conversations about the government and "public affairs."[41]

Both aspects of the New Journalism received frequent articulation. Many observers emphasized the value of human interest stories and other "nonpolitical" items, especially since narrowly defined political items could attract only a small, largely elite audience. W. T. Stead argued that *The Times* had ceased to accord with "the nation at large," as the latter had expanded since the Crimean War. At that time, Stead argued, "the great public was outside the pale. Hence it was a comparatively easy matter for Printing House Square in the old days to keep in accord with the opinion of England."[42] In part, this could mean that the "nation" did not share *The Times*'s political perspective, but it could also mean a call for a more broadly based definition of "news." Another pioneer of the New Journalism, T. P. O'Connor, while holding out the hope that English journalism would not reach the "low" of American journalism, nevertheless thought it "highly undesirable that politics and politics alone should sell a journal." He continued, "Why should not the public be told of how the party of Mrs. Smith went off; of how Miss Robinson looked; of the dress Miss Jones wore? . . . they are the subjects about which we talk over the dinner-tables; and it is the sound principle to which we shall all come at last in literature and journalism, that everything that can be talked about can also be written about."[43]

Interestingly, O'Connor presented the "commonplace" in strictly feminine terms. This association occurred repeatedly, underscoring the common presumption that the female sphere was not that of politics. Nor did all observers welcome the inclusion of female readers. E. M. Phillipps noted that he

"Oh no, we never mention her!
Her name is never heard!"
SHE HAD BEEN TO THE STATE BALL—AND HER NAME WAS OMITTED IN EVERY LIST NEXT MORNING! "IS LIFE WORTH LIVING?"

The New Journalism's focus on commonplace events rather than politics was often seen by critics as the "feminization" of the press. From *Punch*, 8 June 1889.

expected soon to see a "ladies' page" in *The Times*. Already, he wrote, the "leading daily papers have an occasional column, and all but the most serious among the weeklies think it incumbent on them to satisfy the feminine appetite with a little babble about clothes and knicknacks."[44] Similarly, in his satirical pamphlet *An Argument against the Abolition of the Daily Press,* Cecil Headlam wrote that there existed a general agreement that newspapers were "trivial, personal, inaccurate, and harmful." Headlam acknowledged that he agreed with the first two charges but insisted that "it may be of some advantage [to readers] to be kept in touch with the views of their valets and the style of their ladies' maids."[45]

Commentators on the press often cast the New Journalism as a blurring of the distinction between the public (masculine) and private (feminine) spheres. Their observations thus effectively illustrate the sociologist Adam Seligman's argument that not only did the "devolution of the public sphere [entail] a concomitant destructuring of the private . . . the opposite process is also at work. In lieu of the public the private is projected into the public arena, is made public, in an attempt to reconstitute itself through its representation in that sphere."[46] According to critics as well as defenders, that is, in the New Journalism, topics that had recently been regarded as "private" or "domestic" became the subject of news and comment. A distinction between the two spheres had been made by Mr. Hutchinson during the parliamentary discussion of the Newspaper Libel Act of 1881, when he argued that a newspaper was "the record and expression of what took place in public . . . everything outside the domain of strictly domestic intercourse."[47] In the minds of contemporary observers, this distinction was increasingly flouted as the decades progressed. We have already seen that Frank Fox, writing a quarter-century later on the New York human interest story that so many feared represented the future of British journalism, pointed out that its "foundation is the principle that the romantic or humorous happenings of the 'common people' are, properly treated, as vividly interesting to the newspaper reader as dynastic changes or great battles." Going so far as to call the human interest story "good reading, and, moreover, edifying reading," Fox nevertheless admitted that in the yellow journals it tended to "degenerate into 'keyhole journalism'—into grossly offensive spyings on domestic privacy."[48]

In large part, this insistence that the public and private spheres were merging, or that the private was parading itself in public, betrayed an uneasiness about the increasing prominence of a "social" sphere.[49] Massingham lamented in 1892 that a "revolution in a foreign state stirs but languidly the pulse of the British citizen," while a "foul crime in his own city or a ghastly exposure of 'immorality in high life' sends him hot-footed for the paper." Later in the same book, Massingham praised the *Daily Telegraph* for avoiding the "curious and characteristic fault of most English daily newspapers that they conceive the world to be mainly interested in politics." Instead, it appealed to the "everyday life of the clerk, the shopkeeper, and also to the great mass of villadom."[50] As a journalist, Massingham noted that the *Daily Telegraph* managed better than many newspapers to represent the demands of a popular consituency. Yet his association of this newspaper with particular (lower) classes, coupled with his earlier lamentation of popular reading habits—in addition to his lingering educational approach—suggests that he was far from pleased with this emerging social sphere.

The above quotations from Massingham's book suggest that the social sphere in journalism was typically associated in the elite mind with the newspapers of the lower classes. This association contributed to a fragmentation of the hypothesized public sphere. It is worth remembering that elite observers may have overstated the novelty of the New Journalism. Raymond Williams rightly points out that in many cases all that was new was that the longstanding practices of the popular Sunday papers had made their way into the daily press. In addition, audience fragmentation was hardly new; in the early nineteenth century, various periodicals had created distinct audiences.[51]

Nevertheless, in the late nineteenth century the mid-Victorian notion of a unified public sphere tended to receive fewer proponents. Increasingly, commenators understood that a paper had to find its niche and could not address a mythical public of all readers. Moreover, this fragmentation could have class implications. In the 1901 *Newspaper Press Directory*, for example, the *Pall Mall Gazette* advertised itself as "THE EVENING PAPER OF THE BUSINESS MAN, THE CLUB MAN, THE POLITICIAN, THE WEST-END RESIDENT, THE SOCIETY MAN AND WOMAN, AND THE BEST PEOPLE EVERYWHERE. . . . AN IDEAL MEDIUM FOR REACHING THE AFFLUENT CLASSES."[52] Similarly, Massingham distinguished the *Daily Telegraph* as the newspaper of certain of the lower classes, from *The Times*, which spoke the "average mind of the Englishmen of the governing classes . . . the men I see in the first class railway carriage, on the floor of the Stock Exchange, in the stalls of London theatres, on the green benches of the House of Commons, in great town houses, and in cool villas by the sea." Fitzroy Gardner noted that *The Times* was the paper of the wealthy only; "its price debars it from influencing the people at large." Francis Hirst identified the market for the "cheap and nasty Weekly" as the "baser sort."[53]

Many of the themes explored in this chapter came together in R. A. Scott-

James's 1913 book *The Influence of the Press:* representing the people, the democratization of the press, the fragmentation of the public sphere. Scott-James, whose journalistic experience included working for the radical editors A. G. Gardiner and H. W. Massingham, posited multiple publics rather than the single and potentially inclusive public that the mid-Victorians had identified. Scott-James reaffirmed the mid-Victorian image of their period's press; he argued that because the mid-Victorian newspapers aimed at only a small portion of the community, rather than the millions, "there was no need to depart from the essentials of the established tradition."[54] Prior to the 1870 Education Act—that is, before the creation of a new class of readers supposedly forced newspaper owners to introduce the methods of the New Journalism—all newspapers were able to treat "seriously their function of giving information—that is to say, not mere sensation, but reports of those public events which might be expected to interest enfranchised citizens—speeches by public men, proceedings in the law-courts, scientific discoveries, etc."[55]

In discussing his own era, by contrast, Scott-James identified two distinct publics. On the one hand, the mid-Victorian "liberal" public continued to exist; on the other hand, a new and larger public had emerged, centering around the half-penny press. Any journalist who wished to succeed in his or her profession needed to recognize this division. In Scott-James's words, "the professional journalist must be content to select and limit his audience if he is to satisfy the influential few; he will be tempted to diversify and sensationalize his paper if he would appeal to the variegated many." Scott-James identified the *Daily Mail* as the newspaper of the larger, uneducated but literate public, whereas "the public which [for example] is interested in the dextrous interpretation, day by day, of official Liberalism, is the public which is faithful to the *Westminster Gazette*."[56]

Scott-James saw the smaller, "influential" public of such papers as the *Westminster Gazette* very much in the same light as he saw the mid-Victorian public; its members wanted opinions, well-argued and developed at length. He believed that the larger, newly created, uneducated but literate public, however, wanted something more similar to the American-style yellow journalism: "coloured 'funny' pictures . . . colossal headlines . . . exaggerated phraseology." Moreover, foreshadowing current debates about "tabloidization," he feared that the success of the half-penny papers that appealed to this public was prompting owners of the "serious" papers to imitate the former, thus threatening the few remaining papers of mid-Victorian quality. Scott-James held to a liberal or educational theory in his analysis of the serious political press and echoed much of contemporary criticism of the commercial threat to the existence of this type of paper.[57] At the same time, however, his discussion of the press's role in the political system was not one-sided. In discussing the function of the half-penny papers, he echoed and expanded upon the theme of the press as a Fourth Estate. Referring to the American press, which he saw as the model for the British half-penny press, he argued that these papers did not help "the crowd" to think but nevertheless insisted that "it was something that [the crowd] could be made to gasp simultaneously, even at the order of an interested millionaire. The appearance of the Yellow Press was a recognition of the fact that the majority of the nation not only existed, but that it might have opinions, that it certainly had tastes, that it possessed a *consciousness* of life. A popular Press—that is to say, a Press which can appeal to the least persons in a nation, and to all of them—is at least a step towards the democratic ideal of an articulate nation."[58]

Scott-James credited the American press and its imitator, the British half-penny press, with helping to create a national political community comparable to a Greek polis. The latter had been smaller and had been based on the principle of personal communication, whereas the modern political community, the "organic state," was based upon the publication and diffusion of information. Nevertheless, even if the readers of a newspaper did not participate in the political life of the nation in the same face-to-face manner as the citizens of a polis, Scott-James believed that not only did the press ensure that their interests were represented but that it actually integrated them into the nation by making them "articulate."

When Scott-James uses the word "articulate," however, he does not employ it in a mid-Victorian, liberal sense. He did not, for example, envision a "marketplace of ideas" in which every citizen expressed his or her opinions, however far-fetched they might seem to others, in order that the "true" opinion might triumph in open and rational discussion.[59] Rather, he believed that a person was articulate so long as his or her opinion or interest was expressed publicly by *someone*.[60] The accomplishment of the New Journalism was that it expressed virtually everyone's interests and opinions by dint of its sheer scope and diversity. In Scott-James's words, "The popular Press has at least asserted one very important fact, which is that party politics is only a small part of the whole of public life . . . whereas, if, on the contrary, popular sentiment is allowed to play upon all the topics of life, irrespective of party politics, it means that new public interests are thrust forward; that these too must claim the attention of the politician; that it is no longer left to him to choose subjects for legislation; but that legislation is thrust upon him by those who have found independent expression of their needs."[61] Significantly, once again, Scott-James referred to readers not as those who "express their needs" but as those who "have found independent expression of their needs." Nevertheless, he asserts that the press by 1913 had become much more representative of the people than it had ever been in the past.

Unhappily, however, as the success of the half-penny dailies led editors of quality papers like *The Times* to imitate their methods, the "influential" classes found themselves paradoxically in danger of being rendered inarticulate. Like John Stuart Mill, Scott-James worried that pressures toward intellectual conformity could stifle the free expression of minority opinions. He lamented that the press was "not yet capable of dealing with special interests; it [was] still inclined to neglect minorities, even those which are the most profitable, namely, the influential minorities."[62] It is difficult to imagine, within a discussion of the political function of newspapers, a stronger expression of uneasiness toward the rise of a "mass society."

Finally, what did Scott-James really mean by "influence of the press"? He appears to have meant only that the press created a national community of people who were able to know simultaneously about the same national concerns. He explicitly denied the ability of newspapers to operate at the rational level in convincing a reader of the truth of a proposition. He argued that the modern press's ability to shape opinion existed solely at the subrational level. He also believed, however, that the mid-Victorian newspapers, by virtue of their "continuous news," had possessed this ability; modern newspapers had lost this ability because of their presentation solely of sensationalistic and decontextualized snippets. Anticipating Habermas's critique of the bourgeois public sphere, Scott-James insisted that those who wished to be "well informed" had to look elsewhere.[63]

What is the significance of this declining emphasis on the educational or liberal uses of the press and the increasing focus on the press as a representative agent or Fourth Estate? Gareth Stedman Jones has argued that after the 1870s, elite fears of the masses, who were supposedly susceptible to socialist propaganda, led politicians to enact various welfare measures in an effort to win the loyalty of skilled workers and noncasual labor to the existing political system.[64] Following the depression of the 1870s, the rise of the militant and sometimes socialist "new unionism" in the 1880s,[65] and the emergence of the Independent Labour party in 1893, the political elites not surprisingly became less optimistic about the possibility of integrating all the classes into a cohesive social and political nation. The prevailing approaches to understanding the press reflected this growing pessimism. Unlike the older educational ideal, the Fourth Estate or representative model did not presuppose the typical reader's ability to learn to think rationally about his or her interests and those of the state. Rather, the latter model proposed that the journalist *decide* what the people's interests really were. In this sense, the representative or Fourth Estate model was better suited to an era that began to see the state as a benevolent actor that could improve the people's lives for them, an era in which political elites spoke as often about the need for "national efficiency" as about individual liberty, and an era in which many intellectuals became convinced that the problems of modern societies were too complex to be left to individual initiative but required the service of experts or professionals.[66]

Notes

1. This is Alan Lee's argument. See Lee, *Origins of the Popular Press in Britain*, 117–30. The quotation is from Phillipps, "New Journalism," 182.

2. For a useful overview of this theme, see Jones, *Powers of the Press*, 10–27, and Barker, *Newspapers, Politics, and English Society*, 12–21. For a more broadly philosophical approach to this issue, see Keane, *Media and Democracy*, 1–50.

3. [Mill], "Liberty of the Press," 98, 110, 116, 121.

4. Macaulay, *Critical and Historical Essays*, vol. 1, 26–27.

5. On this theme, see Hollis, *Pauper Press*, and Wiener, *War of the Unstamped*.

6. Hollis, *Pauper Press*, 19–25; Johnson, "'Really Useful Knowledge,'" 75–103, esp. 76–8. On *Penny Magazine*, see Anderson, *Printed Image and the Transformation of Popular Culture*, 50–83. Kevin Gilmartin suggests that the radical press helped to create a "counter–public sphere" whose activities centered around opposing the activities of the public sphere, for example through the stamped press. See Gilmartin, *Print Politics*.

7. An exception to this admittedly oversimplified rule occurred in contexts in which the gulf between the "nation" and Parliament seemed more pronounced than usual, for example in debates during the later stages of the Crimean War. See Anderson, *Liberal State at War*, esp. 74, 85, 87–88.

8. Hardman, comp., *Parliament of the Press*, v, 65.

9. Ibid., 155–56.

10. Interestingly, the immediately following sentence was, "Many prominent journalists hold a contrary view, and they can produce confirmatory examples." Reid and MacDonnell, "The Press," 282.

11. Harmsworth, "Daily Newspaper of Today"; Northcliffe to Wells, 21 May 1917, H. G. Wells Papers N-167, University of Illinois at Urbana-Champaign.

12. Symon, *Press and Its Story*, 103.

13. Scotsman, *Story of the Scotsman*, 3–4, 8, 10, 18, 19, 25–26.

14. Pebody, *English Journalism and the Men Who Have Made It*, iv–v.

15. Ibid., 23.

16. Historians have given his career more generous appraisals. See Walkowitz, *City of*

Dreadful Delight, 81–120. Walkowitz interprets Stead's career within the Victorian traditions of melodrama and pornography. See also Baylen, "'New Journalism' in Late Victorian Britain"; Baylen, "W. T. Stead as Publisher and Editor of the Review of Reviews"; Boston, "W. T. Stead and Government by Journalism"; Andrews and Taylor, *Lords and Laborers of the Press,* 1–12; Schults, *Crusader in Babylon.*

17. "Late Mr. W. T. Stead," 17; Stout, "W. T. Stead," 8. Further confirmation of Stead's self-image can be found in his own unpublished words. In an 1893 autobiographical fragment, Stead described his "second conversion" experience, which occurred shortly after writing a prize-winning essay on Cromwell at age nineteen and he was confronted with the possibility of blindness. Realizing that he was partly motivated by an improper desire for fame, he dedicated himself "to work and labour for those around me." W. T. Stead Papers, STED 3/2, Churchill College, Cambridge University.

18. Stead's articles merely elaborated on the point he had made in his criminal defense: "I am charged with conspiracy. What I did was to expose a conspiracy of vice and crime by a combination with the friends of law and virtue." *Armstrong Case,* 2.

19. Stead, "Government by Journalism," 656.

20. Ibid., 653.

21. Ibid., 654–55.

22. Ibid., 655. For the effects of registration requirements on the electorate, see Blewett, "Franchise in the United Kingdom," and Tanner, "Rise of Labour in England and Wales." Of course, women did not attain the vote until after World War I.

23. Stead, "Government by Journalism," 672–73.

24. Ibid., 659.

25. In "The Future of Journalism," Stead proposed a very elaborate mechanism for ascertaining public opinion. Nevertheless, even this article ultimately requires the editor to decide what constitutes public opinion rather than allowing the readers to speak for themselves.

26. See Joyce, *Democratic Subjects,* 204–13, and Walkowitz, *City of Dreadful Delight,* 81–120. See also McWilliam, "Melodrama and the Historians."

27. As Anthony Wohl has reminded us, however obviously evil the Turks' bayoneting of babies might have been, the "realist" approach to foreign policy was a respected tradition whose merits could be seriously argued. See Wohl, "'Dizzi-Ben-Dizzi,'" 385.

28. See, for example, *The Journalist,* 3 December 1886; *The Journalist and Newspaper Proprietor,* 8 March 1889.

29. Greenwood, "Newspaper Press," 836–37, 842.

30. Havighurst, *Radical Journalist.*

31. Massingham, *London Daily Press,* 191–92.

32. Ibid., 70. Five years earlier, William Morris had noted in a letter to the *Daily News* that the paper disapproved of the police breaking up a "Gladstonian meeting" but approved of similar action when the participants were a "few unhappy people thrust out of work, or degraded beyond power of seeking work by the economical conditions of our faultless society." Henderson, ed., *Letters of William Morris to His Family and Friends,* 276–27.

33. C. P. Scott to Ramsay MacDonald, 27 May 1924, *Manchester Guardian* Archives 336/

121, John Rylands Library, University of Manchester; Kingsley Martin to Harold Wilson, 8 May 1965, Kingsley Martin Papers 14/5, University of Sussex.

34. Walsh, *Moral Damage of War*, 1–38.
35. Ibid., 199–200, 206.
36. Falkirk Herald, *Jubilee of the Falkirk Herald*, 9–11.
37. Ibid., 11–12.
38. Ibid., 56–57.
39. Hoggart, *Uses of Literacy*, 338.
40. Jones, *Languages of Class*, 179–238.
41. For an excellent discussion of this theme in a late twentieth-century context, see Sparks, "Goodbye Hildy Johnson." See also Chalaby, *Invention of Journalism*, 190–93.
42. Stead, *Journalist on Journalism*, 83–84. See also Stead, "Press in the Twentieth Century," for a discussion of the triumph of the nonpolitical popular press in the 1890s.
43. O'Connor, "New Journalism," 429–30.
44. Phillipps, "New Journalism," 186.
45. Headlam, *Argument against the Abolition of the Daily Press*, 7.
46. Seligman, *Idea of Civil Society*, 134.
47. *Hansard's Parliamentary Debates*, 11 May 1881, cols. 261, 218–20.
48. Fox, "New York Journalism," 258–59.
49. On this theme, see Arendt, *Human Condition*, 38–49. Arendt describes "society" as "that curiously hybrid realm where private interests assume public significance" (35).
50. Massingham, *London Daily Press*, 14, 91–93.
51. Williams, *Long Revolution*, 218–19; Klancher, *Making of English Reading Audiences*.
52. *Newspaper Press Directory, 1901*, 40.
53. Massingham, *London Daily Press*, 20–21; Gardner, "Tory Press and the Tory Party," 360; Hirst, "English Newspapers and Their Authority," 145. Before Harmsworth/Northcliffe, no one embodied the trend toward "narrow casting" and audience segmentation more than George Newnes, whose 1890s empire incorporated audiences male and female, elite and popular, political and nonpolitical. See Jackson, *George Newnes and the New Journalism in Britain*.
54. Scott-James, *Influence of the Press*, 126.
55. Ibid., 131.
56. Ibid., 137–38, 194–95, 212.
57. Ibid., 160, 248–50. For Scott-James's discussion of the commercial pressures on the press, see ibid., 239–42.
58. Ibid., 160–61.
59. The classic expression of this mid-Victorian liberalism is John Stuart Mill's *On Liberty*.
60. Scott-James, *Influence of the Press*, 215.
61. Ibid., 278.
62. Ibid., 286. Scott-James explicitly linked this inability to the press's increasing subservience to advertisers.
63. Ibid., 284–85. Habermas argues that around the turn of the twentieth century, the press ceased to provide a forum for the creation of public opinion. Henceforth, "opin-

ion" was developed in nonpublic forums such as in think tanks. In "public," preformed opinions were now "presented" for "consumption." See Habermas, *Structural Transformation of the Public Sphere,* chaps. 20–22.

64. Jones, *Outcast London.*
65. See Pelling, *History of British Trade Unionism,* 89–120.
66. See Wiener, "Unloved State," Searle, *Quest for National Efficiency,* Harris, *Private Lives, Public Spirit,* 180–219, and Perkin, *Rise of Professional Society,* 116–70.

5. Persuasion or Propaganda? Thinking about the Press in Britain, 1914–50

The British in the interwar years inherited two distinct, competing, and yet sometimes overlapping theories of the press. The educational ideal was born in optimism; the emergence of a general cultural pessimism not surprisingly helped to undermine the ideal. Following the great depression of the 1870s, the rise of militant New Unionism, the emergence of a mass reading public and a mass electorate, and the unsettling of widely accepted gender roles, it became increasingly difficult to advocate bringing more and more readers into a politics by public discussion. In addition, it became questionable whether newspapers could serve as a forum for such a public discussion. As the press became more commercialized, its ownership became more concentrated, and the role of advertising revenues became more prominent, the practice of journalism changed. In the mid-nineteenth century, daily papers contained scant news but offered strong opinion. News was confined largely to verbatim or extensive transcriptions of parliamentary debates and speeches by prominent political figures. Beginning in the 1880s, news became increasingly the emphasis, and from the perspective of concerned observers the news was often sensationalistic. Collectively, these changes were often referred to as the "New Journalism."

In the era of the New Journalism, beginning in the 1880s, theorists of the press became less willing to attribute educational qualities to it. Instead, it became more common to refer to the press as a "representative" vehicle. Rather than influencing the people or drawing them into a politics by public discussion, the press was seen to represent readers' interests and desires. This formulation typically disavowed the idea that the press could influence readers or shape public opinion. Instead, conventional wisdom began to assert that the press reflected or mirrored public opinion. These broad theories of the press formed the intellectual tradition inherited by the twentieth century. The debates and positions outlined thus far continued to define the debates about the press, although in very different conditions.

These changed conditions included the further commercialization and concentration of the press and the resulting visible power of the Press Barons. Beyond these factors, however, other developments in British society increased the perceived importance of the debate about the press and helped to shape it in particular directions. For many cultural conservatives, the press was an artifact of modernity that threatened to overwhelm the cultural elite with its mediocrity. Such critics' concerns went beyond the fear of popular newspapers' effects on their audience; they entailed a worry that more "cultured" papers would give up their calling and imitate the popular press. F. R. Leavis, writing in 1930 in his pamphlet *Mass Civilisation and Minority Culture,* credited the press with helping to create a positively hostile environment for the tiny elite charged with preserving British culture. According to Leavis, only a "very small minority" was "capable of unprompted, first-hand judgment," and only a "small minority, though a larger one," was "capable of endorsing such first-hand judgment by genuine personal response." According to Leavis, the press, beginning with Lord Northcliffe, threatened the continuation of both of these groups. Similarly, the economist F. A. Hayek in 1944 blamed the wartime vogue for "planning," which he saw as the "road to serfdom," on the fact that propaganda could effectively capture the allegiance of the masses, "the least original and independent, who will be able to put the weight of their numbers behind their particular ideals." Against such numbers, the intelligent and highly educated individuals whose "views and tastes are differentiated" and who would thus resist intellectual conformity had little hope.[1]

The perspective of the political Left was shaped by its historical expectations of the press and franchise reform. Deian Hopkin has shown that socialists and radicals had generally believed in the press's power to influence politics. They believed that it could shape workers' views, educating them to see where their interests lie. Hopkin shows, however, that at the turn of the century, socialists often saw the existing press "in terms of a crude conspiracy theory" in which the attacks of the "capitalist press" stifled the labor movement.[2] In the 1860s, Robert Lowe had predicted that the extension of the franchise would lead directly to a labor government. Following the Second and Third Reform Bills, this had not happened, partly because the Conservative and Liberal parties remade themselves, at least to a limited extent.[3] After the Representation of the People Act in 1918, many on the Left believed that Labour party rule was the natural and inevitable state of affairs, a view that has helped to shape Labour party historiography for much of the twentieth century.[4] When the inevitable failed to materialize, charges of "false consciousness" were heard, and the popular press was often implicated.[5]

In the period considered here, most public discussion of the press came from a critical perspective, informed by cultural traditionalists or the political Left, sometimes united in the same person. These critiques demonstrated that the educational ideal did not disappear, however much it had come under challenge and waned during the era of the New Journalism. These critiques kept the educational ideal alive, though often only negatively, by pointing out the extent to which the ideal was smashed by reality. The cultural traditionalists kept alive a commitment to Matthew Arnold's vision of the "best which has been thought and said in the world," or what they took as traditional journalistic practices. The political Left continued to see the press as an arena of potentially rational political discussion. Even the pro-business camp often objected to the intrusion of business imperatives into editorial decisions.

These perspectives generated most of the volume of public commentary on the press, but they did not possess a monopoly in the debates. An alternative theory existed, one voiced less frequently and mainly in response to direct challenges, but one that possessed considerable institutional power. This was the Press Barons' perspective, what we might call a market or libertarian view, in which any state intervention in the affairs of the press was inherently tyrannical and a violation of centuries of hard-won press reform. The British press (with all its imperfections) was the best in the world. True, some aspects of the popular press were regrettable, but after all, the people got the press they wanted, in true democratic fashion. If the nation were ever going to have a better press, it would happen only when improved education raised the public's standards of expectations for their newspapers.

The Press Barons' market ideology effectively co-opted the representative ideal that had become so pervasive in the three decades before World War I. By claiming to give the people the newspapers they wanted, proprietors could cast themselves as the voice of democracy, in contrast to the paternalistic or snobbish defenders of an educational press. Moreover, whereas Stead's vision of "government by journalism" had relied on editorial integrity and ability, by the 1930s, early polling techniques lent newspapers' claims to represent their readers the trappings of social-scientific legitimacy—trappings whose shallowness was noted by critics. A 1940 Mass-Observation report regarded these polls with suspicion, claiming that "the press seems to use them rather to assure its readers are being taken into account, than to make any deductions from them." While some polls were "held genuinely in order to find out what people think," others were held "merely to gain support for the paper's own policy." Richard Hoggart noted the same trend in 1957: "The popular papers, always identifying themselves with 'the people,' conduct polls on this matter and questionnaires on that matter among their readers, and so elevate the counting of heads into a substitute for judgment." Even more ingeniously, he noted, weekly magazines increasingly solicited copy from readers "in the form of contributed snippets." Not only did this practice potentially save money, it further increased the appearance of papers representing their readers.[6]

The market view served the interests of the Press Barons, and we need neither question nor accept their sincerity in arguing it. Certainly, proprietors such as Northcliffe, Rothermere, or Beaverbrook did not think in purely democratic or commercial terms but would use their papers to pursue their own pet agendas from time to time. Still, as Jean Chalaby has argued, the Press Barons tended to see newspapers as commodities and as commercial property more than as political tools.[7] For this reason, many who articulated a market/libertarian position often demonstrated an equal willingness to resist state interference on grounds of economic freedom as on grounds of political freedom.

As with the other theories conveyed in this book, the market/libertarian theory can be seen as posturing, but again, it was *public* posturing, and its success reflected the fact that it drew on deeply felt ideals about the press. This period begins only a couple of generations after 1855, and not surprisingly there still existed a widespread wariness of state interference in the press. As we will see, even such an important critic of press commercialization as Kingsley Martin could also see the need to write a pamphlet attacking state interference in the press.[8] Moreover, in an era in which Bloomsbury writers such as Lytton Strachey and Virginia Woolf exposed the hypocrisies of the Victorian period, it was easy to see the stuffiness of the nineteenth-century press as just one more priggish display. Even critics from the political Left generally recognized the inevitability of the Northcliffe revolution.[9]

Having outlined in brief form what we might call the Press Barons' perspective, or the market theory of the press, the remainder of this chapter will concern itself mainly with the critical perspectives. We will see the market theory asserted on certain occasions, such as in response to the Royal Commission on the Press. In general, however, it was assumed or inferred rather than stated, and when it was articulated, it was often given voice by critics who wished to use it as a foil. In short, the educational theory's attack on state control of the press and the representative theory's democratic posturing had been so successful that they had become part of a new implicit orthodoxy that critics had to modify if they were to achieve further press reform.

* * *

The critique of the press in the interwar period drew on a belief in the educational ideal, however skeptical one was about its implementation. A commitment to an educational press accounted in part for the difficulty of the early *Daily Herald* in appealing to working-class readers. Ernest Bevin articulated his view of the *Herald*'s purpose in 1919: "Labour's press must be a real educational factor, provoking thought and stimulating ideas. In addition it must not be full of the caprices of princes, the lubricities of courts and the sensationalism produced by display of the sordid. All these things are but passing phases and are the products of an evil system which is rotten at the base." By the early 1920s, however, J. H. Thomas warned the *Herald*'s directors that perhaps "you had better stop providing the workers with something they do not want." Responding to this logic, in April 1923 the *Herald* announced its new plan to "appeal to everybody, whether they are interested in the politics of the Labour Movement or not; and while it will deal very fully with politics its first cause will be to see that the *Herald* is a complete newspaper, giving each day the full history of yesterday."[10] In other words, the *Herald* would attempt to learn some of the lessons of the New Journalism in order to build the larger circulation it needed to survive.

This tension between "elevating" a working-class audience and providing it with a mass culture it actually wanted also confronted the BBC under John Reith. In developing a "public service" ideal, Reith constantly had to choose between programs reflecting working-class tastes and those of an "elevating" nature that would, unfortunately, probably alienate much of the intended audience.[11] Reith's ability to make this public service ideal economically viable derived largely from the BBC's status as a protected monopoly that did not derive income from advertisements. This difference in the commercial positions of the BBC and newspapers made the former a largely irrelevant model for the press, unless its sacrosanct "independence" was compromised by state interference.[12]

Where the educational ideal did survive, it often did so almost as a form of nostalgia. We have already seen Robert Ensor's 1930 discussion of the Victorian press and its "destruction" at the hands of the New Journalism. Recall the following quotation, describing the press of the period before 1886: "But the reader was at least fairly given the facts, on which he could form his own judgment. Editorial opinion was more or less confined to the leading articles. . . . Propaganda was made by open argument; not, as in the twentieth century, by the doctoring of news."[13] Ensor, a former staffer on the *Manchester Guardian,* here used the Victorian press as a foil for critiquing the press of his own era. In doing so, he drew particular attention to the contemporary press's failure to attempt rationally to persuade readers, as the Victorian press had done. Writing in an era in which most British adults took at least one paper, Ensor had to acknowledge that in the venerated Victorian era the press was addressed to a very limited readership, in contrast to the mass press of the 1930s. His historical account of the period 1870–1914 is also indirectly about the interwar years in which it was written, and in his account of the press he could not avoid pining after a journalistic practice that had all but disappeared. He affirmed the educational ideal, that is, by lamenting its disappearance.

The editor of the *Daily News,* A. G. Gardiner, exhibited a similar yet more explicit nostalgia in an essay written on the death of C. P. Scott, the longtime editor and proprietor of the *Manchester Guardian.* By the time of his death, Scott had come to embody the liberal conscience; Walter Lippmann dedicated his 1920 volume, *Liberty and the News,* to Scott. Gardiner began his essay by claiming, "No personal event since the death of Gladstone has touched the Liberal thought of the world more profoundly than the passing of Charles Prestwich Scott of the *Manchester Guardian.*"[14]

In this essay, Gardiner made claims about the Victorian press that were similar to Ensor's. He acknowledged that Scott was attuned to the business side of journalism. "The remarkable and sustained commercial success his paper achieved under his administration was evidence of that." Yet, unlike Northcliffe, Scott "saw that journalism was not merely a business, in the sense that brewing or tailoring or soap-making is a business. As the by-product of its business activities it had a profound influence upon the public mind. It was the chief instrument in the formation of public opinion, and it was this fact that distinguished it from all other forms of business, and imposed on the journalist a very special responsibility." According to Gardiner, Scott willingly sacrificed his commercial interests when his conscience demanded.[15] Sometimes his paper conflicted with prevailing sentiments, but he "had no passion for conflict for the sake of conflict, and"—in good Mill-like fashion—"was never happier than when the victory of reason over prejudice was won." More generally, his "feelings were always under the governance of the intellect."[16]

Even though, as Gardiner pointed out, Scott outlived Northcliffe by several years, Gardiner linked Scott to the "old journalistic tradition," whereas Northcliffe represented the new. For Gardiner, Scott did not reflect the spirit of the times but was an almost anachronistic character. Northcliffe had led a revolution that was "in a sense inevitable." This revolution had applied to the daily press the discovery that "what the democracy wanted was not instruction, but amusement and thrills . . . every issue must be as full of 'turns' as a music-hall programme." The success of Northcliffe's papers affected all papers, for they had to change to compete. "Before this tornado the old tradition withered away." Scott, however, continued to follow the old tradition. Specifically, he did not seek the largest circulations but aimed at the "best minds of his time all over the world."[17] Scott resisted the pressures of the day by courting a selective audience. The old tradition was increasingly unrealistic and could only be maintained by shunning the masses. All of the most important aspects of the Victorian educational ideal are present in Gardiner's assessment of Scott: sobriety, reason, influence, and a selective audience. Gardiner reaffirmed this ideal by noting how generally it had passed away—even its anachronistic living embodiment had finally died.

At the same time that this educational approach faltered in the face of the reality of popular tastes, the idea of an "influential" media was revived, but as sinister and irrational rather than edifying and rational. Certainly, the notion of the irrational, undesirable influence of the media was not completely new in the interwar period. Aled Jones has traced its presence in mid-Victorian understandings of the press, and theories of nonrational communication were among the factors helping to undermine the educational ideal in the late nineteenth century. In 1913, R. A. Scott-James likened the "influence" of the popular press to "the pattering of rain which wears down rocks." In general, the notion of *rational* influence became more problematic as leading social theorists began to note the social construction of ideas.[18]

Yet it was only after World War I that observers began to credit the press as well as new media with the power to overwhelm a passive audience with irrational "persuasion."[19] In part this derived from the continuing development of theories of the irrationality of communication for yet another generation between 1886 and 1918, through the ongoing diffusion of the ideas of T. H. Green, F. H. Bradley, and others, joined shortly by continental writers like Freud, Le Bon, and Bergson. By the end of the First World War, though, the beginnings of the advertising industry and what Thomas Richards has called a "commodity culture" added further evidence of the manipulability of the masses.[20] In addition, this greater apprehensiveness derived from the development of sophisticated government propaganda techniques. During the First World War, the government had created a Ministry of Information to project the British virtues domestically and abroad. This sort of propaganda was widely regarded as contrary to British tradition. Although Philip M. Taylor has argued that most British elites by the end of the interwar period had come to accept propaganda as "an essential ingredient of British peacetime diplomacy,"[21] this does not change the fact that the government's wartime propaganda activities were disconcerting to many observers.

Unlike in subsequent totalitarian countries, however, in Britain many observers feared the "propaganda" of individuals and corporations more than the state itself. Even during the war the greater fear was that government propaganda was not even emanating directly from the elected government but from unelected, power-hungry Press Barons like Lord Northcliffe. Northcliffe, instrumental in the fall of Asquith's ministry in 1916, was brought into the government as head of the British War Mission to the United States in May 1917.[22] Fear of Northcliffe's political aspirations was widespread, and for good reason. In a letter to H. G. Wells in May 1916, prior to Asquith's fall, Northcliffe offered his thoughts on bringing down the government: "I quite agree with you when you say that 'if any considerable section of the Press decided to make a list of a score or so of men of to-morrow and noticed them unostentatiously, steadily and fully, an alternative government would follow quite naturally.' It is only when one looks through the world with the microscope of a newspaper that one sees how reputations are made. Unfortunately, owing to the manipulation of the Press by self-advertising quacks, the wrong men often rise to the surface." He went on to indicate that Sir Edward Carson and David Lloyd George were the only politicians who took the war as seriously as they should.[23]

Even after bringing down one government, Northcliffe did not rest on his laurels, continuing to use his papers' influence to force the hand of the Lloyd George administration that he ostensibly served. Northcliffe's opponents often accused him of overstepping journalism's proper function. In January 1918, *The Spectator* cautioned, "In spite of its faults, we have no desire to see Mr. Lloyd George's Administration destroyed by a Press typhoon." The writer elaborated, holding out the fanciful prospect of Northcliffe's actually taking the government's helm. In doing so, the writer explained the proper purpose of the press: "The function of the Press—and it may be a public service of untold good—is to act as critic and watchman, to be perpetually warning the country of the dangers that beset the State. But no one in a moment of great danger takes the watchman away from his patrol and places him inside the building."[24] W. T. Stead had envisioned "Government by Journalism"; *The Spectator*'s writer rejected this principle's concrete manifestation in an imagined "Northcliffe Ministry."

Even in a less extreme scenario than an actual Northcliffe ministry, *The Spectator*'s writers feared that in wartime, government by journalism was becoming too much of a reality. Several times in early 1918, *The Spectator* referred to repeated "coincidences" between the government's will and earlier newspaper proposals. In February, that journal acknowledged Lloyd George's denial that he was in any Press Baron's pocket but argued that "the fact remains that there has been an extraordinary series of coincidences between the will of the Government and the operations of certain owners of newspapers who are closely allied with the Government." The article repeated its earlier insistence that the press's duty is to serve as a "watchdog which barks in order to warn" but not to rule the country.[25] The following month, *The Spectator* again referred to "the long series of coincidences between Press campaigns and Government policy." These "coincidences" were the subject of the "greatest uneasiness" among the members of the House of Commons and had been the subject of a parliamentary debate. This article concluded that Lord Northcliffe did not deserve the blame—"if we may assume, as we do, that Lord Northcliffe thinks he is saving the country"—but that Lloyd George deserved blame for yielding to Northcliffe's pressure.[26] Again, Stead had seen government by journalism as democratic because of the editor's proximity to the people; by contrast, faced with Northcliffe's wartime actions, *The Spectator* saw the press as the subverter of a democratically elected government.

Three weeks later, *The Spectator* referred yet again to the "series of coincidences," this time describing Northcliffe's method: "A certain number of papers, which may be generally described as the Northcliffe Press, agitated violently in favour of particular positions, or against particular persons, and shortly afterwards it was discovered that the adoption of those policies, or the removal of those persons, was the will of the Government."[27]

It is difficult to imagine a more exact restatement of Stead's principle that the press had become the "chamber of initiative"—in this case, however, it was condemned rather than praised. Part of the difference in opinion, no doubt, was due to difference in perspective. Stead had written as a self-promoter on the heels of a "progressive" victory for his paper. By contrast, *The Spectator,* an independent conservative journal with close ties to leading politicians, denounced one of these politicians' most important antagonists. More importantly, however, important changes had occurred in the "business" of the press since Stead wrote in 1886. Most significantly, the concentration of the press had reached the point that a handful of proprietors like Lord Northcliffe had little external competition. No proprietor before or since has dominated circulation to the extent that Northcliffe did. Moreover, the increased importance of advertising revenues blurred the line between the business and editorial sides of the newspaper. It should not escape our notice that Stead's vision depended upon editorial control; in the case of the Northcliffe press, however, it was the proprietor rather than the editor who seemed to be the driving force.[28]

These business concerns threatened the existence of an independent press. James Curran has shown that, however large its circulation, a radical paper in the twentieth century would have a prohibitively difficult time surviving. Alan J. Lee has shown that even a liberal paper, if sufficiently committed to independent opinions, would face nearly insurmountable obstacles.[29] Before the First World War, the critique of press concentration had developed only slightly. In the mid-nineteenth century, the constitutional theorist Walter Bagehot was unconcerned about the ability of the "propertied class" to influence the press. As he expressed it, because "'its weight is always in favour of the order and decency without which political life soon becomes a mad strife of factions, it is well that it should.'"[30] Yet in 1863, when Bagehot wrote, the industrialization of the press was only beginning. Before the war, the most important statement of this critique had come from J. A. Hobson as part of his attack on imperialism and jingoism.[31] During the interwar period, however, this critique became much more prominent, culminating in 1947 to 1949 in the first Royal Commission on the Press.

The interwar critique of press concentration can only be understood in the context of continuing attachment to the doctrine of liberty of the press. We have seen in previous chapters that this principle had evolved over centuries, serving as a rallying cry in the war of the unstamped of the 1830s and the campaign to repeal the taxes on knowledge in the 1850s. For the most part, Victorian commentators after 1855 wrote as if the question of press freedom had been resolved once and for all in Britain. Most discussions of press freedom had a self-congratulatory air.

In the interwar period, however, and particularly after Hitler came to power in Germany in 1933, critics on the Left began to note potential threats to press freedom from the state. Harold Laski, for example, wrote to the *New Statesman and Nation* in 1931 in defense of *Daily Worker* printers and journalists convicted for inciting members of the armed forces to mutiny. Laski pointed out that no mutinous act was actually traced to these men, thus qualifying their conviction as an egregious government abridgment of press freedom. Citing A. V. Dicey, Laski argued that "[a]ny emphatic effort to apply the Seditious Libels Act in this country would . . . make political controversy impossible; it is only because it is rarely invoked that the Opposition can hope effectively to criticise the Government of the day."[32] That this episode did not turn into a major cause célèbre is no doubt at least partly due to the *Daily Worker*'s status as a communist organ. Indeed, the jailing of a communist journalist by a popularly elected government can be seen as a classic example of John Stuart Mill's idea of the "tyranny of the majority."

In the late 1930s, as Hitler's intentions aroused increasing suspicion on the Left, the British ideal of liberty of the press became a prominent theme in the writing of Kingsley Martin, the editor of the *New Statesman and Nation*. Martin was one of the most prominent champions of an educational press and chose journalism only after considering an academic career. After impressing C. P. Scott with his early historical writing, Martin signed on as political columnist for the *Manchester Guardian;* he would later regard Scott's example as one of the formative influences in his journalism.[33] Although Martin became one of the strongest critics of the capitalist press, he most frequently argued during the 1930s on behalf of press freedom from government restrictions rather than against the influence of the Press Barons. In his 1938 pamphlet *Fascism, Democracy, and the Press,* Martin argued that most of Germany's neighboring nations had already been intimidated into restricting press freedom to appease Hitler: "In one country after another we read that political parties opposed to Fascism have been suppressed in the hope of buying Hitler's goodwill." Although Britain had not yet reached that point, Martin wrote, "the same tendencies are at work."[34] Prime Minister Neville Chamberlain had publicly expressed his displeasure with press criticism, and his government had repeatedly attempted to suppress dissent through informal measures. Martin carefully disavowed the suggestion that Chamberlain "likes or approves of Fascist methods," but he saw signs "that he envies the advantages, from a Government's point of view, of not being subjected to criticism, and that he may fall into an easy acceptance of the Fascist doctrine that the Government and nation are identical." Martin argued that "[t]o object to criticism on the ground that it is damaging to the nation is to jump the chasm that divides Democracy from Fascism." He invoked seventeenth-century British history to attack the notion that "criticism is treason" and argued that the ultimate tendency of Chamberlain's attack on criticism was for Parliament to exist "for the same purpose as the Reichstag—to register approval of the *fait accompli.*"[35] Martin's attack on Chamberlain involved a rhetorical flourish; a British government did not need the fascist example to equate patriotism with its own immunity to criticism, as C. P. Scott's experiences as an antiwar editor during the Boer War had made clear.[36] Still, it is significant that even one of the most prominent critics of press concentration as a threat to liberty of the press could easily shift his attention to the state's interferences.[37]

This short pamphlet was primarily concerned with the state's threat to the freedom of the press; it only briefly acknowledged the problems of concentrated ownership. According to Martin, the freedom of the press "is a technical term. It means that the Englishman is free at Common Law to print what he wishes without prior censorship, prohibition or restriction by the Government."[38] Admittedly, concentration had proceeded apace during the past generation: "Forty years ago we had innumerable newspapers primarily concerned with politics; their circulations were limited and their contents, by modern standards, deplorably dull; to-day we have a few vast commercial enterprises owned by a handful of millionaires, and greatly influenced by the commercial needs of their advertisers."[39]

Martin continued, acknowledging that "[i]n such circumstances the average man to-day may be inclined to scoff at the liberty his grandfather extolled. . . . In short the liberty to start a paper sounds rather like the legal liberty which even the unemployed enjoy to live at the Ritz." Despite these practical constraints to press freedom, however, Martin defended the existing British press. Asking if it mattered whether Britain had a state-controlled press or one dominated by a few individuals, Martin concluded that "it matters a great deal to the citizen, who must in a democratic country have access to news not exclusively selected from one point of view." Despite the concentration, the British press continued to provide a "considerable variety of views and a choice between different treatments of news."[40] In short, the threat of state interference in the press exposed for Martin the limitations of the threat by the "monopoly press." Notwithstanding a generation of critique of press concentration, Martin argued that "[t]here is a world of difference between a country where plutocracy only controls most of the big papers, while non-commercial papers continue to appear, and a country, such as Germany, where all the propaganda is under a single control, so that even those who do not believe what they read cannot find any alternative source of information. In a Fascist country the press and the wireless all speak all the time with a single voice. In a demoplutocracy the fact that independent newspapers appear and a variety of opinions are freely expressed means that there is continuous controversy. Conflict of opinion is the stuff of political life."[41] The balance of the pamphlet addressed the threat to press freedom posed by backstairs government influence, for example through selectively inviting journalists to press conferences, and the abuse of legal restrictions such as libel laws and the Official Secrets Act.

While Martin was publishing this pamphlet, his journal, the *New Statesman and Nation*, echoed this same theme. Again, the focus was on Chamberlain's expressing that one advantage of totalitarianism was the government's exemption from criticism. Martin's journal saw potential government threats to press freedom in the context of Hitler's Germany and England's seventeenth-century absolute monarchy. According to the *New Statesman and Nation,* Chamberlain "seems, like Hitler, to identify the Premier with the nation and thus to cross at a bound the chasm that divides the democratic and totalitarian ideas of society. We in England fought a war, beheaded one king and drove another from the throne in order to vindicate the opposite principle—that the Government is the servant, not the master of the people, and that free and frank criticism is the proper duty of an Opposition, since the nation lives and may live more healthily even when the Government of the moment is killed by attacks upon its policy and administration."[42]

Compared to Martin's pamphlet, the much shorter article in the *New Statesman and Nation* focused more on the government's informal or "indirect" methods of "influence" rather than on heavy-handed legal measures. It was at this point that the traditional concept of press freedom, as freedom from state repression, merged with the critique of press concentration: "'influence' is often enough, where you have a press predominantly in the hands of a few rich men."[43] In addition to holding press conferences open to selective audiences, Chamberlain's government held the threat of war over the heads of the British people, "so that we shall be intimidated into giving up those very rights of free speech and publication which are of the essence of the democracy we are supposed to be defending."[44]

One month later, in reviewing Martin's pamphlet, Aylmer Vallance wrote in the same journal, "When Thomas Jefferson declared that it would be better to have newspapers without a Government than a Government without newspapers, he was only exaggerating a sentiment which is deeply rooted in the minds of the British people." Like Martin, Vallance saw Britain's "mass-circulation capitalist press" as better and more free than a state-dominated press would be: "there remains, as between rival ownerships, a vigorous individuality of opinion, an eagerness to be 'first with the news,' whose consequence is that a proportion of the reading public—one day in this paper, another day in that—is given an approximation to the truth, no matter how distasteful to the Government."[45]

Leftist critics were the most vocal in attacking the increased concentration of press ownership as a threat to press freedom. Even they, however, remained wary of state interference in the press and contributed to the scare literature. It is therefore not surprising that the attempt to link capitalist control of the press with an unfree press and to look to the state to ensure freedom of the press would face an uphill battle. While many leftist critics remained amenable to the critique of state interference in the press, others proved even more wedded to that tradition. B. Ifor Evans, for example, insisted that "whatever may be the evils of irresponsibility, they are less than the evils of censorship."[46] This equation of state intervention with tyranny appeared in surprising places, such as when the science magazine *Nature* worried, early in the Second World War, that wartime restrictions on the press might stifle scientific inquiry and free criticism. Though wary of censorship of scientific discoveries that might be of use to the enemy, *Nature* did not ignore freedom of opinion: "It is, however, in the matter of leading articles that NATURE is perhaps most deeply concerned in the freedom of the Press. A rigidly controlled Press is a characteristic feature of totalitarian rule, echoing with fulsome monotony the official view. It is equally characteristic of the democratic system that officialdom is open to criticism, out of which comes further progress. . . . It is a hardly won privilege, which we have used, and shall continue to use, with a keen sense of responsibility."[47]

Such sensitivity to encroachments by the state was also stimulated by wartime press controls in both world wars, particularly the second. The Communist *Daily Worker* and *The Week* were both closed in 1941; the ban on the *Daily Worker* was lifted in August 1942, more than a year after the USSR had become Britain's close ally. The government closed both journals by ministerial decree rather than prosecuting them through the law courts. Even more mainstream leftist papers such as the *Daily Herald* attracted the wartime government's attention, though this paper was pressured through the Trades Union Congress rather than overtly censored.[48] This continuing antagonism to state repression of the press, reaffirmed by wartime press restrictions, stifled any developing visions of using the state to rein in the excesses of capitalism.

The interwar critique of press concentration belonged to the liberty-of-the-press tradition but rested uneasily within it. Interwar critics could make the case that they were animated by the same concerns as Milton, Macaulay, James Mill, and Feargus O'Connor but that the primary threat was now in corporate rather than royal or aristocratic hands. In this regard, these critics were analogous to those twentieth-century liberals—from the former party of Cobden—who contemplated increased state intervention in the economy.[49] Their animating spirit of antagonism to all threats to individual freedom shifted advanced liberal focus over the course of a century from Old Corruption to private monopoly and the social causes of poverty. As Harold Laski wrote in 1940, mainstream liberalism was in decline because it had not successfully adapted to changing conditions: "For liberalism, let us remember, was not developed by its makers as a system *in vacuo;* it was a fighting creed seeking to attain specific objectives. It sought, as all human creeds have sought, to make its particulars universal. . . . The weakness of liberalism, historically, did not lie in the fundamental method of its approach; it lay in its inability to recognize how to adapt that approach to a new world for which it was unprepared."[50] According to Laski, the nineteenth-century middle class had accepted the specific reforms accorded by Benthamite principles without following the principles to their logical conclusion: "For when the middle class had wrested from Benthamite principles the changes it desired, it was tempted to believe that the main work of liberalism had been done."[51] These early liberals, wrote Laski, "thought of liberty above all as freedom from [state] interference. . . . They did not understand that in any society where economic power is possessed by a small part of the population, there cannot be the effective enjoyment of liberty by the many. They did not understand, either, that men think differently who live differently, and that a simple faith in the power of reason to win common ground will not do because between those who live so differently there is not, in fact, a common language."[52]

Laski credited T. H. Green with articulating the distinction between positive and negative liberty and the role of government in promoting both: "Negatively, it must remove the hindrances to the good life; positively it must promote those things, especially public education, which enable the citizen to do and to enjoy those things which are worth doing and enjoying." Green, wrote Laski, "brought his age face to face with the problem of social organization and the relations it imposes. He showed that men are not free, as the earlier liberalism deemed them free, because they have the vote and can read the daily press."[53]

This particular version of Laski's analysis of liberalism was not published until 1940, but I have quoted it here because it so forcibly states the basic distinction between the old and new liberalisms. A similar distinction existed, as already noted, between old and new versions of the liberty-of-the-press ideal; the persistence of the older version often helped to impede acceptance of the updated version. As the historian Tom O'Malley has written, "One consequence of the Liberal theory was that it could have the effect of equating all forms of government involvement in the press with actual or potential interference with press freedom."[54] We have already seen that J. A. Hobson developed a critique of press concentration at the turn of the century. In the early 1920s, only a year after the death of Northcliffe, Norman Angell noted a growing concern about "newspaper monopoly." Angell, the socialist, friend, and admirer of the late Lord Northcliffe and former editor of the *Continental Daily Mail*—as well as a pioneer of the League of Nations and the future winner of the Nobel Peace Prize—looked not to the state but to journalists' professional organizations for a solution to "the Press Problem."

"If the public are to accept a newspaper monopoly," he wrote, "they must feel that that monopoly is giving them the news." He saw the inherent danger of censorship as preventable, even without breaking up the monopoly. "It should be as impossible for a newspaper proprietor to assume that he can doctor and tamper with the judgment of a journalist who is reporting, say, the happenings in the Ruhr, as it would be for the owners of a convalescent home to expect its doctors so to treat the inmates that their stay in the institution would be prolonged."[55] How should journalists combat this danger? In his words, "The professional organizations of journalists should fight for a completely new conception of the obligations of the journalist. That obligation is not primarily to the man who pays him, any more than the judge's obligation is primarily to the Government that pays his salary. The obligation is to the public—and to professional conscience."[56] Given the weakness of newspaper professional organizations at that time, Angell's suggestion seems inadequate, even naïve. For our present purposes, the most salient point is that Angell, like other critics, had begun to see press concentration as a threat to liberty of the press; press freedom could be endangered by powerful individuals or corporations as well as by the state.

An article in *The Spectator* in 1923 reaffirmed this broader point. Readers liked newspaper competition because "they know it secures them that freedom of choice which they desire. The reader likes to feel he can, if he so desires, go elsewhere. But we are approaching the point when to go elsewhere means finding the same newspaper under an *alias!*"[57] This author argued that the great danger was that the powerful newspaper owners were wealthy from nonpress concerns and thus could afford to own newspapers not to make a profit but to promote their own politics.[58] Not all interwar critics accused the Press Barons of subsidizing their political interests, however. According to a writer in *The Spectator* in 1935, the mantra "freedom of the press" was misused by proprietors in defense of their commercial interests when this freedom legitimately belonged to editors, leader writers, and other journalists. Wrongly employed, the "so-called Freedom of the Press" often amounted not to the freedom of journalism "but the freedom of finance to exploit journalism and to diminish the status of journalists."[59]

Antibusiness arguments did not go unanswered. E. T. Good, writing in 1920, flatly denied that the "capitalist press" was unfair to labor. He offered no evidence beyond his own authority: "I am sure there is not a man my age who has read and watched more papers or written for more papers than I have. I really can claim to have full knowledge of the subject of the Press and Labour." Based on this vast experience, he claimed that the press was "not merely fair, but very indulgent" to labor; indeed, the "cry against the 'capitalist' Press comes mainly from those who cannot stand fair criticism, and who will not believe that anybody but a Socialist can be honest."[60]

More convincingly, Reginald Wilson, the general secretary of the British Empire Union, wrote in 1922 that the Trades Union Congress's support of the *Daily Herald* constituted a breach of freedom. He argued that this union funding was "compulsory, not voluntary" on the part of the union's members. Developing a market argument, Wilson wrote, "If the *Herald* were really the organ of the workers, it should have no difficulty in attaining a circulation that would make it not only a self-supporting, but an extremely profitable concern. . . . In short, the *Herald* is enabled to preach its extremist views at the expense of large numbers of workers who entirely disagree with them."[61] Wilson thus employed the language of democracy to denounce support for press diversity; his logic steadfastly equates press freedom with consumer sovereignty.

We will return to the theme of press concentration in the context of the Royal Commission on the Press. First, however, we will consider critics' fears of propaganda and mass manipulation by this concentrated press. We have already seen the waning of the educational ideal as many commentators ceased to believe in the efficacy of rational persuasion. For a time it was even common to deny that newspapers could influence readers at all; instead, they reflected public opinion. In the interwar period, however, it became common to warn of *irrational* influence, which threatened to turn readers into the playthings of the Press Barons.

* * *

If the First World War had alerted critics to the increased power or influence of proprietors like Lord Northcliffe, and the related ongoing concentration of press ownership had equally begun to catch their attention, then it is not surprising that critics grew increasingly distraught at the thought that the press was engaging in propaganda that manipulated the helpless masses. This distress predated Hitler's rise to power in Germany, but it only became exacerbated by this event abroad. Given that Britain was not a totalitarian country, however, it is also not surprising that the critique of the press as propaganda focused not so much on the state's activities as on business's. It was during the early interwar years that business propaganda, or "public relations," began to assume its modern form. Stuart Ewen has told this story in an American context, where the development of "spin" perhaps advanced most quickly. As Ewen makes clear, however, this was an international development, growing out of continental social psychology and Graham Wallas's Harvard lectures (attended by the young Walter Lippmann), among other influences.[62]

In Britain, the emergence of newspaper propaganda met a critical response that further weakened the lingering prewar educational ideal. Writing in 1921 in his apocalyptically titled *The Salvaging of Civilization,* H. G. Wells defended a Victorian liberal ideal of education. In describing the proper function of the college, he wrote that "the young man and the young woman begin to think for themselves, and the college education is essentially the supply of stimulus and material for that progress." Wells elaborated, stating that college was "essentially the establishment of broad convictions." To establish these convictions "firmly and clearly," Wells wrote, "it is necessary that the developing young man or woman should hear all possible views and see the medal of truth not only from the obverse but from the reverse side." Wells did not identify particular beliefs that should constitute these adolescents' "broad convictions"; in this context, he was clearly more interested in developing reasoning skills. Properly stimulated, the student should spend the rest of his or her life "confirming, fixing or modifying his or her general opinions."[63]

Like the mid-nineteenth-century educationalists, Wells saw the newspaper as helping to fulfill this function, particularly because "for the generality of people the daily newspaper, the Sunday newspaper, the magazine and the book constitute the only methods of mental revision and enlargement after the school or college stage is past." Wells held to an educational view of the press, which served as a standard by which to judge the contemporary press. On the whole, he found much to praise in the British press, especially compared to the Soviet press. Most importantly, the British press was produced by an "unorganized multitude of persons." It was not "centralized" or "controlled." By contrast, in Russia, the Communist party had taken control of paper, printing, and book distribution. "Free discussion—never a very free thing in Russia—has now on any general scale become quite impossible."[64] Wells ended his discussion of the British press optimistically.

In a chapter conveying overwhelming optimism, however, Wells expressed a few misgivings that heralded the direction of the new critique. "Modern newspapers," he wrote, "have been described, not altogether inaptly, as sheets of advertisements with news and discussions printed on the back."[65] In this sentence, which stands almost isolated in his essay, Wells revealed the growing perception that advertising was now the real business of the newspaper, with news and views as a clearly subordinate feature. The question was not merely one of emphasis. Wells also intimated, in a somewhat lengthier discussion, that the business priority took precedence over truth: "I am inclined to think that there has been a considerable increase of deliberate lying in the British press since 1914, and a marked loss of journalistic self-respect. . . . Quite half the news from Eastern Europe that appears in the London press is now deliberate fabrication, and a considerable proportion of the rest is rephrased and mutilated to give a misleading impression to the reader." Moreover, further illuminating business's control of press content, Wells wrote that a "considerable proportion of the industrial and commercial news is now written to an end." Wells's only grounds for optimism derived from his belief that "people cannot be continuously deceived in this way" and that, as a consequence, the newspaper was losing its credibility. According to Wells, "this swamping of a large part of the world's press by calculated falsehood and partizan propaganda is a temporary phase in the development of the print nexus." Nevertheless, it was "a very great inconvenience and danger." As long as the press constituted such propaganda, "Reality is horribly distorted. Men cannot see the world clearly and they cannot, therefore, begin to think about it rightly."[66]

Wells gave remarkably little grounds for his faith in the reemergence of a critical public, and subsequent critics would echo his critiques more than his optimistic conclusions. A decade later, in an address to the Liberal Summer School at Oxford, Wells himself would, after restating his case for a "freely critical" liberalism, assert that in Great Britain and France, "[l]iberalism is made practically inaudible to the mass of people by a more and more reactionary Press."[67] Wells now thought that the intellectual environment had changed sufficiently so that liberalism, characterized by "freedom of criticism," free speech, and the belief that "accepted opinion is provisional," could no longer follow older or "conservative" methods. If liberalism was to survive, Wells insisted, "I suggest you study the reinvigoration of Catholicism by Loyola. . . . I am asking for a Liberal Fascisti, for enlightened Nazis; I am proposing that you consider the formation of a greater Communist Party, a Western response to Russia."[68] Wells's assessment of the extent of press propaganda had changed dramatically, if his defense of liberalism now entailed copying the methods of the Counter-Reformation, the Fascists, Nazis, and Communists.

Wells was not alone in his increasing pessimism about the prospects of an educational press or a politics by (journalistic) public discussion. Immediately after the First World War, the critique of the press as propaganda began to escalate. Lord Northcliffe was often blamed for altering the character of the press, but the motives assigned to the Press Baron were varied. Although it seemed clear that Lord Northcliffe represented the takeover of a potentially liberal medium by big business and that this was distasteful, critics could not agree on either the source of this transformation nor precisely what it meant. For E. T. Raymond, writing in 1919, Northcliffe was a businessman, pure and simple: "He knows exactly what the public wants, or rather what the public would want if it knew how to make its wants known. A good many caterers in his line are shrewd enough judges of what the common man says and feels to-day. It is Lord Northcliffe's special gift that he knows what the common man will be saying the day after to-morrow, and says it in advance."[69] For Raymond, Northcliffe's skills appeared less as influencing the masses than as reflecting their desires; Northcliffe was not so much manipulating as following them. A page later, though, Raymond argues that he used exactly this talent to "enslave" the masses. Raymond saw Northcliffe as a composite of two of his heroes, Dickens and Napoleon. Like Northcliffe, Dickens had "aimed at the heart of the masses," and Northcliffe "has also the Napoleonic gift of enslaving the intellects of other men without recourse to vulgar tyranny." In Raymond's view, Northcliffe hated politics and yet wished to play a part in it; more than a decade before Stanley Baldwin made this assessment of the Press Barons famous, Raymond asserted that Northcliffe sought "power without responsibility."[70]

A. G. Gardiner had earlier explored Northcliffe's ability to exert an undue influence in politics by following public opinion. In an open letter to Northcliffe printed in *The Star* in 1914, Gardiner told Northcliffe that "you represent no idea, no passion, no policy, no disinterested enthusiasm." On domestic issues, Northcliffe had supported whichever side he took to be more popular, willingly switching sides as he saw fit; he had "spent [his] life in an infamous servitude to the changing passions of the hour." By preaching a war in 1914 that he believed to be popular, "Next to the Kaiser, Lord Northcliffe has done more than any other living man to bring about the war." Even during the Boer War, according to Gardiner, Northcliffe had advocated war not out of a hatred of the Boers but simply to sell newspapers.[71] Eight years later, an anonymous obituary writer in the New York–based *Nation* asserted that, having acquired *The Times* and the *Evening News* as well as retaining the *Daily Mail,* Northcliffe altered the opinions and even the correspondence "to suit the supposed taste of the particular clientele of each newspaper."[72] Well before Rupert Murdoch's English and Scottish papers preached British nationalism and Scottish devolution, respectively, Northcliffe mastered the art of self-contradiction.

Similar charges were leveled in Arnold Bennett's 1909 play, *What the Public Wants,* against the fictitious Northcliffe figure, Sir Charles. Early in the play, Sir Charles tells his brother, Francis, that his only principle is "give the public what it wants." He elaborates: "Don't give the public what you think it ought to want, or what you think would be good for it; but what it actually does want. I argue like this. Supposing you went into a tobacconist's and asked for a packet of cigarettes, and the tobacconist told you that cigarettes were bad for you, and that he could only sell you a pipe and tobacco—what should you say?" He goes on to deny that "because it's newspapers I sell, and not soap or flannel" any other principle should inform his business. Later in the play, his other brother, John, charges him with inconsistency; in justifying his publication of morally dubious material in a popular Sunday paper, Sir Charles claims to be only a businessman, but in his elite paper he poses as a moral guardian. After the argument has developed for several pages, John angrily asserts, "You've got too many principles, Charlie. That's what's the matter with you. You've got one for the Mercury, and another for this Sunday rag." Sir Charles acknowledges this charge: "Don't be childish! You surely ought to be able to see, with your brains, that I can't be the same in forty different papers. I've no desire at all to ram my personal ideas down the throats of forty different publics. I give each what it wants. I'm not a blooming reformer. I'm a merchant."[73]

Nothing could be a greater challenge to the liberal ideal of promoting a politics of public discussion. Northcliffe's commercial instincts led him to shun the forceful presentation of his own opinions, which would risk alienating potential customers; instead, he gave his customers what he believed they wanted, even if this meant contradicting himself in various venues. Ultimately, the greatest danger Northcliffe presented was not that his politics were wrong but that they were vacuous; he did not appear to have an independent political vision. As one anonymous writer put it, "It cannot be said that his mind *works* in any direction. It is not a trained mind. It does not know how to think and cannot support the burden of trying to think."[74]

Whether or not they specifically blamed Northcliffe, critics increasingly pointed to the dominance by business's bottom-line concerns and the press's means of controlling the opinions of readers. Massingham wrote in 1923, shortly after his resignation as editor of *The Nation*, that press owners were "good trade-psychologists." He compared them to "the people who 'dress' shop-windows, write or draw advertisements, compose trade circulars, and invent or alter trade models."[75] This being the case, it was not surprising that newspaper stories borrowed the methods of advertising: "The Rothermere Press rarely reasons about anything. It excites and suggests. Its opinions are dressed up with its news, or are presented pictorially, by headlines or epithets, or huge display posters, which, appearing simultaneously in slightly varied forms, give the false idea of an independent research of voices in place of a single gramophoned-utterance." Massingham went on to call journalism a "*masked* power," a "*mo-*

nopoly power," and a "*non-moral* power" and to call the Rothermere press a "dangerous trade, poisoning the minds of the English, as other industries, still unfavourably known to the law, used to poison their bodies."[76]

The same year, 1923, Gardiner echoed Massingham's linking of business motivations and mass manipulation. In an article titled "The Rothermere Press and France," Gardiner called the late Lord Northcliffe's brother the "most powerful individual in the State" and accused him of abusing his power in a way that threatened world peace. Rothermere's powerful weapon, wrote Gardiner, "consists of the great machine for manufacturing mob opinion, which he chiefly inherits from his brother." Gardiner continued: "There has never been, in this or any other country, so tremendous an engine for stamping the public thought with the bias of a single mind as that controlled by Lord Rothermere to-day." How did Lord Rothermere effect this "manufacturing," this "stamping"? Gardiner's vision of Rothermere's practice is reminiscent of Massingham's:

> Leaders have ceased to have importance in this journalism of stunts and apoplectic seizures; but the news columns have been saturated with the prejudices and policies which the Harmsworths sought to impose on the public mind. . . . But in the case of the systematic manipulation of the news, the suppression of facts that seem to support the purpose in view, the public have no such corrective at command. They do not, being for the most part simple and ignorant people, suspect the enormous fiction of which they are the sport. They accept what they read in good faith, and innocently suppose that they have themselves conceived the opinions which have been insinuated into their minds by the daily trip of the Rothermere press.[77]

All of the familiar elements of mind control are present in this quotation: the absence of reason (represented in leading articles), the use of emotional devices (stunts), the imposition of official views, the "manipulation of news," and simple and ignorant people. Again, however, this mind control did not emanate from the government but from a businessman. Gardiner concluded, "Whatever the motive, we are in the presence of a deliberate and impudent attempt to destroy Parliamentary government and to substitute the dictatorship of a lawless mob, inflamed with passion and subject to an irresponsible power which is great in virtue of nothing but the control of a machine of publicity, and which we do not elect and cannot bring to judgment. . . . Are we to drift into Fascism with Lord Rothermere or his Man Friday, Mr. Lovat Fraser, as its Mussolini?"[78]

Britain did not succumb to Rothermere's or anyone else's brand of fascism, but in an atmosphere of popular discontent and economic instability, at home and abroad, Gardiner can perhaps be forgiven for hyperbole. Moreover, although not all critics of the Press Barons held out the prospect of fascism,[79] Gardiner's critique would become increasingly familiar. Norman Angell offered a substantially similar critique of the press, but with a different emphasis. Writing also in 1923, Angell fundamentally blamed the readers, the masses themselves—or at least their circumstances—for the character of the press. The industry "simply could not exist on a 'Manchester Guardian' basis of circulation," he wrote. Whenever the mass-circulation *Daily Mail* or the Hearst papers addressed politics, they were forced to do so in a way that

> will appeal most readily to the tens of millions, to the tea-shop waitress or the schoolgirl typist. That is to say, it must touch some feeling easily aroused; must not puzzle them by upsetting conceptions that have become familiar; and must present so simple a case that it will hold attention in competition with the rattle of Tube and factory, or the fatigue of the day's end. And though the waitress or typist may be as capable, inherently and potentially, of sound political judgment as the country parson and the retired colonel who were such large constituents of public opinion a generation ago, modern conditions, both as they affect the readers and the newspaper industry itself, not only give native common sense and individual judgment less chance against mass suggestion than did conditions a generation or two ago, but the unwisdom of the million is politically much more serious and dangerous now than it was then.[80]

In this quotation, the prospect of fascism was at most implicit ("serious and dangerous"), and Angell held out the common socialist hope that if only they were freed from drudgery, the common workers might embrace high culture.[81] Yet his vision of press propaganda did not differ fundamentally from Massingham's and Gardiner's. Like theirs, his interpretation envisions mass manipulation by hidden means. Even presumably apolitical papers like *The Sketch* or *The Mirror,* he wrote, contained a political angle. "Every story about the wickedness of Germans, every picture showing Monsieur Poincaré being cheered by the French crowds, every cartoon revealing the Hun as a sly and fraudulent debtor, means crystallizing certain opinions, the stiffening of a certain attitude on social questions."[82] As Massingham wrote on Northcliffe's death, in the journalism of this "destroying angel" there was "[n]o need to argue or state; a nickname—'Huns,' 'Cuthberts,' 'Wait and See'—would do as well, or a catchword, such as 'Kitchener Must Go,' yield the derisive or pictorial effect which was required."[83] David Low made a similar point in his 1936 cartoon "Seeing Red," in which he accused the press of painting the Spanish Republicans with the Bolshevik brush to support a pro-Franco position.[84]

Persuasion or Propaganda? 153

SEEING RED

David Low portrays the western press's hostility to the Spanish Republic. Anyone sympathetic to the republic is branded a "red." From the *Evening Standard*, 20 August 1936.

For critics like Angell, Massingham, and Gardiner, as well as for George Binney Dibblee and R. A. Scott-James writing on the eve of the First World War, views were routinely smuggled into news. Or, as J. J. Astor put it, "It would indeed appear that the majority of newspaper readers are unconscious of their own susceptibility to newspaper suggestion, and unaware of the extent to which their neighbours are affected by it." During the war, the Wellington House propagandist Sir Gilbert Parker had drawn on a similar assumption, noting the efficacy of using dispassionate, seemingly "objective" language to persuade readers; in his view, German publicists had alienated American opinion by failing to disguise their propaganda. To take another example, in 1930 the journalist George Blake noted that "the British public seems to cherish to this day a childlike faith in the veracity of whatever it sees in public print. 'I saw it in the paper'—as who should say in Holy Writ—is still used as a clinching argument in support of statements of the more fantastic sort."[85] Again, not all observers have been convinced that print contained inherently rational qualities.

The primary means of effecting subrational "persuasion," according to many critics, were distortion and suppression. The Catholic cultural traditionalist and French emigré Hilaire Belloc argued that "false ideas are suggested by false news and especially by news which is false through suppression." He took such suppression in the daily press for granted, claiming that the interesting question was the "degree to which news can be suppressed or garbled, particular discussion of interest to the common-weal suppressed, spontaneous opinion boycotted, and artificial opinion produced."[86] Others made similar observations. *The Saturday Review* in 1931 spoke longingly of the past, when "no respectable newspaper made any effort to edit its news, and its views were to be found set out at length in the leading article." Those days were past, and now the news was "warped in some way, so as to convey the editorial standpoint upon the subject with which it deals."[87] According to David Ockham, writing in 1931, "news is carefully winnowed; the primary functions of the Press have become those of distortion and suppression, and the daily paper is the daily dope." For Evelyn Waugh's fictional journalist, Corker, newspapers' distortion justifies multiple correspondents and news agencies: "It gives them a choice. They all have different policies so of course they have to have different news."[88] Not all commentators agreed, however. Ivor Thomas, a Labour MP and formerly an editor on *The Times* and leader writer on the *News Chronicle,* wrote in 1943 that the provincial press generally confined its politics to the leader columns: "in its treatment of news and features [it] is nearly always scrupulously fair to all parties." Even advertisers' power over newspaper content was limited, not least because advertisers were as dependent on newspapers as the papers were on them. Thomas acknowledged that complete objectivity was impossible but insisted that any "distortion is more often unconscious than conscious. Critics are apt to attribute to deliberate malice what is more probably due to the speed at which newspaper staffs work."[89]

Notwithstanding a dissenting voice such as Thomas's, the overwhelming assessment was that distortions in the news influenced readers at a subrational level. As Harold Laski wrote in his 1931 book, *Politics,* "Events like the Russian Revolution, a great strike, the operation of a nationalized industry, are distorted so as to produce an unfavourable impression of their nature upon the citizen who learns of their character from his newspaper. He gets his facts as through a mirror in which their perspective is out of proportion to suit a special interest." As the Mass-Observation director Tom Harrisson would state nearly a decade later in 1940, people "are often not sufficiently skeptical about news," though they had become "definitely skeptical" about editorial comment.[90] For Norman Angell, this potential for mass manipulation further solidified the bifurcation of public opinion, which had already been noted by writers like Scott-James, into high/low, elite/popular, or masculine/feminine. In a paragraph that surely owed more than a little to Walter Lippmann's writings, Angell asserted that the English public had been divided into two groups with "diametrically opposed views of policy: on the one side, the relatively tiny group who know the facts, more or less, and see the rocks on to which we are drifting; and on the other side, the enormous majority of the British nation, violently opposed to the views of the smaller group, not knowing the facts, not seeing the dangers."[91] For Lippmann, this mass ignorance was the product of "stereotypes," and the solution was governmental administration by an apolitical expert elite. Echoing the diagnosis, Angell seemingly went out of his way to avoid such a solution.[92]

This emphasis on the distortions of language appeared in contexts not specifically concerned with the press. In his 1946 essay "Politics and the English Language," George Orwell argued that political writing in his era was generally bad because it largely consisted of the "defence of the indefensible." Unlike Massingham, however, Orwell emphasized the use of language not to achieve a particular mental image (of "Huns," for example) but to suppress such images. According to Orwell,

> political language has to consist largely of euphemism, question-begging and sheer cloudy vagueness. Defenceless villages are bombarded from the air, the inhabitants driven out into the countryside, the cattle machine-gunned, the huts set on fire with incendiary bullets: this is called *pacification*. Millions of peasants are robbed of their farms and sent trudging along the roads with no more than they can carry: this is called *transfer of population* or *rectification of frontiers*. People are imprisoned for years without trial, or shot in the back of the neck or sent to die of scurvy in Arctic lumber camps: this is called *elimination of unreliable elements*. Such phraseology is needed if one wants to name things without calling up mental pictures of them.[93]

Critics in the interwar period were well aware of the conflict between their own press ideals and the newspapers that the readers would accept. Jean Chalaby has argued that the repeal of the taxes on knowledge created the "journalistic field" in which newspapers became primarily a commodity. Before 1855 and for some time afterwards, newspaper owners and writers were chiefly "publicists," not "journalists"; they wrote to advocate their politics, not primarily to sell newspapers and thus survive in a fierce competition.[94] Whether or not one accepts Chalaby's entire argument, it is clear that after 1855 the commercialization of the press began apace, and by the interwar period any journalistic strategy had to take full measure of the intensely short-term desires of readers.

This capitulation to readers' wants could be presented as mere realism, a principle of sound business. Speaking to the Institute of Journalists in 1929, Lord Riddell, owner of the *News of the World*, argued, "The newspaper reader buys his paper for several reasons. He wants the ordinary bread and butter news, such as markets, stock exchange intelligence, law reports, racing and sports results, and the outstanding news of the day, but he also wants interesting reading. He wants something startling and fresh presented in attractive form. Therefore, the journalist is compelled, hour by hour and day by day, to strain for what will interest the reader."[95] Similarly, a writer in *The Spectator* a decade later, admitting that many abuses in popular journalism derived from the profit motive, nonetheless assigned primary blame to the readers themselves. If newspapers often exploited the worst aspects of popular taste, this "would not happen if the public were more discriminating in what it buys and reads," in other words, "if it were better educated." As Northcliffe's longtime manager Kennedy Jones argued, the "new class of readers" invented by the 1870 Education Act were "the children, the grandchildren and the great grand-children of a people accustomed to public hangings, public whippings, pillories, ducking-stools, and stocks.... Was the taste engendered by such sights during the centuries to be outbred by the cheap schooling of a single generation?" Even Angell, in his 1922 book *The Press and the Organisation of Society*, had to acknowledge that if Northcliffe had not exploited the popular audience in the way he did, someone else would have, and "the control of big circulations—and in certain crises national destinies—would be in other hands."[96]

Most leftist critics saw this market approach as too simplistic or too glibly evasive of a newspaper's public duty. We have already seen, in a couple of different contexts, Angell's concern for treating popular taste as a problem rather than an excuse. He called upon journalists to follow the examples of other professionals in refusing to allow the piper to call the tune. This demand became increasingly common.

Other critics believed that the public was becoming more rather than less discriminating. As early as 1918, *The Spectator* argued that "[a]s education spreads and deepens, the popular Press will steadily respond to the demand for fuller and more trustworthy news and more serious and responsible comment."[97] In light of *The Spectator*'s frequent willingness to blame the reader for journalism's excesses, this argument reads like a defense of continued laissez-faire. Yet the Labour politician George Lansbury concurred, writing of the popular press that had emerged (in his view) with the 1870 Education Act, "After fifty years, the dope is not working quite so well." This assessment echoed that of an anonymous writer in the left-liberal *Nation and the Athe-*

naeum, who claimed in 1922 that "we may already discern a certain reaction against the most disheartening signs of popular journalism—the colored telegrams, the elaborately worked-up sensations, the hysterical politics, and the trivial gossip of passion." According to this writer, this reaction "perhaps" derived from the "sobering influences" of the First World War.[98] Norman Angell noted a similar reaction but less optimistically called it a mere interlude. For Robert Graves, anyone who had fought in the war had already learned to distrust the press; they were far from the helpless masses portrayed by Gardiner, Massingham, and Angell. In *Good-Bye to All That,* Graves wrote that from the perspective of the returning soldier, "civilians talked a foreign language; and it was newspaper language." Graves and Alan Hodge wrote in 1940 that the "official propaganda machine, under Lord Northcliffe's direction," had completely fooled "the Rest," those who had not fought in the war, but for those who had fought, "who knew the facts," the press's dishonesty during the war had "undermined their simple faith in the printed word." Malcolm Muggeridge, discussing Stanley Baldwin's famous 1931 denunciation of Press Barons as harlots, claimed that the public may read Beaverbrook and Rothermere papers but had "so engrained a distrust of their judgment and motives that it will not be influenced by them, except contrariwise."[99] Similarly, a 1934 article in *The Spectator,* while calling for more sober journalism in place of sensationalism and lamenting that most newspaper readers took in only a single favorite newspaper, nonetheless took comfort in the "apparent resistance of the average reader" to the influence of the press.[100]

Some believed that the presence of alternative new media such as the BBC would encourage readers to demand better of the press.[101] By early 1941, BBC Listener Research discovered that "I heard it on the wireless" tended to settle all disputes about the news, while readers had become increasingly skeptical of what they read in newspapers: "it has not been on the wireless, so it is probably newspaper talk."[102] For other critics it was the Second World War that led readers to seek a more "responsible" press. As *The Spectator* wrote in March 1940, "Today the whole nation is in the mood for sober common sense."[103]

These opinions received apparent empirical confirmation in the surveys of Mass-Observation, which commenced in 1937. A December 1938 report noted that, far from passively accepting newspapers' "facts" at face value, 37 percent of readers objected to their own daily paper "on grounds of political bias or unreliability," while 30 percent objected that their paper "lacks culture, or is trivial or sensational." Such readers typically bought their particular newspaper for a favored feature or writer. Moreover, people read newspapers in ways that perhaps differed from the intentions of the journalists.

Newspaper reading was a "habit" whose function was "largely to make people feel they are in touch with the outer world"—in other words, to enable them to "talk to other people about it and to feel a sense of participation." Another reason for newspaper reading, more common among female readers, was escapism, "a means of getting away from the world rather than keeping in touch with it and using it in the same way as a novel or magazine."[104] A subsequent report stated directly that "[g]eneral doubt of newspapers on the grounds of propaganda and concealment militates against their effect as opinion-forming instruments."[105] Following a summary of an interview with an informant, the report concluded: "What emerges from this conversation is that thinking people—and it should be clear from the other evidence in this report that many more people are thinking people than politicians or editors currently suppose—prefer newspapers that appear to report facts impartially, uninfluenced by either party considerations or the need for greater and greater sales. And it is precisely because there are few such newspapers that people have become distrustful of the press as a whole."[106] This conclusion neatly sidestepped the problem, already noted by Dibblee, of papers that might appear unbiased but smuggle opinion in the news. Nonetheless, these and other Mass-Observation reports showed that readers were capable of appropriating newspapers for their own cultural purposes and reading them with a degree of sophistication.

Despite these signs of a critical readership, for many on the Left the crucial problem of the press was the difficulty of conveying complexity to an audience that, on a daily basis, preferred simplicity and amusement. The American Walter Lippmann most strongly developed this argument in his 1922 book *Public Opinion*; Norman Angell (a sometime contributor to Lippmann's *New Republic*), Kingsley Martin, and others echoed it for a British audience. According to Lippmann, the environment in which modern people lived was "altogether too big, too complex, and too fleeting for direct acquaintance." Between a person and this environment existed a "pseudo-environment," comprising fictions, or manmade representations of the environment. One acted in the complicated environment, yet one's actions were guided by response to the simplified pseudoenvironment.[107]

Lippmann argued that ordinary people necessarily apprehended the world through stereotypes, which were convenient shortcuts for making sense of a more nuanced world. According to Lippmann, people's public opinions—the "pictures inside the heads of . . . human beings, the pictures of themselves, of others, of their needs, purposes, and relationships"—often misled them in their interactions with the outside world. Unlike the straightforward, often personalized, stereotyped pseudoenvironment, the complex real world consisted of many factors hidden to ordinary people, hidden by "censorship and privacy at the source, by physical and social barriers at the other end, by scanty attention, by the poverty of language, by distraction, by unconscious constellations of feeling, by wear and tear, violence, monotony." According to Lippmann, "democracy in its original form never seriously faced the problem which arises because the pictures inside people's heads do not automatically correspond with the world outside." If representative government was to survive in the modern world, society had to create an "independent, expert organization for making the unseen facts intelligible to those who have to make the decisions." Many democrats expected newspapers to perform this feat; Lippmann argued, however, that "newspapers necessarily and inevitably reflect, and therefore, in greater or lesser measure, intensify, the defective organization of public opinion." Representative government thus depended on finding a way to organize public opinions "for the press if they are to be sound, not by the press as is the case today."[108]

British observers noted a similar gap between the modern world's complexity and the simplicity of its depictions in the press. According to the *Nation and the Athenaeum* in 1921, an oversimplified, commodified depiction of the leisure classes, or "Kensington," threatened to undermine working-class loyalty to the society that these "betters" dominated. The *Nation and the Athenaeum* argued that workers acquired their understanding of Kensington primarily through the Sunday papers. These papers essentially portrayed "murders with violence, adulteries in high places, indecent assaults, unnatural crime." Even the cleaner papers "create the impression of great classes giving their lives merely to the luxurious pursuit of enjoyment"; during the present economic adversity, this was difficult for workers to accept. Workers' loyalty to the existing social order was compromised: "while pictures, gossip, and advertisement still record the doings of a fairyland seemingly utterly unmoved by their present plight, they find themselves lectured on the need for the cutting of their wages to the bone, in order, as it appears to them, that fairyland may still persist in its fascinating, irrelevant life."[109] This brief article merely implied that reality was more complex than this "fairyland" picture; presumably, the upper classes gave their lives to something more worthwhile than the papers let on, and workers were not actually immiserated for the sake of Kensington's high life.

Other critics made their point more overtly, and not merely from a leftist perspective. The *Quarterly Review* in 1931 faulted statesmen with unwillingness to tell voters unpleasant truths. If statesmen failed, so did the press, and for an obvious reason: "for the press to join in any such crusade would strike at their advertisement revenue as well as their readers' usual complacency."

The press's inability to tell hard truths, the author wrote, allowed the Trades Union Congress to conduct a "fiery class-war against the nation." Britain was engaged in a serious, complicated financial crisis, and the author called upon the press to stop focusing on "levity or even ... ordinary features of public interest and distinction" and to focus on explaining the crisis with "an all-daring lead in such vital matters as class-cleavage and labour costs; a drastic economy in spending both public and private funds, together with every sort of sleight and ingenuity to unite and rouse our people in a concerted effort to restore the nation's lost prestige. ... Whole columns and pages of play-ball should forthwith disappear, so should the racing and betting news."[110] The specific remedy offered echoed the political perspective that leftist critics found all too pervasive in the capitalist press. Yet the significance of this passage for our current purpose is that it called for serious attention to complicated matters in lieu of a merely superficial explanation drowned in a sea of frivolity. Unfortunately, however, "the root causes of Britain's crumbling credit are not only complex to the layman, but of poor 'news-value' to the Press."[111] Harold Nicolson echoed this sentiment more than a decade later: "Never in our history has it been so important to inform the public; and never has the sovereign been so ill-informed." Part of the problem was the paper rationing resulting from postwar austerity, but newspapers compounded it by "entertaining and flattering their readers rather than instructing them."[112]

Nobody developed this theme for a British audience more thoroughly than Norman Angell. In his 1922 book *The Press and the Organisation of Society,* Angell explicitly echoed Lippmann, citing the *Atlantic Monthly* essays that became Lippmann's *Liberty and the News.* For his part, Lippmann wrote to express his unqualified endorsement of Angell's study.[113] Angell's broader interests diverged somewhat from Lippmann's. In his introduction, Angell revealed as one of his concerns that the existing capitalist press would stifle the labor movement so that even if a Labour government were elected, the capitalist press would render their victory "nugatory." "While 'Labour' might constitute the Government, it would find that the forces which made and unmade Governments were still in the hands of those outside the ranks of Labour."[114] In this regard, one of Angell's key interests was the harmfulness of press concentration.

Angell's book moved beyond mere questions of "press bias," however, in ways that derived directly from Lippmann. For Angell, the Press Barons did not possess an unmitigated sway over the public mind; the originating and defining condition of the press was the character of the reader and social psychology. For this reason, Angell saw the press as "conservative" not in the sense of protecting the interests of the Conservative party, though it might do that, but in the sense of buttressing a conceptual status quo. The press acted in this way, in turn, because readers preferred such a press.

According to Angell, people had a genuine capacity for rational thought. For most of them, however—indeed, for "natural man"—contemplating ideas contrary to their own passions and instincts was distasteful, however necessary for social progress.[115] Thus their "first" thoughts, the "instincts and emotions that can be most rapidly excited," were often the most "anti-social." Unfortunately, in the highly competitive search for profits, newspapers were forced to appeal to such "first" thoughts instead of the more reasoned "second" thoughts. Angell wrote of an example of Gresham's Law, whereby the bad currency drives out the good, and claimed that if Northcliffe had not appealed to these baser instincts, someone else would have done so and filled his position as the most influential Press Baron. Such readers, in a commercial environment, thus tended to prefer papers that supported the conceptual status quo or the "stereotyping of all those social and political conceptions which involve easily aroused passion and feeling—those that are rooted not necessarily in the deepest instincts, but in the most easily awakened ones." Since people naturally disliked ideas that challenged their current beliefs or assumptions, "Every attempt at revision encounters somewhere the primitive tribal instinct or passion. All revision of conceptions in the past has been the work of small minorities, of individual minds, of a few heretics, encyclopaedists or pamphleteers, able to reach other minds for a sufficient length of time to break down the first prejudice." Because of this law, the sufficient length of time was impossible to attain. Thus, "The modern Press is likely to make our conceptions of the State, Nationalism, individual right, international obligation, and institutions that depend thereon, all but impossible of reform."[116]

The conservative nature of the press thus derived from the nexus between readers' own prejudices and journalism's commercial imperative to exploit them. The press owners were not innocent bystanders, however. We have already seen that, for Angell, newspaper owners were themselves prosperous capitalists who had every incentive to support the same status quo that appealed to readers' instincts. These owners would be willingly complicit in encouraging the prevailing stereotypes, appealing to the first instead of the second thought.

That is not to say that a proprietor never wished to support an unpopular idea. Angell acknowledged the debate between those who saw the Trust Press as a mere "barometer" that "registers the weather and has no part in determining it" and those who believed that the best way to carry a political agenda was the "conversion of Northcliffe."[117] Without resolving this controversy over whether the press influenced or reflected public opinion, Angell maintained that the importance of the Press Barons was in determining the very news upon which ordinary people thought: "Obviously what England thinks is largely controlled by a very few men, not by virtue of the direct expression of any opinion of their own, but by controlling the distribution of emphasis in the telling of facts: so stressing one group of them and keeping another group in the background as to make a given conclusion inevitable."[118] Angell provided an example in the Paris Peace Conference, an occasion that called for difficult truths rather than easy stereotypes. The public, however, "did not want to be informed, did not want the truth." Instead of the truth the public received stories of German atrocities that confirmed their prejudice. Angell cited this as an example of distortion through selective truth telling; the atrocities may all have "happened," yet "they were, as selected by the Press, less than half the truth. To get the whole truth—to achieve the state of mind necessary for making a real peace at Paris—it would have been necessary to tell with equal emphasis of the humane actions of the enemy, and of the atrocities committed even by the allies; and to remind ourselves that if Americans were not to be 'outlawed from civilisation' for the weekly burning of negroes, or the British for Irish reprisals and Indian repression, the Germans could not be outlawed for conduct no more atrocious."[119]

Angell would often return to this theme of readers' antisocial instincts crowding out their more reasoned second thoughts. Writing fifteen years later, in 1937, he argued that the effect of the popular press had often been "extremely evil," not because of intention but because of intense competition and "the present state of general education." Specifically, the press had to be called to account for the First World War. Before 1914, British readers needed a true picture of Europe, including nationalism and states' concern for security and "fears which expanding peoples were beginning to have about possible exclusion from their share of the earth's resources." Some writers did their best to give this picture, but "most of the Press, practically the whole of the popular section of it, was busy creating a mood which made it impossible for the public to see that picture, much less consider it." Unfortunately, the complicated picture did not make a good "news story"—"the sort of 'story' which circulation managers would regard as likely to sell the paper to ever more millions." Instead, readers preferred, or were thought to prefer, stories of "secret German plots directed at the invasion of this country and destruction of the Empire, the discovery of plans of invasion, stories of what would happen when it had been brought off, disquisitions on the evil character of the Germans, quotations from Nietzsche, Treitschke and Bernhardi—it was that sort of emotion-feeding matter which built up big circulations." In this journalistic atmosphere, "sober consideration" was drowned out by "the competitive exploitation of the emotions of melodrama, spiced with fear and prejudice."[120]

Kingsley Martin developed this theme in his 1947 study, *The Press the Public Wants.* Unlike Lippmann's *Public Opinion,* in which the press surfaced as a leading site of the creation of public opinions and the pseudoenvironment, Martin's book, written in the context of the Royal Commission, focused widely on most aspects of press history, economy, and politics. Like most commentators, Martin saw a large disjunction between the Victorian press and its twentieth-century counterpart; in his own era the press was highly commercialized, and he had no illusions that education could ever triumph over such commercialization. "Naturally we get recreation for which we are prepared to pay rather than instruction which we think we ought to get free. We put into the hands of the people most clever at entertaining us the enormous weapon of propaganda."[121]

In the present context, what stands out is Martin's use of Lippmann's concept of "stereotypes." Martin did not believe that the public was infinitely malleable in the realm of domestic news; according to him, the newspaper reader

> forms his political outlook from his environment; he may vote Conservative or Liberal or Labour because his father did before him or, perhaps equally frequently, because his father voted the opposite way. He takes his politics from the company he keeps; his opinions reflect the gossip of his club or the political affiliation of his trade union; he hears speeches, talks in trains, likes or dislikes the personality of the candidate and to-day takes good account of things said on the wireless. He cannot picture the country as a whole nor completely understand the political or economic situation, but he has personal knowledge of a random sample which is generally some guide to a domestic issue.[122]

This quotation reveals a more nuanced assessment than the often remarked Frankfurt School interpretation of masses all but helpless before scientific propaganda and commercialized mass culture. Moreover, it anticipates more recent studies of the "influence of the media" that downplay the media's influence in areas in which the reader, listener, or viewer has independent knowledge and highlight the greater influence of friends and acquaintances.[123] Lippmann argued that for most people, much of the world constituted an environment beyond their experience; he thus called for a greater role for nonpartisan expertise. By contrast, Martin preferred a more localized society, for "the smaller the area in which an individual participates actively, the more free he will be from the menace of second-hand information and valueless news, and the better chance he will have to know what he is doing, to judge honestly and to live creatively."[124]

Although his proposals differed from Lippmann's, we see the same emphasis on an environment mediated for most people by stereotypes. While people remained relatively immune to press manipulation in domestic affairs, international affairs were another matter entirely. Even in domestic affairs, people relied to a great extent on symbols and stereotypes to make sense of reality, "But in home affairs we accept this symbol critically." By contrast, in international affairs, "comparatively few people have the knowledge or the critical training to free them from the tyranny of symbols. Nations become good or bad, gangsters or saints." Martin continued to show the uses of stereotypes historically in promoting wars.[125]

For Martin, like Lippmann, the basic problem of modern democracy was the scale of the modern world: "Politics were less and less about what ordinary people understood, and more and more about a world too complex to understand and too big to imagine. The citizen grew up in an artificial, second- or tenth-hand world, reacting not to facts which he had experienced, but to a picture of those facts painted for him by people who might or might not have an interest in presenting them fairly, but who in any case had to make them intelligible and interesting by tricks of simplification, by symbols, catchphrases, and dramatisation."[126]

We have seen throughout this chapter a fundamental tension between perceptions of "the press the public wants" and the press that a democracy required. This tension mirrored that between freedom-of-the-press ideologies that focused on the state and those that focused on private corporations. While leftists like Angell and Martin called for more "responsible" newspapers, as an antidote to mass manipulation or propaganda, conservatives and Press Barons could counter that, in giving the public what they wanted, *they* were the real democrats.

* * *

For analytical purposes, this chapter has distinguished between the commercial interests and political views of the business elite. Clearly these are not the same thing, however much they may overlap. In 1942, Ernest Barker claimed, "Money treats the press in terms of dividends; of a large circulation, to be secured by any means; of a large advertisement revenue. Left to itself, it will provide any views—if only they pay; and it will incline to demagogy rather than reaction." James Curran has rendered this view untenable; all things being equal, "money" would clearly choose the publications with congenial views. Mere circulation was not enough; the paper had to attract advertisers, and advertisers, as Hilaire Belloc noted in 1918, did not merely follow circulation. The advertiser "would not advertise in papers which he thought might by their publication of opinion ultimately hurt Capitalism as a whole; still less in those whose opinions might affect his own private fortunes adversely." Not only would such considerations affect the editorial "line" of a paper, Belloc argued, they would on occasion lead to the suppression of news. Writing in 1939, F. P. Bishop took pains to deny that advertisers possessed this kind of power. While it was certainly no longer the case that the editor could "cultivate a self-conscious ignorance of half the contents of his paper," the influence of advertisers over editorial content was limited by, among other factors, the advertisers' own self-interest. A paper's chief value to an advertiser lay, after all, in the public's perception of its independence.[127] Kingsley Martin, by contrast, believed that even to raise the question of advertisers' influence over the press already missed the point: "It assumes a conflict of interest where no conflict exists. If the proprietor of a newspaper with a million circulation does not offend his advertisers it is not because he cannot afford to, but because he does not wish to do so. The big advertisers are his friends; they have a common interest in the success of his newspaper, a common social and political outlook, and a common approach to the public. They are both advertisers, one of goods, the other of news, and there is no conflict of interest between them. Why should anyone try to bribe a millionaire in order to make him a capitalist?"[128]

Although there is a clear analytical distinction between the business elite's political views and commercial interests, this is not a distinction that most critics of the popular press tended to develop very precisely during the interwar years. Rather, a composite picture emerged in which the "bad politics" of the Press Barons consisted of their desire to put business ahead of "the truth," their willingness to manipulate the masses politically and commercially—that is, to "sell out" to the advertisers as well as promote their own maverick politics, which, if traced to their source, usually led back to financial bottom lines. We are accustomed to employing different words, "propaganda" and "advertising" (or "public relations"[129]), depending on whether such activities emanate from the state or private companies. In the interwar critique, this distinction was rejected by critics of the popular press—by conscious decision, it would seem. The difference between propaganda and advertising could appear as only one of categorical convenience. As George Peel expressed it in the *Contemporary Review* in 1944, "budding propagandists are taught, as a matter of routine, how to 'sell' their convictions and their coun-

THE AIMS OF THE TIMES

To be the first but not the hastiest with the news; to be serious without dullness or solemnity; to persuade and not to dogmatize; to be emphatic without becoming hysterical; to be graphic without sensationalism; to give the story and to reject the "stunt"; to miss nothing that is amusing and to keep the trivial in proportion; to give the news faithfully and fully without "featuring" the worst side of human nature—these have been the aims of *The Times* for generations, and these are its aims to-day.

THE TIMES

THE TIMES WEEKLY EDITION • THE TIMES LITERARY SUPPLEMENT • THE TIMES EDUCATIONAL SUPPLEMENT • THE TIMES REVIEW OF INDUSTRY
THE TIMES LAW REPORTS

PRINTING HOUSE SQUARE, LONDON, E.C.4

In this ad, *The Times* asserts its continued allegiance to the educational ideal and its rejection of the worst qualities of the New Journalism. From *Newspaper Press Directory and Advertisers' Guide 1949* (London: Benn Brothers, Ltd., 1949).

try on exact principles, and how to combat, by the aid of science, the 'sales-resistance' of recalcitrant minds."[130] A political idea, like soap, was a product that could be sold, and citizens were primarily consumers to be cajoled.

* * *

British theories of the press, as they developed in the nineteenth and early twentieth centuries, were intimately tied to prevailing attitudes toward "the people" and the emerging mass democracy. In the mid-nineteenth century, optimism about integrating the people into the political nation fueled the equally optimistic educational ideal; in the late nineteenth century, economic uncertainty and the rapid extension of the franchise, combined with the onset of the New Journalism, tended to discourage this ideal and foster instead a representative ideal. Following World War I, the representative ideal became the foundation for the defense of a market or libertarian view of the press that was congenial to Press Barons' interests. At the same time, this vision of the press tended to retreat among the Left, discredited for many by Lord Northcliffe's actions during the war. Hopes for an educational media lingered and reasserted themselves repeatedly, but the predominant trend was toward a rejection of this ideal, both because of a general nervousness about "democratic culture" and influence and more specific worries about the changing nature of the media.

In this anxious atmosphere, few critics still held out much hope for an independent commercial press. Late in World War I, *The Spectator* had called upon the government to resist its takeover by Lord Northcliffe. By the end of World War II, critics were calling upon the state to intervene in the interests of freedom of the press. In a commercial environment and in a democratic society, the more optimistic nineteenth-century press ideals, while helping to structure the debates, no longer compelled assent.

Notes

1. Leavis, *Mass Civilisation and Minority Culture*, 3–4, 7–8; Hayek, *Road to Serfdom*, 152. For the broader context of this aversion to mass culture and attempts to preserve high culture from being engulfed by democracy, see LeMahieu, *Culture for Democracy*. See Rubin, *Making of Middle Brow Culture*, for an American comparison.

2. Hopkin, "Socialist Press in Britain," 294–95.

3. See, for example, Cornford, "Transformation of Conservatism in the Late Nineteenth Century," Green, *Crisis of Conservatism*, and Clarke, *Lancashire and the New Liberalism*.

4. The literature is, of course, voluminous. Cronin's *Labour and Society* and Addison's *Road to 1945*, in different ways, have both problematized the link between class and Labour politics in the twentieth century.

5. See, for example, Labour Research Department, *The Press,* and O'Malley, "Labour and the 1947–9 Royal Commission on the Press," 136–38.

6. "Report on the Press: Contents of Newspapers; Control of Press; Reading Public; Belief in News; Opinion Formation," 10, 12, File Report 126, May 1940, Mass-Observation Archive, University of Sussex; Hoggart, *Uses of Literacy.* 180, 182.

7. Chalaby, *Invention of Journalism,* 48–53. Jeremy Tunstall argues, however, that the Press Barons displayed a greater willingness to put politics ahead of commercial interests than do today's "media moguls." See Tunstall, *Newspaper Power,* 79–94. In addition, Beaverbrook offered his own view of this question to the Royal Commission on the Press, claiming, "I ran the paper purely for the purpose of making propaganda and with no other object." See *Royal Commission on the Press, Minutes of Evidence Taken before the Royal Commission on the Press, Twenty-Sixth Day, 18 March 1848,* 4, in Lord Beaverbrook Papers BBK/H/37, House of Lords Record Office, London.

8. Martin, *Fascism, Democracy, and the Press.*

9. See, for example, "From Essay to Stunt," 679.

10. Richards, *Bloody Circus,* 12, 47, 50.

11. LeMahieu, *Culture for Democracy.*

12. The BBC's monopoly status was initially founded on airwave scarcity. For the early history of the BBC, see Briggs, *History of Broadcasting in the United Kingdom,* and Briggs, *The BBC.*

13. Ensor, *England 1870–1914,* 144.

14. Gardiner, "C. P. Scott and Northcliffe," 247.

15. Ibid., 254. For confirmation of Gardiner's point, see Hampton, "Press, Patriotism, and Public Discussion."

16. Gardiner, "C. P. Scott and Northcliffe," 255.

17. Ibid., 249, 250, 251, 254, 255.

18. Jones, *Powers of the Press,* 73–97; Hampton, "'Understanding Media'"; Scott-James, *Influence of the Press,* 13; Harris, *Private Lives, Public Spirit,* 246.

19. According to James Curran, Michael Gurevitch, and Janet Woollacott, "To a remarkable extent, there was a broad consensus during the inter-war period—to which many researchers, writing from a 'right' as well as a 'left' perspective subscribed—that the mass media exercised a powerful and persuasive influence." Curran, Gurevitch, and Woollacott, "Study of the Media," 11.

20. Richards, *Commodity Culture of Victorian England.*

21. Taylor, "British Official Attitudes Towards Propaganda Abroad," 23–49, esp. 25.

22. On Northcliffe's press campaigns during World War I, see Thompson, *Politicians, the Press, and Propaganda.*

23. Northcliffe to Wells, 8 May 1916, H. G. Wells Papers, N-167, University of Illinois at Urbana-Champaign.

24. "Northcliffe Ministry," 76–77.

25. "Government and the Press," 197.

26. "Position of the Prime Minister," 277.

27. "Warning," 368.

28. For a Press Baron's view of Northcliffe's role in the government, see Beaverbrook's unpublished manuscript "Lord Northcliffe," which explicitly echoes the representative

ideal. Northcliffe was a "great patriot: he has placed his independent judgment against the official experts, faced the outcry, and in nine cases out of ten he has proved right. He has watched with a sedulous and meticulous care, and used his great influence for the advancement, glory, and betterment of the realm." Lord Beaverbrook Papers, BBK/C/261, House of Lords Record Office, London.

29. Curran, "Press History"; Lee, "Franklin Thomasson and 'The Tribune.'"
30. Quoted in Harrison, *Transformation of British Politics,* 140.
31. Hobson, *Psychology of Jingoism;* Hobson, *Imperialism.*
32. H. J. Laski, letter to the editor, *New Statesman and Nation,* 12 December 1931, 743.
33. "Ruminations," 20 April 1927, Kingsley Martin Papers 7/17; Personal Diary, 1935, Kingsley Martin Papers 7/26; Scott to Martin, 15 March 1927, Kingsley Martin Papers 15/1, University of Sussex.
34. Martin, *Fascism, Democracy, and the Press,* 3.
35. Ibid., 5–6.
36. Hampton, "Press, Patriotism, and Public Discussion."
37. No doubt these views resurfaced in his mind a year later when he forced H. G. Wells to remove a passage that might offend Mussolini. (See chapter 1.)
38. Martin, *Fascism, Democracy, and the Press,* 8.
39. Ibid., 9.
40. Ibid., 9.
41. Ibid., 10.
42. "Muzzled Britain," 756.
43. Ibid., 756.
44. Ibid., 757.
45. Vallance, "Muzzling Democracy," 958–59.
46. Evans, "Lessons of the *Areopagitica,*" 345.
47. "Function of the Press," 139–40.
48. Curran, "Press History," 59–70.
49. See Freeden, *New Liberalism;* Freeden, *Liberalism Divided.*
50. Laski, *Decline of Liberalism,* 5–6.
51. Ibid., 9.
52. Ibid., 14–15.
53. Ibid., 11–12.
54. O'Malley, "Labour and the 1947–9 Royal Commission on the Press," 128.
55. Angell, "Problem of the Press," 269–70.
56. Ibid. See also Evans, "Lessons of the *Areopagitica,*" 345.
57. "Press Combinations," 544.
58. Ibid.
59. "False Freedom of the Press," 680.
60. Good, "Labour and the 'Capitalist' Press," 808–9.
61. "'Daily Herald' and 'Compulsory Propaganda,'" 620.
62. Ewen, *PR!* 131–73.
63. Wells, *Salvaging of Civilization,* 170, 172–73, 178.
64. Ibid., 184, 186, 187.
65. Ibid., 185. This theme is prominent in Evans, "Decay of News," 486–87.

66. Wells, *Salvaging of Civilization*, 188–89.
67. Wells, "Liberalism and the Revolutionary Spirit," 18–19, 23.
68. Ibid., 18–24.
69. Raymond, *Uncensored Celebrities*, 160.
70. Ibid., 161, 162–64.
71. Gardiner, *Daily Mail and the Liberal Press*, 2, 11, 12, 14. For another argument that the press helped to bring about World War I, see Raleigh, *War and the Press*. According to R. D. Blumenfeld, however, in 1933, "the idea that newspapers make wars is an illusion." See Blumenfeld, *Press in My Time*, 46–47.
72. "Lord Northcliffe," 180. Similar accusations were leveled against Lords Rothermere and Beaverbrook; see "Press and the Elections," 833.
73. Bennett, *What the Public Wants*, 22–23, 117, 122.
74. *Mirrors of Downing Street*, 52.
75. Massingham, "Journalism as a Dangerous Trade," 839.
76. Ibid., 839–40.
77. Gardiner, "Rothermere Press and France," 567–68.
78. Ibid., 568–69. He developed this theme further a few weeks later: see Gardiner, "Press and the State," 736–37.
79. To give one of the Press Barons his due, Beaverbrook wrote to H. G. Wells that "Rothermere also offers us Mussolini, though, poor man, his newspapers would be the first to suffer suppression under such a regime. He would soon be found in retirement in the USA." Beaverbrook to Wells, 11 December 1928, Lord Beaverbrook Papers, BBK/C/321a, House of Lords Record Office, London.
80. Angell, "Commercialisation of Demagogy," 114. In a letter to W. T. Stead in 1909, Angell had articulated similar themes, although with more than a hint of self-interest. He complained that his pamphlet demonstrating the interdependence of modern nations had been ignored by the press, which continued to write from the perspective that "political and military power is able to achieve for those nations excercising it commercial, industrial, financial and social advantages. National wealth is presumed to need protection against the aggression of other nations." His letter implied that his more nuanced view was considered too complicated for the newspapers, citing not political bias but the prominence of human interest stories, including "the result of a world-shaking billiard match" or the "difficulty of the post office in dealing with boxes containing ladies' hats," as the reason for his pamphlet's exclusion from the press. It is instructive that in evidently trying to shame Stead into mentioning his pamphlet in the *Review of Reviews*, Angell opened his letter with the twin claims that newspaper editors "are always to be keen to know 'what the public wants'" (and he, Angell, was a member of the public thus entitled to speak) and that "Liberal newspapers are supposed to place their ideals just a little higher and to be something of an educative force." Angell to Stead, 25 November 1909, STED 1/1, W. T. Stead Papers, Churchill College, Cambridge University. See also Angell to Stead, 1 December 1909, STED 1/1, in which Angell thanked Stead for promising to review Angell's pamphlet *Europe's Optical Illusion*.
81. For a wider discussion of this theme, see Waters, *British Socialists and the Politics of Popular Culture*.
82. Angell, "Commercialisation of Demagogy," 181.

83. Massingham, "Journalism of Lord Northcliffe," 674.

84. *Evening Standard,* 20 August 1936.

85. Astor, "Independent Journalism," 685; Blake, *Press and the Public,* 5; Sir Gilbert Parker, "The United States," in *Second Report of the Work Conducted for the Government at Wellington House* (1 February 1916), 23, INF 4/5, Public Records Office, London. Of course, Parker's report was not intended for public consumption.

86. Belloc, *Free Press,* 4, 31.

87. "Misrepresentation of News," 329.

88. Ockham, "Is the Press an Evil?" 754; Waugh, *Scoop,* 90.

89. Thomas, *The Newspaper,* 8–9, 24–25, 27–28.

90. Laski, *Politics,* 126; Harrisson, "Popular Press?" 172.

91. Angell, "Commercialisation of Demagogy," 181.

92. Ibid., 182.

93. Orwell, "Politics and the English Language," 136. For an interesting study that lends much support to Orwell's argument, see Wilkinson, *Depictions and Images of War in Edwardian Newspapers.*

94. Chalaby, *Invention of Journalism,* 9–53.

95. Riddell, "Psychology of the Journalist," 113.

96. "Democratic Press," 1117; Jones, *Fleet Street and Downing Street,* 310; Angell, *Press and the Organisation of Society,* 29–30. See also Political and Economic Planning, *Report on the British Press,* 80–81.

97. "Endowed Press," 199.

98. Lansbury, *Miracle of Fleet Street,* 25; "From Essay to Stunt," 680.

99. Angell, *Press and the Organisation of Society,* 35; Graves, *Good-Bye to All That,* 228; Graves and Hodge, *Long Week-End,* 14; Muggeridge, *Thirties 1930–1940 in Great Britain,* 102.

100. "People and the Press," 492. In what seems to have been a tongue-in-cheek quip, the article claimed that many *Spectator* readers dutifully read papers of both the Left and Right before forming their views on public questions.

101. See, for example, Ervine, "Coming Decade in Journalism," 746.

102. Nicholas, "All the News That's Fit to Broadcast," 140.

103. "Responsible Press," 318.

104. "Motives and Methods of Newspaper Reading: An Inquiry by Mass-Observation," 1, 16, File Report A11, December 1938, Mass-Observation Archives, University of Sussex.

105. "Report on the Press," Section 5: "Is the Press Opinion-Forming," 9, File Report 126, May 1940, Mass-Observation Archives, University of Sussex.

106. Ibid., 9, 26.

107. Lippmann, *Public Opinion,* 10–11.

108. Ibid., 18, 19, 48–49.

109. "Fairyland," 51–52.

110. "Leadership and the Press," 339, 342, 349, 354.

111. Ibid., 350.

112. Nicolson, "Marginal Comment," 107.

113. Lippmann to Angell, 25 July 1922, box 17, Norman Angell Papers, Ball State University.

114. Angell, *Press and the Organisation of Society*, 12.

115. Ibid., 21.

116. Ibid., 21, 23, 36, 37.

117. Ibid., 26.

118. Ibid., 27.

119. Ibid., 39.

120. Angell, "Press and Propaganda," 890. See Wilkinson, *Depictions and Images of War in Edwardian Newspapers,* for confirmation of Angell's point.

121. Martin, *Press the Public Wants*, 93.

122. Ibid., 76–77.

123. See Seaton, "Sociology of the Mass Media."

124. Martin, *Press the Public Wants*, 18.

125. Ibid., 80–81.

126. Ibid., 28–29.

127. Barker, *Britain and the British People,* 168; Curran, "Press History"; Belloc, *Free Press,* 17; Bishop, "Advertiser and the Press," 11–12. T. Russell had made an argument similar to Bishop's in 1907. See Russell, "Supreme Advertising Medium."

128. Martin, *Press the Public Wants,* 45–46. Norman Angell had already developed this argument in 1922. See Angell, *Press and the Organisation of Society,* 51–52.

129. In Ewen's usage, advertising relates to specific products; "public relations" refers to the company or industry more broadly. When Philip Morris promotes its cigarettes, that is advertising; when it promotes the virtues of the company, the harmlessness of tobacco, or the care that the tobacco industry has taken to discourage children's use of cigarettes, that is public relations.

130. Peel, "Science of Propaganda," 268. See also Williams, *Press, Parliament, and People,* 77–84. Williams uses the phrase "public relations" to describe governmental activities.

Epilogue: The First Royal Commission on the Press (and Beyond)

The debates of the previous century culminated in the first Royal Commission on the Press, which lasted from 1947 to 1949. The story of the Royal Commission has been well told, and a detailed retelling need not detain us here.[1] The calling for this Royal Commission late in 1946 intensified the debate that had unfolded throughout the twentieth century, bringing to a head the clash between labor and the capitalist press.

As Tom O'Malley has shown, the Royal Commission has widely but unfairly been perceived as a failure. O'Malley insists that only by interpreting the commission in the context of twentieth-century understandings of the press in society can a fair picture emerge. Most importantly, the Royal Commission clashed with the long-standing ideal of a press independent of the state. In this setting, even to establish the principle that a government could launch such an inquiry, which potentially could have led to statutory restructuring, already constituted a significant accomplishment.[2]

The debates surrounding the first Royal Commission on the Press, as well as the recommendations that resulted from these debates, reveal the contradictions and tensions inherent in simultaneous commitments to editorial diversity, an educational and representative press, and "liberty of the press," all in a commercial environment. In petitioning the Labour government to appoint a Royal Commission, the president of the National Union of Journalists (NUJ), Clement Bundock, denied partisanship. Rather, he claimed, "as journalists, we are concerned only that the best possible supply of fact and news about national and international affairs shall be at the disposal of our people that they may form their judgment on sound knowledge and shall be well and truly informed." Bundock called for a Royal Commission to inquire whether the "present tendencies in newspaper production move to that end." Drawing on both the educational and representative ideals, Bundock maintained that the function of the press—"a highly important function—is to reflect the opinion of the country and to keep the country instructed in current affairs. . . . It would be harmful to the public interest should anything like estrangement appear between the House of representatives of the people [Parliament] and the organs of the press, which should be the voice of the people." Reflecting and instructing public opinion, goals long attributed to the press, required the "free right of criticism." Bundock continued, drawing on themes we have seen developed by Kingsley Martin and others: "A careful selection from the facts and an equally careful choice of news items designed to present a false picture for a political purpose is not in keeping with our journalistic traditions and is definitely against the public interest. Complete freedom of criticism in the editorial columns and complete and disinterested presentation of affairs in the news columns, is we consider the correct balance." Bundock argued that these requirements were threatened by the tendency toward monopoly: "the freedom of the press we claim from the Government of the day must not be choked by the concentration of the country's newspapers in the hands of two or three powerful commercial groups."[3]

Bundock's argument depended on a recognition of the conflict between the idea of the press as a public service and the reality that it was a commodity and that journalists were typically employees. Monopolistic tendencies, therefore, threatened not only editorial diversity; they threatened to create a commercial environment in which the pursuit of profits forced journalists to violate practices that should be simple professionalism. For example, intrusive methods of news gathering and photography should be eschewed not only by journalists but by their employers.[4]

Not surprisingly, the Royal Commission met with considerable resistance. *The Times* argued on 27 March 1947, "It is far from certain that, with the best will in the world, the commissioners will be able to add much that is really new and significant to what is already known, though perhaps not very widely, about the Press." The editorial raised the problem of trying to address "monopolistic tendencies" by state intervention without at the same time unjustifiably restricting the "free expression of opinion" that the NUJ ostensibly wished to protect. The best hope *The Times* could offer was that the Royal Commission might, ironically, "expose and remove many of the fallacious opinions about the Press which have led to its own appointment."[5]

Such resistance came not only in newspapers but also in newspaper managers' replies to the Royal Commission's inquiries. The Northcliffe Group argued, in its evidence to the Royal Commission, that chains did not necessarily reduce the numbers of newspapers, since chains sometimes saved papers that, left to their own devices, would be forced out of business. In addition, it argued that by drawing on "common services," papers in chains could "provide a better service" than if they remained independent. As to charges of distortion in the press, the Northcliffe Group's evidence stated unambiguously that editors were never subject "to control or direction to influence or determine" either news or opinions. Nor were the Northcliffe Group's newspapers guilty of "distortion": "While it is not—particularly in present circumstances of restricted sizes of newspapers—possible to publish . . . reports in full, the condensed versions give an accurate representation of their main purport. Some reports unfortunately have to be omitted entirely, but these are judged to be the least important." In addition, the Northcliffe Group insisted that it kept news and opinion strictly separated in its papers and that any "advertiser who tried to influence editorial policy in any of our papers would receive short shrift."[6] This final argument fails to address Kingsley Martin's point that advertisers did not need to "influence" newspaper proprietors per se because they were from the same social class and saw the world in much the same terms.

It is perhaps not surprising that the Northcliffe Group answered the Royal Commission's inquiry in this way. We would be mistaken, however, to see the weakness of the eventual proposals and their general neglect by newspapers as evidence of press groups' ability to steamroll over journalistic democracy. The conglomorates' spokespeople were able to stave off a thorough restructuring of the press not because of their undue influence but because their argument for freedom from interference resonated with so much of British thought on the press. Those who thought of the press as commercial property naturally wished to see it unregulated. Others, regarding journalism as a profession, wished to maintain self-regulation rather than statutory control. Many journalists, in keeping with long-standing tradition, saw any intervention by the state as a potential threat to rather than a protection of press freedom. For all of these reasons, the proposal to create a press council to enforce particular standards in press content received a great deal of opposition.[7]

Many of those who supported the creation of a press council, moreover, wished to restrict its membership to journalists, in other words, to keep outsiders from having a voice in the conduct of the press. Murray Watson, the president of the Institute of Journalists, argued in September 1948 that a statutory body was a bad idea and that allowing members of the public to serve on it was even worse, "for then the appointment of the public so-called would get into the hands of the Government of the day sooner or later, and frankly no Government could be entrusted with such powers." He continued, arguing that however "well-intentioned such a proposal might be," it could become "the means of inserting the wedge of State control, and before we knew where we were, the freedom of the Press might be undermined and curtailed." Lady Violet Bonham Carter quipped in response that although Watson referred to himself as a "public servant," he "regards the presence of public representatives on the Press Council as an unwarrantable intrusion." M. E. Aubrey concurred, noting that "it is plain that journalists who a few months ago were desirous of securing public representatives as prospective allies against the proprietors and 'monopolists' now seem as alarmed as any at the prospect of close public scrutiny and judgment." He argued that the public had an interest in the press not only because of "dictation of suppression of news, and bad taste in dealing with private and personal matters, and the steady drip-drip of biassed opinion on unreflective minds," but also because in the postwar scarcity, the supply of newsprint meant that "other needs may have to be denied." Unfortunately, however, the NUJ, which had called for the Royal Commission, had now "taken a new line similar to that of most editors and proprietors," in other words, to protect its profession from any public oversight.[8]

Significantly, the commission concluded in 1949 that "nothing approaching monopoly" existed in the press and that the period from 1921 to 1948 saw a "marked tendency away from concentration of ownership in the national Press." In the provincial press, a trend toward concentration between 1921 and 1929 had subsequently stabilized or even reversed. The commission further concluded that the "present degree of concentration in ownership" was "not so great as to prejudice the free expression of opinion or the accurate presentation of news or to be contrary to the best interests of the public." If the conclusions were largely complacent, the recommendations were tepid. The commission recommended a General Council of the Press with 20 percent lay members "to safeguard the freedom of the Press; to encourage the growth of the sense of public responsibility and public service amongst all engaged in the profession of journalism—that is, in the editorial production of newspapers—whether as directors, editors, or other journalists; and to further the efficiency of the profession and the well-being of those who practise it." Although the commission specified ten subcategories of the General Council's role, what was left unsaid was more significant: no mention was made of whether or not the General Council's recommendations would have statutory force.[9]

The Royal Commission's conclusions and recommendations reflected the state of British elite understandings of the press at midcentury. These understandings derived from the debates of the previous century, and they continued to shape discussion of the press and other mass media in the subsequent half-century (including in two additional Royal Commissions in 1962 and 1977). At the beginning of the twenty-first century, journalists continue to resist statutory regulation, maintaining a self-regulation through a Press Complaints Commission, even as large sections of the public clamor for privacy laws and statutory "right of reply." While journalists continue to cite their quasi-constitutional political function as a watchdog, the increasingly relentless pursuit of profits by papers owned by multinational, nonmedia conglomerates has led to cost-cutting measures that seriously hamper any sort of investigative journalism. In this atmosphere, governments as well as business have become increasingly sophisticated in their approaches to information management. Moreover, although most of the popular press, including Rupert Murdoch's *The Sun,* has supported Tony Blair's New Labour, this support seems thin and conditional and has not erased the perception on the part of many observers of several decades of tabloid sabotage of the Labour party.[10]

Michael Schudson has observed that "[o]bjectivity is a peculiar demand to make of institutions which, as business corporations, are dedicated first of all to economic survival."[11] This observation might be extended: depth, seriousness, and parliamentary reporting are peculiar demands to make of business corporations. Looking at the press from a different direction, governments are in the business of governing, and it is not shocking that they would attempt to manage the information circulated about matters that concern them. In the early nineteenth century the methods of choice were imprisonment, bribery, and taxation; today political press officers take advantage of overburdened journalists' need for copy to pursue the best possible presentation of their client's personality and agenda.[12]

As calls for statutory regulation continue to attract support, scholars and policy makers would do well to consider the history of thinking about the press in Britain, as well as the context in which various ideas have arisen and waned.[13] The educational ideal of the press, so powerfully articulated in the mid-nineteenth century, reflected confidence in the possibilities of "elevating" the popular classes, but this confidence depended in great part on idealized assumptions about readers that have not always been borne out by the subsequent century. Moreover, the verbatim parliamentary reports of the 1860s were just as much a response to the commercial demands of that era as David and Victoria Beckham stories are to today's commercial environment. Although words like "education" and "instruction" are still bandied about in public relations for the mass media, it is clear that the model of entertainment has long since captured the popular press, and many observers worry about its ongoing importation into the "quality" press as well. Moreover, as Todd Gitlin has recently pointed out, the present media "supersaturation," which is deeply embedded in modern cultures and societies, is inherently biased in favor of "fun."[14] The mid-Victorian educational ideal is attractive and an excellent starting point for thinking about what kind of press might be created, but it requires adapting to very different conditions if it is to have any use in contemporary Britain.

The representative ideal of the press lingers. Yet this ideal, so radical and evocative during the 1820s and 1830s when the working classes had no vote, and so potentially reformist in the hands of a crusader like W. T. Stead (or an American muckraker), risks becoming a mere legitimizing charade in today's commercial environment.[15] The image of a Woodward and Bernstein bringing down a corrupt government bears little resemblance to the daily work of journalists, but it allows media moguls to cast themselves as the champions of the people. Moreover, by equating audiences with voters, or consumers with citizens, the representative ideal undergirds the claim that those giving readers "what they want," even if that means escapist, depoliticized scandal stories, are "democratic," whereas those clamoring for the "serious" and contextualized political news and argument necessary for a functioning democracy are "elitist."[16]

Notes

1. O'Malley, "Labour and the 1947–9 Royal Commission on the Press"; Curran, "Liberal Theory of Press Freedom."

2. O'Malley, "Labour and the 1947–9 Royal Commission on the Press," 126–27. Remembering Norman Angell's 1922 prediction that the capitalist press could undermine any Labour political victory, we should not be surprised that opponents of the inquiry charged that Labour politicians had initiated the inquiry simply because they could not accept criticism. The press's treatment of the Labour government beginning in 1945 was likely a factor in Herbert Morrison's decision to launch the inquiry. See O'Malley, "Labour and the 1947–9 Royal Commission on the Press," 138–41.

3. "Deputation from N.U.J. to Lord President of the Council, Rt. Hon. Herbert Morrison, P.C., M.P., July 1946," 1, Mss. 86/1/NEC/21, National Union of Journalists Archives, Modern Records Office, University of Warwick. Predictably, the president of the rival Institute of Journalists, John Gordon, charged the NUJ with being "more concerned with Left Wing politics than with the stature, honour, and well-being of journalism." See Gordon, "Burst Bubble."

4. "Deputation from N.U.J. to Lord President of the Council, Rt. Hon. Herbert Morrison, P.C., M.P., July 1946," 3. The NUJ had adopted a Professional Code in 1935. See Mss.

86/1/NEC/10, National Union of Journalists Archives, Modern Records Office, University of Warwick.

5. "Press and Public," *The Times,* 27 March 1947, 5C.

6. "Summary of Evidence Submitted to the Royal Commission on the Press on Chain Ownership of Newspapers," Home Office 251/3, Public Records Office, London.

7. All of these themes are abundant in the "Summary of Oral Evidence Opposed to a Press Council or Institute," in Home Office 251/101, Annex C, Public Records Office, London.

8. "Presidential Address, IOJ, Mr. Murray Watson, September 15, 1948, Advance Copy," Home Office 251/101; "Notes by Lady Violet Bonham Carter" and "Comments by Mr. M. E. Aubrey," Paper 253, Home Office 251/101, Public Records Office, London. Kingsley Martin was a notable example of a witness who welcomed public representatives on a press council. The NUJ's position in 1948 was as follows: "The NUJ is not committed to any proposal. Some members see objections to a Press Council. . . . [They] do not want anything 'onerous in so far as daily work of journalists is concerned.'" See "Summary of Oral Evidence in Favour or Not Opposed to a Press Council or Institute," Home Office 251/101, Annex B, Public Records Office, London.

9. *Royal Commission on the Press 1947–1949,* 175–79. The other recommendations included a requirement that chain newspapers publicize their common ownership on the front page and that nonjournalistic forms of competition be indefinitely prohibited.

10. See Franklin, *Newszak and News Media,* 25–66; Tunstall, *Newspaper Power.*

11. Schudson, *Discovering the News,* 3.

12. For an extensive description of methods of information management in contemporary Britain, see Barnett and Gaber, *Westminster Tales,* 96–115.

13. O'Malley and Soley, *Regulating the Press,* makes the most interesting, historically informed, and up-to-date case for regulation of the British press. McChesney's *Rich Media, Poor Democracy* provides an equally compelling case for regulating the American media.

14. Gitlin, *Media Unlimited.*

15. For an interesting American attempt to revive something resembling the representative ideal, see Rosen, *What Are Journalists For?* For a rare example of a first-rate investigative journalist who discomfits the powerful, see Palast, *Best Democracy Money Can Buy.* As Palast points out, his employers, *The Guardian, The Observer,* and the BBC, are able to support his investigative efforts because they are somewhat sheltered from the naked market.

16. "The popular as representative of the people, certainly in the contemporary era, only has currency when that is reflected in a mass appeal. Authenticity is now economically marked, not by some reference to a set of criteria unrelated to number. That battle was lost with the liberalization of the newspaper markets in Europe and the United States." Conboy, *Press and Popular Culture,* 179. See also Sparks, "Goodbye Hildy Johnson." For a persuasive critique of present-day market-populist fundamentalism, see Frank, *One Market under God.*

Bibliography

Archives Consulted

C. P. Scott Papers, British Library Manuscript Collections
George Cadbury Papers, University of Birmingham Library
H. G. Wells Papers, University of Illinois at Urbana-Champaign
Kingsley Martin Papers, University of Sussex
Lord Beaverbrook Papers, House of Lords Record Office, London
Lord Northcliffe Papers, British Library Manuscript Collections
Manchester Guardian Archive, John Rylands Library, University of Manchester
Mass-Observation Archive, University of Sussex
National Union of Journalists Archives, Modern Records Centre, University of Warwick
New Statesman Archives, University of Sussex
Norman Angell Papers, Ball State University, Muncie, Indiana
Public Records Office, London
Robert Blatchford Papers, Central Library, Manchester
Robert Blatchford Papers, British Library Manuscript Collections
Robert Donald Papers, House of Lords Record Office, London
W. T. Stead Papers, Churchill College, Cambridge University

Published Sources

The Aberdeen Journal. *The Aberdeen Journal and Its History: The Men Who Made It*. Aberdeen: The Aberdeen Journal, 1894.
———. *Our 150th Year: A Unique Journalistic Record; Newspapers Old and Young, Historic Survey 1748–1897*. Aberdeen: The Aberdeen Journal, 1897.
About Newspapers: Chiefly English and Scottish. Edinburgh: St. Giles Printing Co., 1888.
"About the Daily News." *British and Colonial Printer and Stationer*, 26 July 1883, 1–2.
Adams, William Edwin. *Memoirs of a Social Atom*. 2 vols. London: Hutchinson, 1903.
Addison, Paul. *The Road to 1945: British Politics and the Second World War*. Rev. ed. London: Pimlico, 1994.

Aird, Andrew. *Reminiscences of Editors, Reporters, and Printers during the Last Sixty Years.* Glasgow: Aird and Coghill, 1890.

Aitken, William Maxwell (Baron Beaverbrook). *Politicians and the Press.* London: Hutchinson and Co., 1926.

Alterman, Eric. *What Liberal Media? The Truth about Bias and the News.* New York: Basic Books, 2003.

Altholz, J. L. "Anonymity and Editorial Responsibility in Religious Journalism." *Victorian Periodicals Review* 24 (Winter 1991): 180–86.

———. *The Religious Press in Britain, 1760–1900.* New York: Greenwood Press, 1989.

Altick, Richard Daniel. *The English Common Reader: A Social History of the Mass Reading Public, 1800–1900.* 2d ed. Columbus: Ohio State University Press, 1998.

———. "The Sociology of Authorship: The Social Origins, Education, and Occupations of 1,100 British Writers, 1800–1935." *Bulletin of the New York Public Library* 66 (June 1962): 389–404.

"The American Press." *British Quarterly Review* 53 (January 1871): 1–26.

Anderson, Olive. *A Liberal State at War: English Politics and Economics during the Crimean War.* New York: St. Martin's Press, 1967.

Anderson, Patricia. *The Printed Image and the Transformation of Popular Culture, 1790–1860.* Oxford: Clarendon Press, 1991.

Andrews, Alexander. *The History of British Journalism, from the Foundation of the Newspaper Press in England to the Repeal of the Stamp Act in 1855.* 2 vols. London: Richard Bentley, 1859.

Andrews, Linton, and H. A. Taylor. *Lords and Laborers of the Press: Men Who Fashioned the Modern British Newspaper.* Carbondale: Southern Illinois University Press, 1970.

Angell, Norman. "The Commercialisation of Demagogy." *The Nation and the Athenaeum* 34 (20–27 October 1923): 113–15, 180–82.

———. "Place of the Press." *The Spectator* 143 (23 November 1929): 758–59.

———. "The Press and Propaganda." *The Spectator* 159 (19 November 1937): 890–91.

———. *The Press and the Organisation of Society.* London: Labour Publishing Co., 1922.

———. "The Problem of the Press: Salvation through the Trust?" *The Nation and the Athenaeum* 34 (17 November 1923): 269–70.

Annand, James. "The Re-Organisation of Liberalism." *New Review* 13 (November 1895): 494–503.

Anonymous Journalism. London: J. Ridgway, 1855.

Arendt, Hannah. *The Human Condition.* Chicago: University of Chicago Press, 1958.

The Armstrong Case: Mr. Stead's Defense in Full; Reprinted, with Notes and Elucidations, from the "Pall Mall Gazette." London: H. Vickers, 1885.

Arnold, Matthew. *Culture and Anarchy.* 1869. Ed. Samuel Lipman. New Haven, Conn.: Yale University Press, 1994.

———. "Up to Easter." *The Nineteenth Century* 21 (May 1887): 629–43.

Ashton, Harold. *First from the Front.* London: Pearson, 1914.

Aspinall, Arthur. *Politics and the Press, ca. 1780–1850.* London: Home and Van Thal, 1949.

———. "The Social Status of Journalists at the Beginning of the Nineteenth Century." *Review of English Studies* 21 (July 1945): 216–32.

Astor, J. J. "Independent Journalism." *The Spectator* 131 (10 November 1923): 685.

Atkins, John Black. "C. P. Scott: A Great Editor." *The Spectator* 148 (9 January 1932): 40.

———. *The Life of Sir William Howard Russell, the First Special Correspondent.* 2 vols. London: John Murray, 1911.

———. "The Work and Future of War Correspondents." *Monthly Review* 5 (September 1901): 81–90.

"Autobiography of the Rev. Jonathan Edmondson, A.M., with Notes by the Rev. Jacob Stanley, Sen." *Wesleyan Methodist Magazine* 4.6 (January–February 1850): 1–16, 113–23.

Ayerst, David. *Garvin of the Observer.* London: Croom Helm, 1985.

———. *The Manchester Guardian: Biography of a Newspaper.* Ithaca, N.Y.: Cornell University Press, 1971.

Baker, Alfred. *The Newspaper World: Essays on Press History and Work, Past and Present.* London: Pitman, 1890.

Baldasty, Gerald. *The Commercialization of the News in the Nineteenth Century.* Madison: University of Wisconsin Press, 1992.

Ball, W. Valentine. *The Law of Libel as Affecting Newspapers and Journalists.* London: Stevens and Sons, 1912.

Barber, Benjamin. *Jihad vs. McWorld: How Globalism and Tribalism Are Reshaping the World.* New York: Ballantine Books, 1996.

Barclay, Sir Thomas. *Thirty Years: Anglo-French Reminiscences (1876–1906).* London: Constable, 1914.

Barker, Ernest. *Britain and the British People.* London: Oxford University Press, 1942.

Barker, Hannah. *Newspapers, Politics, and English Society, 1695–1855.* Harlow: Longman Books, 2000.

Barnett, Steven, and Ivor Gaber. *Westminster Tales: The Twenty-First-Century Crisis in Political Journalism.* London: Continuum, 2001.

Barrie, Sir James Matthew. *When a Man's Single: A Tale of a Literary Life.* In *The Works of J. M. Barrie, Peter Pan Edition.* Vol. 3. New York: Charles Scribner's Sons, 1929.

Barrow, Logie. "The Socialism of Robert Blatchford and the 'Clarion.'" Ph.D. dissertation, University of London, 1975.

Baylen, J. O. "Matthew Arnold and the *Pall Mall Gazette*." *South Atlantic Quarterly* 68 (Autumn 1969): 543–55.

———. "The 'New Journalism' in Late Victorian Britain." *Australian Journal of Politics and History* 18.3 (1972): 367–85.

———. "W. T. Stead as Publisher and Editor of the Review of Reviews." *Victorian Periodicals Review* 12.2 (1979): 70–84.

Beatty-Kingston. *A Journalist's Jottings.* 2 vols. London: Chapman and Hall, 1890.

Beetham, Margaret. *A Magazine of Her Own? Domesticity and Desire in the Woman's Magazine, 1800–1914.* London: Routledge, 1996.

Bell, Lady Florence. "What People Read." *Independent Review* 7 (December 1905): 426.

Bell, Walter George. *Fleet Street in Seven Centuries.* London: Pitman, 1912.

Belloc, Hilaire. *The Free Press.* London: Allen and Unwin, 1918.

Benn, Caroline. *Keir Hardie.* London: Hutchinson, 1992.

Bennett, [Enoch] Arnold. *Journalism for Women: A Practical Guide.* London: John Lane, 1898.

———. *What the Public Wants.* New York: George H. Doran, 1911.

Bernstein, George. *Liberalism and Liberal Politics in Edwardian England.* Boston: Allen and Unwin, 1986.

Besant, Walter. "The Amusements of the People." *Contemporary Review* 45 (March 1884): 342–53.

———. *The Pen and the Book.* London: Thomas Burleigh, 1899.

Berridge, Virginia. "Popular Journalism and Working-Class Attitudes, 1854–86: A Study of Reynold's Newspaper, Lloyd's Weekly Newspaper, and the Weekly Times." Ph.D. dissertation, University of London, 1976.

———. "Popular Sunday Papers and Mid-Victorian Society." In *Newspaper History: From the Seventeenth Century to the Present Day.* Ed. George Boyce, James Curran, and Pauline Wingate. 247–64. London: Constable, 1978.

Betts, Raymond. *Assimilation and Association in French Colonial Theory, 1890–1914.* New York: Columbia University Press, 1961.

Bevir, Mark. "The Long Nineteenth Century in Intellectual History." *Journal of Victorian Culture* 6 (Autumn 2001): 313–35.

———. "The Rise of Ethical Anarchism in Britain, 1885–1900." *Historical Research* 69 (June 1996): 143–65.

Biagini, Eugenio. *Liberty, Retrenchment, and Reform.* Cambridge: Cambridge University Press, 1992.

———, ed. *Citizenship and Community: Liberals, Radicals, and Collective Identities in the British Isles, 1865–1931.* Cambridge: Cambridge University Press, 1996.

Biagini, Eugenio, and Alastair Reid. *Currents of Radicalism: Popular Radicalism, Organized Labour, and Party Politics in Britain, 1850–1914.* Cambridge: Cambridge University Press, 1991.

Billington, M[ary]. F[rances]. "Leading Lady Journalists." In *Sell's Dictionary of the World's Press, 1897.* 95–103. London: Sell, 1897.

Bishop, F. P. "The Advertiser and the Press." *The Spectator* 162 (6 January 1939): 11–12.

Black, Jeremy. *The English Press, 1621–1861.* London: Sutton, 2001.

Blake, George. *The Press and the Public.* London: Faber and Faber, 1930.

Blatchford, Robert. *Merrie England.* 1893. London: Journeyman Press, 1976.

———. *My Eighty Years.* London: Cassell and Co., 1931.

Blease, W. Lyon. *A Short History of English Liberalism.* London: T. Fisher Unwin, 1913.

Blewett, Neal. "The Franchise in the United Kingdom, 1885–1918." *Past and Present* 32 (December 1965): 27–56.

Blowitz, Henri de. "Journalism as a Profession." *Contemporary Review* 63 (January 1893): 37–46.

———. *My Memoirs.* London: Edward Arnold, 1903.

Blumenfeld, R. D. *The Press in My Time.* London: Rich and Cowan, 1933.

Bohemian Days in Fleet Street, by a Journalist. London: John Long, 1913.

Boston, Ray. "W. T. Stead and Government by Journalism." In *Papers for the Millions: The New Journalism in Britain, 1850s to 1914.* Ed. Joel H. Wiener. 91–106. New York: Greenwood Press, 1988.

Boswell, H. A. *About Newspapers: Chiefly English and Scottish.* Edinburgh: St. Giles, 1888.

Bourne, H. R. Fox. "The Cheapening of Journalism." In *Sell's Dictionary of the World's Press, 1899.* 25. London: Sell, 1899.

——— . *English Newspapers: Chapters in the History of Journalism*. 2 vols. London: Chatto and Windus, 1887.

——— . "The Institute of Journalists." In *Sell's Dictionary of the World's Press, 1899*. 17. London: Sell, 1899.

Boyce, George. "The Fourth Estate: The Reappraisal of a Concept." In *Newspaper History: From the Seventeenth Century to the Present Day*. Ed. George Boyce, James Curran, and Pauline Wingate. 19–40. London: Constable, 1978.

Boyce, George, James Curran, and Pauline Wingate, eds. *Newspaper History: From the Seventeenth Century to the Present Day*. London: Constable, 1978.

Boyd, Kelly. *Manliness and the Boys' Story Paper in Britain: A Cultural History, 1855–1940*. London: Palgrave, 2003.

Boyle, Frederick. *The Narrative of an Expelled Correspondent*. London: Bentley, 1877.

Bradley, F. H. *Ethical Studies: Selected Essays*. 1876. Indianapolis: Bobbs-Merrill, 1951.

Brake, Laurel. *Print in Transition, 1850–1910: Studies in Media and Book History*. London: Palgrave, 2001.

Braham, Peter. "How the Media Report Race." In *Culture, Society, and the Media*. Ed. Michael Gurevitch, Tony Bennett, James Curran, and Janet Woollacott. 268–86. London: Methuen, 1982.

Brake, Laurel. *Subjugated Knowledges: Journalism, Gender, and Literature in the Nineteenth Century*. London: Macmillan, 1994.

Brake, Laurel, Aled Jones, and Lionel Madden, eds. *Investigating Victorian Journalism*. London: Macmillan, 1990.

Brendon, Piers. *The Life and Death of the Press Barons*. New York: Atheneum, 1983.

Briggs, Asa. *The Age of Improvement*. London: Longmans, Green, 1960.

——— . *The BBC: The First Fifty Years*. Oxford: Oxford University Press, 1985.

——— . *The History of Broadcasting in the United Kingdom*. Vols. 1–4. London: Oxford University Press, 1961, 1965, 1970, 1979.

——— . *Press and Public in Early Nineteenth-Century Birmingham*. Oxford: Printed for the Dugdale Society, 1948.

——— . *Victorian People: A Reassessment of Persons and Themes, 1851–67*. Chicago: University of Chicago Press, 1955.

Briggs, Asa, and Peter Burke. *A Social History of the Media: From Gutenberg to the Internet*. Cambridge: Polity, 2002.

"The Bringing Forth of the Daily Newspaper." *Chambers's Journal* 2 (26 August 1854): 129–33.

Brittain, Sir Harry Ernest. "The First Imperial Press Conference." In *Newspaper Press Directory, 1910*. 5–11. London: Mitchell, 1910.

Brodrick, George Charles. *Memories and Impressions, 1831–1900*. London: J. Nichols, 1900.

——— . "What Are Liberal Principles?" *Fortnightly Review* 25 (1 February 1876): 174–93.

"Broken Pledges." *The Spectator* 116 (18 March 1916): 372–73.

Bromley, Michael, and Tom O'Malley, eds. *A Journalism Reader*. London: Routledge, 1997.

Brown, David. "Compelling but Not Controlling? Palmerston and the Press, 1846–1855." *History* 86 (January 2001): 41–61.

Brown, Ivor. "C. P. Scott." In *The Post Victorians*. London: Nicholson and Watson, 1933.

Brown, Lucy. *Victorian News and Newspapers*. Oxford: Clarendon Press, 1985.

Bruce, Steve. *Pray TV: Televangelism in America.* London: Routledge, 1990.
Bunce, J. Thackray. "Church and Press." *National Review* 23 (November 1893): 387–93.
Bundock, Clement. *The National Union of Journalists.* Oxford: Oxford University Press, 1957.
Bussey, Harry Findlater. *Sixty Years of Journalism: Anecdotes and Reminiscences.* Bristol: J. W. Arrowsmith, 1906.
"The Byways of Literature? Reading for the Million." *Blackwood's Edinburgh Magazine* 84 (August 1858): 200–16.
Cadett, Herbert. *The Adventures of a Journalist.* London: Dands and Co., 1900.
Calhoun, Craig, ed. *Habermas and the Public Sphere.* Cambridge: MIT Press, 1992.
Campbell, Duncan. *Reminiscences and Reflections of an Octagenarian Highlander.* Iverness: Northern Counties Newspaper and Printing and Publishing Co., 1910.
Campbell, Theophilia Carlile. *The Battle of the Press, as Told in the Story of Richard Carlile.* London: Bonner, 1899.
Camrose, Viscount. *British Newspapers and Their Controllers.* London: Cassell and Co., 1947.
Carey, John. *The Intellectuals and the Masses: Pride and Prejudice among the Literary Intelligentsia, 1880–1939.* Chicago: Academy Chicago Publishers, 2002.
Carnie, William. *Reporting Reminiscences.* 3 vols. Aberdeen: Aberdeen University Press, 1902–6.
Carson, William English. *Northcliffe, Britain's Man of Power.* New York: Dodge Publishing Co., 1918.
Catling, Thomas. "The Founder of Lloyd's." *Lloyd's Weekly News*, 30 November 1902, 8.
———. *My Life's Pilgrimage.* Intro. Lord Burnham. London: John Murray, 1911.
———, ed. *The Press Album.* London: John Murray, 1909.
Catterall, Peter, Colin Seymour-Ure, and Adrian Smith, eds. *Northcliffe's Legacy: Aspects of the British Popular Press, 1896–1996.* London: Macmillan, 2000.
Chalaby, Jean. *The Invention of Journalism.* London: Macmillan, 1998.
———. "No Ordinary Press Owners: Press Barons as a Weberian Ideal Type." *Media, Culture, and Society* 19 (October 1997): 621–41.
———. "Northcliffe: Proprietor as Journalist." In *Northcliffe's Legacy: Aspects of the British Popular Press, 1896–1996.* Ed. Peter Catterrall, Colin Seymour-Ure, and Adrian Smith. 27–44. London: Macmillan, 2000.
Chisholm, Anne, and Michael Davie. *Lord Beaverbrook: A Life.* New York: Alfred A. Knopf, 1993.
Christian, Harry, ed. *The Sociology of Journalism and the Press. Sociological Review* Monograph no. 29. Keele: University of Keele Press, 1980.
Chomsky, Noam. *Necessary Illusions: Thought Control in Democratic Societies.* London: Pluto Press, 1989.
Chomsky, Noam, and Edward Hermann. *Manufacturing Consent: The Political Economy of the Mass Media.* New York: Pantheon, 1988.
Clarke, John. "Pessimism versus Populism: The Problematic Politics of Popular Culture." In *For Fun and Profit: The Transformation of Leisure into Consumption.* Ed. Richard Butsch. 28–44. Philadelphia: Temple University Press, 1990.

Clarke, John, Chas Critcher, and Richard Johnson. *Working-Class Culture: Studies in History and Theory.* London: Hutchinson and Co., 1979.

Clarke, Peter. *Lancashire and the New Liberalism.* Cambridge: Cambridge University Press, 1971.

———. *Liberals and Social Democrats.* Cambridge: Cambridge University Press, 1978.

Clarke, Tom. *My Northcliffe Diary.* London: Cassell, 1959.

Cliff, N. D. "The Press and Germany." Letter to the editor. *The Spectator* 160 (25 March 1938): 522.

Clowes, Alice. *Charles Knight.* London: R. Bentley and Sons, 1892.

Cobden, Richard. *Speeches on Questions of Public Policy.* Ed. John Bright and James E. Thorold Rogers. London: Macmillan, 1878.

Cockett, Richard. *Twilight of Truth: Chamberlain, Appeasement, and the Manipulation of the Press.* New York: St. Martin's Press, 1989.

Collet, Collet Dobson. *History of the Taxes on Knowledge: Their Origin and Repeal.* 2 vols. Intro. George Jacob Holyoake. London: T. Fisher Unwin, 1899.

Collini, Stefan. *Liberalism and Sociology: L. T. Hobhouse and Political Argument in England, 1880–1914.* Cambridge: Cambridge University Press, 1979.

———. *Public Moralists: Political Thought and Intellectual Life in Britain, 1850–1930.* Oxford: Clarendon Press, 1991.

[Collins, Wilkie.] "The Unknown Public." *Household Words* 18 (21 August 1858): 217–24.

Colman, Helen Caroline. *Jeremiah James Colman: A Memoir.* London: Chiswick Press, 1905.

Colomb, P. H. "The Patriotic Editor in War." *National Review* 29 (April 1897): 253–63.

Coltham, Stephen William. "The *Bee-Hive* Newspaper: Its Origins and Early Struggles." In *Essays in Labour History,* vol. 1. Ed. Asa Briggs and John Saville. 174–204. London: Macmillan, 1960.

———. "English Working-Class Newspapers in 1867." *Victorian Studies* 13 (December 1969): 159–80.

Compton-Rickett, A. "Some Personalities of Fleet Street." *Bookman* 84 (August 1933): 240–41.

Conboy, Martin. *The Press and Popular Culture.* London: Sage Publications, 2002.

Concerning Three Northern Newspapers: Their Rise and Progress, 1748–1900. Aberdeen: Process and Colour Printing, 1900.

Conrad, Joseph. *The Secret Agent.* 1907. New York: Random House, 1998.

"Contemporary Literature—Journalists." *Blackwood's Edinburgh Magazine* 124 (December 1878): 641–62.

"Contemporary Literature—Newspaper Offices." *Blackwood's Edinburgh Magazine* 126 (October 1879): 472–93.

A Contributor. "Editors." *National Review* 27 (June 1896): 505–15.

Cook, Sir Edward Tyas. *Edmund Garrett: A Memoir.* London: Edward Arnold, 1909.

Cooper, Charles Alfred. *An Editor's Retrospect: Fifty Years of Newspaper Work.* London: Macmillan, 1896.

Corner, John. "'Influence': The Contested Core of Media Research." In *Mass Media and Society.* 3d ed. Ed. James Curran and Michael Gurevitch. 376–97. London: Edwin Arnold, 2000.

Cornford, James. "The Transformation of Conservatism in the Late Nineteenth Century." In *The Victorian Revolution: Government and Society in Victoria's Britain*. Ed. Peter Stansky. 287–318. New York: Franklin Watts, 1973.

Courlander, Alphonse. *Mightier Than the Sword*. London: T. Fisher Unwin, 1912.

Courtney, L. "The Making and Reading of Newspapers." *Contemporary Review* 79 (March 1901): 365–76.

C. P. Scott, 1846–1932: The Making of the Manchester Guardian. London: Frederick Muller, 1946.

Cranfield, Geoffrey Alan. *The Development of the Provincial Newspaper, 1700–1760*. Oxford: Clarendon Press, 1962.

———. *The Press and Society: From Caxton to Northcliffe*. London: Longman, 1978.

Crawford, Emily. "Journalism as a Profession for Women." *Contemporary Review* 64 (September 1893): 362–71.

Crawfurd, John. *Taxes on Knowledge: A Financial and Historical View of Taxes Which Impede the Education of the People*. London: Charles Ely, 1836.

[Croal, David.] *Early Recollections of a Journalist, 1832–1859*. Edinburgh: Elliot, 1898.

Cronin, James. "Class, Citizenship, and Party Allegiance: The Labor Party and Class Formation in Twentieth-Century Britain." *Studies in Political Economy* 21 (Autumn 1986): 107–35.

———. *Labour and Society in Britain, 1918–1979*. New York: Schocken, 1984.

Crossick, Geoffrey. *An Artisan Elite in Victorian Society: Kentish London, 1840–1880*. London: Croom Helm, 1978.

———, ed. *The Lower Middle Class in Britain, 1870–1914*. London: Croom Helm, 1977.

Crowe, Sir Joseph Archer. *Reminiscences of Thirty-Five Years of My Life*. London: John Murray, 1895.

Cunningham, Hugh. "Jingoism in 1877–78." *Victorian Studies* 14 (June 1971): 429–53.

———. "The Language of Patriotism? 1750–1914." *History Workshop Journal* 12 (Autumn 1981): 8–33.

Curran, James. "The Liberal Theory of Press Freedom." In *Power without Responsibility: The Press and Broadcasting in Britain*. 5th ed. Ed. James Curran and Jean Seaton. 287–301. London: Routledge, 1997.

———. "Media and the Making of British Society, ca. 1700–2000." *Media History* 8 (December 2002): 135–54.

———. "Mass Media and Democracy: A Reappraisal." In *Mass Media and Society*. 3d ed. Ed. James Curran and Michael Gurevitch. 120–54. London: Edwin Arnold, 2000.

———. "The Press as an Agency of Social Control: An Historical Perspective." In *Newspaper History: From the Seventeenth Century to the Present Day*. Ed. George Boyce, James Curran, and Pauline Wingate. 51–73. London: Constable, 1978.

———. "Press History." In *Power without Responsibility: The Press and Broadcasting in Britain*. 5th ed. Ed. James Curran and Jean Seaton. 5–108. London: Routledge, 1997.

———. "Rethinking the Media as a Public Sphere." In *Communication and Citizenship: Journalism and the Public Sphere*. Ed. Peter Dahlgren and Colin Sparks. 27–57. London: Routledge, 1991.

Curran, James, Michael Gurevitch, and Janet Woollacott. "The Study of the Media: Theoretical Approaches." In *Culture, Society, and the Media.* Ed. Michael Gurevitch, Tony Bennett, James Curran, and Janet Woollacott. 11–29. London: Methuen, 1982.

Curran, James, and Michael Gurevitch, eds. *Mass Media and Society.* 3d ed. London: Edwin Arnold, 2000.

Curran, James, and Jean Seaton, eds. *Power without Responsibility: The Press and Broadcasting in Britain.* 5th ed. London: Routledge, 1997.

Curran, James, Anthony Smith, and Pauline Wingate. *Impacts and Influences: Essays on Media Power in the Twentieth Century.* London: Metheun, 1987.

Curtis, L. Perry, Jr. *Jack the Ripper and the London Press.* New Haven, Conn.: Yale University Press, 2001.

Dahlgren, Peter, and Colin Sparks, eds. *Communication and Citizenship: Journalism and the Public Sphere.* London: Routledge, 1991.

"The 'Daily Herald' and 'Compulsory Propaganda.'" *The Spectator* 128 (20 May 1922): 620–21.

Dale, R. W. *The Politics of the Future: A Lecture to the New Electors; Delivered in the Town Hall, Birmingham, on Tuesday Evening, 19 November 1867.* Birmingham: Hudson and Son, Printers, 1867.

"The Dangers of the Country: No. 1—Our External Dangers." *Blackwood's Edinburgh Magazine* 69 (February 1851): 196–222.

Davidson, John. "Fleet Street." In *Fleet Street and Other Poems.* 9–20. London: Grant Richards, 1909.

Davis, Aeron. *Public Relations Democracy: Public Relations, Politics, and the Mass Media in Britain.* Manchester: Manchester University Press, 2002.

Dawson, John. *Practical Journalism: How to Enter Thereon and Succeed; A Model for Beginners and Amateurs.* 2d ed. London: L. U. Gill, 1904.

Deibert, Ronald J. *Parchment, Printing, and Hypermedia: Communication in World Order Transformation.* New York: Columbia University Press, 1997.

Delille, Edward. "The American Newspaper Press." *The Nineteenth Century* 32 (July 1892): 13–28.

"The Democratic Press." *The Spectator* 162 (20 June 1939): 1117–18.

de Nie, Michael. *The Eternal Paddy: Irish Identity and the British Press, 1798–1882.* Madison: University of Wisconsin Press, 2004.

Dibblee, G. Binney. *The Newspaper.* London: Williams and Norgate, 1913.

Dicey, Albert Venn. *Lectures on the Relation between Law and Opinion in England during the Nineteenth Century.* London: Macmillan, 1905.

Dicey, Edward. "Journalism New and Old." *Fortnightly Review* 83 (1 May 1905): 904–18.

Dilnot, Frank. *The Adventures of a Newspaper Man.* London: Smith, Elder, 1913.

Douglas, Susan J. *Where the Girls Are: Growing Up Female with the Mass Media.* New York: Random House, 1994.

Duncan, William. *Life of Joseph Cowen (M.P. for Newcastle, 1874–86).* London: Walter Scott, 1904.

Dunlop, Andrew. *Fifty Years of Irish Journalism.* Dublin: Hanna and Neale, 1911.

Editor. "Contributors." *National Review* 27 (August 1896): 793–801.

Edwards, J. Passmore. *A Few Footprints.* London: Watts and Co., 1906.

Edwards, P. D. *Dickens's "Young Men": George Augustus Sala, Edmund Yates, and the World of Victorian Journalism.* Aldershot, U.K.: Ashgate, 1997.

Eisenstein, Elizabeth L. *The Printing Revolution in Early Modern Europe.* Cambridge: Cambridge University Press, 1983.

Elkins, Charles. "The Voice of the Poor: The Broadside as a Medium of Popular Culture and Dissent in Victorian England." *Journal of Popular Culture* 14 (Fall 1980): 262–74.

Elliott, George. *The Newspaper Libel and Registration Act 1881, with a Statement of the Law of Libel as Affecting Proprietors, Publishers, and Editors of Newspapers.* London: Stevens and Haynes, 1884.

"Endowed Press." *The Spectator* 121 (24 August 1918): 198–99.

Engel, Matthew. *Tickle the Public: One Hundred Years of the Popular Press.* London: Victor Gollancz, 1996.

Ensor, R. C. K. *England 1870–1914.* 1936. Oxford: Oxford University Press, 1992.

———. "News and Communications." *The Spectator* 158 (30 April 1937): 801–2.

Epstein, James A. "'America' in the Victorian Imagination." In *Anglo-American Attitudes: From Revolution to Partnership.* Ed. Fred M. Leventhal and Roland Quinault. 107–23. Aldershot: Ashgate, 2000.

———. "Feargus O'Connor and the *Northern Star.*" *International Review of Social History* 21 (1976): 51–97.

———. *In Practice: Studies in the Language and Culture of Popular Politics in Modern Britain.* Stanford, Calif.: Stanford University Press, 2003.

———. *Radical Expression: Political Language, Ritual, and Symbol in England, 1790–1850.* New York: Oxford University Press, 1994.

Ervine, St. John. "The Coming Decade in Journalism." *The Spectator* 151 (17 November 1933): 744, 746.

Escott, Thomas. "Behind the Scenes in Fleet Street." *London Quarterly Review* 119 (January 1913): 87–100.

———. "John Delane and Modern Journalism." *Quarterly Review* 209 (October 1908): 524–48.

———. "London Pen and Gown in the Sixties and Since." *Fortnightly Review* 57 (1 February 1895): 238–49.

———. *Masters of English Journalism: A Study of Personal Forces.* London: T. Fisher Unwin, 1911.

———. *Platform, Press, Politics, and Play; Being Pen and Ink Sketches of Contemporary Celebrities.* Bristol: J. W. Arrowsmith, 1895.

———. "Politics and the Press." *Fraser's Magazine* 12 (July 1875): 41–50.

———. "Old and New in the Daily Press." *Quarterly Review* 227 (April 1917): 353–68.

Evans, B. Ifor. "The Decay of News." *Saturday Review* 145 (21 April 1928): 486–87.

———. "The Lessons of the *Areopagitica.*" *Contemporary Review* 166 (December 1944): 342–46.

Ewen, Stuart. *Captains of Consciousness: Advertising and the Social Roots of the Consumer Culture.* New York: McGraw Hill, 1976.

———. *PR! A Social History of Spin.* New York: Basic Books, 1996.

"Fairyland." *The Nation and the Athenaeum* 29 (9 April 1921): 51–52.

The Falkirk Herald. *The Jubilee of the Falkirk Herald, 1846–1896.* Falkirk: The Falkirk Herald, 1896.
Fallows, James. *Breaking the News: How the Media Undermine American Democracy.* New York: Vintage, 1996.
"The False Freedom of the Press." *The Spectator* 154 (26 April 1935): 680.
Fenn, George Manville. *George Alfred Henry, the Story of an Active Life.* London: Blackie, 1907.
Ferguson, M. T. "The Late Lord Glenesk and the 'Morning Post.'" *National Review* 53 (July 1909): 796–814.
Ferris, Paul. *The House of Northcliffe: A Biography of an Empire.* New York: New World Publishers, 1972.
Finn, Margot. *After Chartism: Class and Nation in English Radical Politics, 1848–1874.* Cambridge: Cambridge University Press, 1993.
Fisher, Joseph R., and James Andrew Strahan. *The Law of the Press: A Digest of the Law Specially Affecting Newspapers.* London: William Clowes and Sons, 1891.
Fisher, W. J. "The Liberal Press and the Liberal Party." *The Nineteenth Century and After* 56 (August 1904): 199–206.
Fleming, P. "Newspapers, or What You Will." *The Spectator* 157 (20 November 1936): 902–3.
Flint, Kate. *The Woman Reader, 1837–1914.* Oxford: Clarendon Press, 1993.
Forbes, Sir Archibald. *Memories and Studies of War and Peace.* London: Cassell, 1895.
———. *My Experiences in the War between France and Germany.* 2 vols. London: Hurst and Blackett, 1871.
———. *Soldiering and Scribbling: A Series of Sketches.* London: Henry S. King, 1872.
———. "War Correspondence and the Authorities." *The Nineteenth Century* 7 (January 1880): 185–96.
———. "A War Correspondent's Reminiscences." *The Nineteenth Century* 30 (August 1891): 185–96.
Forster, E. M. *Howard's End.* 1910. New York: Random House, 1989.
"The Founders of Modern Liberalism." *Blackwood's Edinburgh Magazine* 116 (October 1874): 501–18.
"The Fourth Estate." *The Gentleman's Magazine* 277 (July 1894): 40–50.
Fox, Celina. "The Development of Social Reportage in English Periodical Illustration during the 1840s and Early 1850s." *Past and Present* 74 (February 1977): 90–111.
———. *Graphic Journalism in England during the 1830s and 1840s.* London: Garland, 1988.
Fox, Frank. "New York Journalism: A Snapshot." *National Review* 54 (October 1909): 258–61.
Frank, Thomas. *One Market under God: Extreme Capitalism, Market Populism, and the End of Economic Democracy.* New York: Random House, 2000.
Franklin, Bob. *Newszak and News Media.* London: Arnold, 1997.
Freeden, Michael. *Liberalism Divided: A Study in British Political Thought, 1914–1939.* Oxford: Clarendon Press, 1986.
———. *The New Liberalism: An Ideology of Social Reform.* Oxford: Clarendon Press, 1978.
Fries, Felix. "The Government and the Press." *The Spectator* 161 (30 December 1938): 1116–17.

"From Essay to Stunt." *The Nation and the Athenaeum* 31 (19 August 1922): 678–80.
Frost, Thomas. *Forty Years' Recollections, Literary and Political*. London: Sampson Low, 1880.
———. *Reminiscences of a Country Journalist*. London: Ward and Downey, 1888.
Fry, Oliver A. "In Defence of the Paragraph." *National Review* 21 (March 1893): 38–43.
"The Function of the Press." *Nature* 146 (13 July 1940): 139–40.
Furniss, Harry. *The Confessions of a Caricaturist*. 2 vols. London: T. Fisher Unwin, 1901.
Fyfe, Henry. *Northcliffe: An Intimate Biography*. New York: Macmillan, 1936.
Gans, Herbert J. *Democracy and the News*. Oxford: Oxford University Press, 2003.
Gardiner, A. G. "C. P. Scott and Lord Northcliffe—A Contrast." *The Nineteenth Century and After* 111 (February 1932): 247–56.
———. *The Daily Mail and the Liberal Press: A Reply to "Scaremongerings" and an Open Letter to Lord Northcliffe*. London: Daily News, Ltd., 1914.
———. *Life of George Cadbury*. London: Cassell, 1923.
———. *Pillars of Society*. London: J. Nisbet and Co., 1915.
———. "The Press and the State." *The Nation and the Athenaeum* 33 (15 September 1923): 736–37.
———. *Prophets, Priests, and Kings*. London: J. M. Dent and Sons, 1914.
———. "The Rothermere Press and France." *The Nation and the Athenaeum* 33 (4 August 1923): 567–69.
Gardner, FitzRoy, et al. "The Tory Press and the Tory Party." *National Review* 21 (May 1893): 357–74.
Gaskell, Elizabeth. *Mary Barton*. 1848. London: Penguin Books, 1996.
Gaskell, J. P. W. "The Decline of the Common Press." Ph.D. dissertation, University of Cambridge, 1956.
Giffen, Robert. "Further Notes on the Progress of the Working Classes in the Last Half Century." *Journal of the Statistical Society* 49 (1886): 28–91.
Gilmartin, Kevin. *Print Politics: The Press and Radical Opposition in Early Nineteenth-Century England*. Cambridge: Cambridge University Press, 1996.
Gissing, George. *New Grub Street*. 1891. Intro. John Gross. London: The Bodley Head, 1967.
———. *The Private Papers of Henry Ryecroft*. 1903. Ed. and intro. Mark Storey. Oxford: Oxford University Press, 1987.
Gitlin, Todd. "Bites and Blips: Chunk News, Savvy Talk, and the Bifurcation of American Politics." In *Communication and Citizenship: Journalism and the Public Sphere*. Ed. Peter Dahlgren and Colin Sparks. 119–36. London: Routledge, 1991.
———. *Media Unlimited: How the Torrent of Images and Sounds Overwhelms Our Lives*. New York: Owl Books, 2003.
Gladstone, William. *Speeches on the Great Questions of the Day*. London: John Camden Hotten, 1870.
Gleason, Arthur. *Inside the British Isles*. New York: Chautauqua Press, 1918.
Goldberg, Bernard. *Bias: A CBS Insider Exposes How the Media Distort the News*. New York: Regnery, 2002.
Goldman, Lawrence. *Science, Reform, and Politics in Victorian Britain: The Social Science Association, 1857–1886*. Cambridge: Cambridge University Press, 2002.

Bibliography

Good, E. T. "Labour and the 'Capitalist' Press." *The Spectator* 125 (18 December 1920): 808–9.

Gordon, John. "The Burst Bubble." *The Journal: The Organ of the Institute of Journalists* 37 (August 1949): 1.

"The Government and the Press." *Blackwood's Edinburgh Magazine* 102 (December 1867): 763–83.

"The Government and the Press." *The Spectator* 120 (23 February 1918): 197.

"Government by Newspaper." *The Spectator* 114 (29 May 1915): 738–39.

"Government, Press, and People." *The Spectator* 163 (4 August 1939): 169.

Gould, Gerald. "In Praise of Journalists." *Saturday Review* 145 (31 March 1928): 386–87.

Grant, James. *The Newspaper Press: Its Origin, Progress, and Present Position.* 2 vols. London: Tinsley Brothers, 1871.

Graves, Robert. *Good-Bye to All That.* 1929. New York: Random House, 1998.

Graves, Robert, and Alan Hodge. *The Long Weekend: A Social History of Great Britain 1918–1939.* 1940. New York: W. W. Norton and Co., 1963.

Green, E. H. H. *The Crisis of Conservatism: The Politics, Economics, and Ideology of the British Conservative Party, 1880–1914.* London: Routledge, 1995.

———. *Ideologies of Conservatism: Conservative Political Ideals in the Twentieth Century.* Oxford: Oxford University Press, 2002.

Green, T. H. *Works of Thomas Hill Green.* 3 vols. Ed. R. L. Nettleship. London: Longmans, Green, and Co., 1900.

Greenwood, Frederick. "The Newspaper Press." *The Nineteenth Century* 27 (May 1890): 833–42.

———. "The Newspaper Press: Half a Century's Survey." *Blackwood's Edinburgh Magazine* 161 (May 1897): 704–20.

———. "The Press and Government." *The Nineteenth Century* 28 (July 1890): 108–18.

[Greg, William Rathbone.] "The Newspaper Press." *The Edinburgh Review* 102 (October 1855): 470–98.

Grew, E. S. "Journals and Journalists of To-Day: VII. Mr. William L. Thomas, of the 'Graphic' and 'Daily Graphic.'" *Sketch: A Journal of Art and Actuality,* 17 January 1894, 637.

Griffiths, Dennis, ed. *The Encyclopedia of the British Press, 1422–1992.* New York: St. Martin's Press, 1992.

Gross, John. *The Rise and Fall of the Man of Letters: A Study of the Idiosyncratic and the Humane in Modern Literature.* New York: Collier, 1969.

Gullace, Nicoletta. *The Blood of Our Sons: Men, Women, and the Renegotiation of Birth Citizenship during the Great War.* Basingstoke: Palgrave, 2002.

Gurevitch, Michael, Tony Bennett, James Curran, and Janet Woollacott, eds. *Culture, Society, and the Media.* London: Methuen, 1982.

Gwynn, Denis. "Advice to Young Journalists." *The Spectator* 139 (5 November 1927): 761–62.

Habermas, Jürgen. *The Structural Transformation of the Public Sphere: An Inquiry into a Category of Bourgeois Society.* Trans. Thomas Burger. Cambridge, Mass.: MIT Press, 1991.

Hajkowski, Thomas. "The BBC, the Empire, and the Second World War, 1939–1945." *Historical Journal of Film, Radio, and Television* 22 (June 2002): 135–56.

Hall, Catherine. "Rethinking Imperial Histories: The Reform Act of 1867." *New Left Review* 208 (November/December 1994): 3–29.
Hall, S. Carter. "The Penny Press." *New Monthly Magazine* 40 (February 1834): 175–84.
Hall, Stuart. *Culture, Media, Language: Working Papers in Cultural Studies, 1972–1979*. London: Hutchinson, 1980.
———. "Notes on Deconstructing the 'Popular.'" In *People's History and Socialist Theory*. Ed. Raphael Samuel. 227–40. London: Routledge and Kegan Paul, 1981.
Hammond, J. L. *C. P. Scott of the Manchester Guardian*. London: G. Bell and Sons, 1934.
Hampton, Mark. "Journalists and the 'Professional Ideal' in Britain: The Institute of Journalists, 1884–1907." *Historical Research* 72 (June 1999): 183–201.
———. "The Press, Patriotism, and Public Discussion: C. P. Scott, the *Manchester Guardian,* and the Boer War, 1899–1902." *Historical Journal* 44 (March 2001): 177–97.
———. "'Understanding Media': Theories of the Press in Britain, 1850–1914." *Media, Culture, and Society* 23 (March 2001): 213–31.
———. "The United Kingdom." In *World Press Encyclopedia: A Survey of Press Systems Worldwide*. 2d ed., vol. 2. 997–1018. Detroit: Thomson, 2002.
Hardcastle, John B. *History of the Wolverhampton Chronicle*. Wolverhampton: The Wolverhampton Chronicle, 1893.
Hardman, Thomas H., comp. *A Parliament of the Press: The First Imperial Press Conference*. Preface Earl of Rosebery. London: Horace Marshall, 1909.
Hardt, Michael, and Antonio Negri. *Empire*. Cambridge, Mass.: Harvard University Press, 2000.
Hargreave, Mary. "Women's Newspapers in the Past." *The Englishwoman* 21 (January/March 1914): 292–301.
Hargreaves, William. *Revelations from Printing-House Square: Is the Anonymous System a Security for Purity and Independence of the Press? A Question for "The Times" Newspaper*. London: William Ridgway, 1864.
Harling, Philip. "The Law of Libel and the Limits of Repression, 1790–1832." *Historical Journal* 44 (March 2001): 107–34.
———. "Leigh Hunt's *Examiner* and the Language of Patriotism." *English Historical Review* 111 (November 1996): 1159–81.
Harmsworth, Sir Alfred. "The Daily Newspaper of Today." *Newspaper Press Directory, 1905*. London: C. Mitchell and Co., 1905.
Harris, Bob. *Politics and the Rise of the Press: Britain and France, 1620–1800*. London: Routledge, 1996.
Harris, Jose. *Private Lives, Public Spirit: A Social History of Britain, 1870–1914*. Oxford: Oxford University Press, 1993.
Harris, Michael. *The London Press in the Age of Walpole: A Study of the Origins of the Modern English Press*. London: Associated University Presses, 1987.
Harris, Michael, and Alan Lee, eds. *The Press in English Society from the Seventeenth to Nineteenth Centuries*. London: Associated University Presses, 1986.
Harris, Robert. *Good and Faithful Servant: The Unauthorized Biography of Bernard Ingham*. In *The Media Trilogy*. London: Faber and Faber, 1994.
Harrison, Brian. *The Transformation of British Politics, 1860–1995*. Oxford: Oxford University Press, 1996.

Harrison, J. F. C. *The Early Victorians, 1832–51.* London: Granada, 1973.
Harrison, Stanley. *Poor Men's Guardians: A Record of the Struggles for a Democratic Newspaper Press, 1763–1973.* London: Lawrence and Wishart, 1974.
Harrisson, Tom. "The Popular Press?" *Horizon* 2 (October 1940): 158–74.
Haslam, J. H. *The Press and the People: An Estimate of Reading in Working-Class Districts.* Manchester: Manchester City News, 1906.
Hatton, J. *Journalistic London: Being a Series of Sketches of Famous Pens and Papers of the Day.* London: Sampson Low, Marston, Searle, and Rivington, 1882.
Havighurst, Alfred E. *Radical Journalist: H. W. Massingham (1860–1924).* Cambridge: Cambridge University Press, 1974.
Hayek, F. A. *The Road to Serfdom.* 1944. Chicago: University of Chicago Press, 1994.
Hayward, F. H., and B. Langdon-Davies. *Democracy and the Press.* Manchester: National Labour Press, 1919.
Headlam, Cecil. *An Argument against the Abolition of the Daily Press.* Oxford: Blackwell, 1904.
Healy, Christopher. *The Confessions of a Journalist.* London: Chatto and Windus, 1904.
Henderson, P., ed. *The Letters of William Morris to His Family and Friends.* New York: AMS Press, 1950.
Henham, Ernest G. "A Newspaper Stopgap." *Cornhill Magazine* 8 (January 1900): 96–111.
"Herr Hitler and the Press." *The Spectator* 160 (11 March 1938): 417.
Heyck, T. W. "From Men of Letters to Intellectuals: The Transformation of Intellectual Life in Nineteenth-Century England." *Journal of British Studies* 20 (Fall 1980): 158–83.
———. *The Transformation of Intellectual Life in Victorian England.* Chicago: Lyceum Books, 1982.
Heyer, Paul. *Communication and History: Theories of Media, Knowledge, and Civilization.* New York: Greenwood Press, 1988.
Hiley, Nicholas. "Making War: British News Media and Government, 1914–1916." Ph.D. dissertation, Open University, 1984.
———. "'You Can't Believe a Word You Read': Newspaper-Reading in the British Expeditionary Force, 1914–1918." In *Studies in Newspaper and Periodical History: 1994 Annual.* Ed. Michael Harris and Tom O'Malley. 89–102. Westport, Conn.: Greenwood Press, 1996.
Hirst, Francis Wrigley. "English Newspapers and Their Authority." In *The Six Panics and Other Essays.* 142–64. London: Methuen, 1913.
———. "Imperialism and Finance." 1900. In *Liberalism and the Empire: Three Essays by Francis W. Hirst, Gilbert Murray, and J. L. Hammond.* Ed. Peter Cain. 1–117. London: Routledge, 1998.
"The History of Newspapers." *Bentley's Miscellany* 27 (June 1850): 596–97.
History of the Sheffield Independent. Sheffield: The Sheffield Independent, 1892.
Hitchman, J. F. "The Newspaper Press." *Quarterly Review* 150 (October 1880): 498–537.
Hobsbawm, Eric. *The Age of Extremes: A History of the World, 1914–1991.* New York: Vintage, 1996.
———. *The Age of Empire, 1875–1914.* New York: Pantheon, 1987.
Hobson, J. A. "The Economic Taproot of Imperialism." *Contemporary Review* 82 (August 1902): 219–32.

———. *How the Press Was Worked before the War*. London: South African Conciliation Committee, 1899.

———. *Imperialism: A Study*. 2d ed. London: George Allen and Unwin, 1905.

———. *The Psychology of Jingoism*. London: Grant Richards, 1901.

———. *The War in South Africa: Its Causes and Effects*. 1900. New York: H. Fertig, 1969.

Hodder, George. *Memories of My Time, Including Personal Reminiscences of Eminent Men*. London: Tinsley, 1870.

Hodgson, George B. *From Smithy to Senate: The Life Story of James Annand, Journalist and Politician*. London: Cassell, 1908.

Hoggart, Richard. *The Uses of Literacy: Changing Patterns in English Mass Culture*. 1957. London: Penguin, 1990.

Hollis, Patricia. *The Pauper Press: A Study in Working Class Radicalism of the 1830s*. London: Oxford University Press, 1970.

Hope, Alexander James Beresford. "Newspapers and Their Writers." In *Cambridge Essays*. 1–27. London: John W. Parker, 1858.

Hopkin, Deian. "Domestic Censorship in the First World War." *Journal of Contemporary History* 5.4 (1970): 151–70.

———. "The Left-Wing Press and the New Journalism." In *Papers for the Millions: The New Journalism in Britain, 1850s to 1914*. Ed. Joel H. Wiener. 225–42. New York: Greenwood Press, 1988.

———. "Socialism and Imperialism: The ILP Press and the Boer War." In *Impacts and Influences: Essays on Media Power in the Twentieth Century*. Ed. James Curran, Anthony Smith, and Pauline Wingate. 9–26. London: Methuen, 1987.

———. "The Socialist Press in Britain, 1890–1910." In *Newspaper History: From the Seventeenth Century to the Present Day*. Ed. George Boyce, James Curran, and Pauline Wingate. 294–306. London: Constable, 1978.

Hopkins, Tighe. "Anonymity." *New Review* 1 (November 1889): 513–31; 2 (March 1890): 265–76.

Houghton, Walter. *The Victorian Frame of Mind*. New Haven, Conn.: Yale University Press, 1957.

Hudson, Derek. *British Journalists and Newspapers*. London: Collins, 1945.

———. "Newspapers." In *Edwardian England, 1901–1914*. Ed. S. Nowell-Smith. 303–26. London: Oxford University Press, 1964.

Hughes, H. Stuart. *Consciousness and Society: The Reorientation of European Social Thought, 1890–1930*. Rev. ed. New York: Vintage, 1977.

Hughes, Spencer Leigh. *Press, Platform, and Parliament*. London: Nisbet, 1921.

Hunt, F. Knight. *The Fourth Estate: Contributions towards a History of Newspapers, and of the Liberty of the Press*. 2 vols. London: David Bogue, 1850.

Hyndman, Henry Mayers. *Further Reminiscences*. London: Macmillan, 1912.

———. *The Record of an Adventurous Life*. London: Macmillan, 1911.

"Independence of the British Press." *The Spectator* 140 (18 February 1928): 216–17.

"The Influence of the Press." *Blackwood's Edinburgh Magazine* 36 (September 1834): 373–91.

"Inquest on the Press." *The Spectator* 177 (1 November 1946): 438.

"Inquiry into the Press." *New Statesman and Nation* 32 (20 July 1946): 39–40.

"Insidious Propaganda." *The Spectator* 125 (24 July 1920): 103–5.

"In the Editorial Chair." *Cornhill Magazine* 12 (June 1902): 792–804.
Jackson, Kate. *George Newnes and the New Journalism in Britain, 1880–1910: Culture and Profit.* Aldershot: Ashgate, 2001.
Jackson, Mason. *The Pictorial Press: Its Origin and Progress.* London: Hurst and Blackett, 1885.
Jamieson, Kathleen Hall. *Packaging the Presidency: A History and Criticism of Presidential Campaign Advertising.* 3d ed. New York: Oxford University Press, 1996.
Janeway, Michael. *Republic of Denial: Press, Politics, and Public Life.* New Haven, Conn.: Yale University Press, 1999.
Jenks, John. "The Enemy Within: Journalism, the State, and the Limits of Dissent in Cold War Britain, 1950–1951." *American Journalism* 18 (Winter 2001): 33–52.
Jerrold, Blanchard. "The Manufacture of Public Opinion." *The Nineteenth Century* 13 (June 1883): 1080–92.
Johnson, Richard. "Educational Policy and Social Control in Early Victorian England." In *The Victorian Revolution: Government and Society in Victoria's Britain.* Ed. Peter Stansky. 199–227. New York: Franklin Watts, 1973.
———. "'Really Useful Knowledge': Radical Education and Working-Class Culture." In *Working-Class Culture: Studies in History and Theory.* Ed. John Clarke, Chas Critcher, and Richard Johnson. 75–102. London: Hutchinson and Co., 1979.
Jones, Aled. *Powers of the Press: Newspapers, Power, and the Public in Nineteenth-Century England.* Hants, U.K.: Scolar, 1996.
———. *Press, Politics, and Society: A History of Journalism in Wales.* Cardiff: University of Wales Press, 1993.
Jones, Gareth Stedman. *Languages of Class: Studies in English Working Class History, 1832–1982.* Cambridge: Cambridge University Press, 1983.
———. *Outcast London: A Study in the Relationship between Classes in Victorian Society.* Oxford: Clarendon, 1971.
Jones, Kennedy. *Fleet Street and Downing Street.* London: Hutchinson, 1920.
Jordan, H. D. "British Press Inquiry." *Public Opinion Quarterly* 11.4 (1947): 558–66.
"Journalism." *Cornhill Magazine* 6 (July 1862): 52–63.
Jouvenel, Henry de, Kingsley Martin, Paul Scott Mowrer, Sanin Cano, and Friedrich Sieberg. *The Educational Role of the Press.* Paris: League of Nations International Institute of Intellectual Cooperation, 1934.
Joyce, Patrick. *Democratic Subjects: The Self and the Social in Nineteenth-Century England.* Cambridge: Cambridge University Press, 1994.
———. *Visions of the People: Industrial England and the Question of Class, 1848–1914.* Cambridge: Cambridge University Press, 1991.
Kaplan, Richard L. *Politics and the American Press: The Rise of Objectivity, 1865–1920.* Cambridge: Cambridge University Press, 2002.
Kaul, Chandrika. *Reporting the Raj: The British Press and India, c. 1880–1922.* Manchester: Manchester University Press, 2003.
Kay, Joseph. *The Education of the Poor in England and Europe.* London: J. Hatchard and Son, 1846.
———. *The Social Condition and Education of the People in England.* New York: Harper and Brothers, 1864.
Keane, John. *The Media and Democracy.* Cambridge: Polity Press, 1991.

Kelly, Richard. *The Law of Newspaper Libel, with Special Reference to the State of the Law as Defined by the Law of Libel Amendment Act, 1888.* London: William Clowes and Sons, 1889.
Kent, Susan Kingsley. *Gender and Power in Britain, 1640–1990.* London: Routledge, 1999.
Kern, Stephen. *The Culture of Time and Space, 1880–1918.* Cambridge, Mass.: Harvard University Press, 1983.
Kinnear, A. "Parliamentary Reporting." *Contemporary Review* 87 (March 1905): 369–75.
Kinnear, J. Boyd. "Anonymous Journalism." *Contemporary Review* 5 (July 1867): 324–39.
Klancher, Jon P. *The Making of English Reading Audiences, 1790–1832.* Madison: University of Wisconsin Press, 1987.
Knight, Charles. *The Case of Authors as Regards the Paper Duty.* London: Fleet Street, 1851.
———. "Education of the People." *London Magazine* 3.1 (April 1828): 1–13.
———. *The Old Printer and the Modern Press.* London: Charles Knight, 1854.
———. *Passages of a Working Life.* 3 vols. London: Charles Knight, 1864.
Knightley, Phillip. *The First Casualty, from the Crimea to Vietnam: The War Correspondent as Hero, Propagandist, and Myth Maker.* New York: Harcourt, Brace, Jovanovich, 1975.
Koss, Stephen. *Fleet Street Radical: A. G. Gardiner and the Daily News.* London: Archon Books, 1973.
———. *The Rise and Fall of the Political Press in Britain.* 2 vols. Chapel Hill: University of North Carolina Press, 1981, 1984.
Labour Research Department. *The Press.* London: Labour Publishing, 1922.
"Lament of a Leader-Writer." *Westminster Review* 12 (December 1899): 656–64.
Lang, A., and "'X,' a Working Man." "The Reading Public." *Cornhill Magazine* 11 (December 1901): 783–95.
Lansbury, George. *The Miracle of Fleet Street: The Story of the Daily Herald.* London: Victorian House Printing Co.; Labour Publishing Co., 1925.
Lasch, Christopher. *The Revolt of the Elites and the Betrayal of Democracy.* New York: W. W. Norton and Co., 1995.
———. *The True and Only Heaven: Progress and Its Critics.* New York: W. W. Norton and Co., 1991.
Laski, H. J. *The Decline of Liberalism.* L. T. Hobhouse Memorial Trust Lectures, no. 10. London: Humphrey Milford, 1940.
———. *Politics.* Philadelphia: J. B. Lippincott Co., 1931.
"The Late Mr. John Edward Taylor." In *Newspaper Press Directory, 1906.* 15. London: Mitchell, 1906.
"The Late Mr. W. T. Stead." In *Newspaper Press Directory, 1913.* 17. London: Mitchell, 1913.
"The Late Sir Wemyss Reid." In *Newspaper Press Directory, 1906.* 13. London: Mitchell, 1906.
Lawrence, Arthur. *Journalism as a Profession.* London: Hodder and Stoughton, 1903.
Lawrence, John. *Speaking for the People: Party, Language, and Popular Politics in England, 1867–1914.* Cambridge: Cambridge University Press, 1998.
Layard, George Somes. *Mrs. Lynn Linton: Her Life, Letters, and Opinions.* London: Methuen, 1901.
Leach, Henry. *Fleet Street from Within: The Romance and Mystery of the Daily Paper.* Bristol: Arrowsmith, 1905.
"Leadership and the Press." *Quarterly Review* 257 (October 1931): 337–54.
"The Leading Article." *Cornhill Magazine* 7 (December 1899): 797–811.

Leahy, Charles Cannon. "The Conditions of British Journalism, 1800–1870." Ph.D. dissertation, University of California, 1977.
Leavis, F. R. *Mass Civilisation and Minority Culture*. 1930. London: Folcroft Library Edition, 1974.
Leavis, Q. D. *Fiction and the Reading Public*. London: Chatto and Windus, 1932.
Lee, Alan J. "Franklin Thomasson and 'The Tribune.'" *Historical Journal* 16 (June 1973): 341–60.
———. "The Management of a Victorian Local Newspaper: The *Manchester City News*, 1864–1900." *Business History* 15 (July 1973): 131–48.
———. *The Origins of the Popular Press in England, 1855–1914*. London: Croom Helm, 1976.
———. "The Radical Press." In *Edwardian Radicalism, 1900–1914: Some Aspects of British Radicalism*. Ed. A. J. A. Morris. 47–61. London: Routledge and Kegan Paul, 1974.
———. "The Structure, Ownership, and Control of the Press, 1855–1914." In *Newspaper History: From the Seventeenth Century to the Present Day*. Ed. George Boyce, James Curran, and Pauline Wingate. 117–29. London: Constable, 1978.
Leigh, John Garrett. "What Do the Masses Read?" *Economic Review* 14 (April 1904): 166–77.
LeMahieu, D. L. *A Culture for Democracy: Mass Communication and the Cultivated Mind in Britain between the Wars*. Oxford: Clarendon, 1988.
Leonard, Thomas C. *News for All: America's Coming of Age with the Press*. New York: Oxford University Press, 1995.
Letham, G. H. "The National Union of Journalists: What It Is and What It Is Doing." In *Sell's Dictionary of the World's Press, 1910*. 528–30. London: Sell, 1910.
Leventhal, F. M. *The Last Dissenter: H. N. Brailsford and His World*. Oxford: Clarendon Press, 1985.
Levine, Philippa. "'The Humanising Influences of Five O'Clock Tea': Victorian Feminist Periodicals." *Victorian Studies* 33 (Winter 1990): 293–306.
Lewes, G. H. "Principles of Success in Literature." *Fortnightly Review* 1 (29 May 1865): 185–96.
Liddle, Dallas. "Salesmen, Sportsmen, Mentors: Anonymity and Mid-Victorian Theories of Journalism." *Victorian Studies* 41 (Autumn 1997): 31–68.
"The Limits of Press Power." *The Spectator* 124 (6 March 1920): 297–98
Lippmann, Walter. *Liberty and the News*. 1920. New Brunswick, N.J.: Transaction Publishers, 1995.
———. *Public Opinion*. 1922. New York: Free Press, 1997.
Lodge, T. C. Skeffington. "Why I Voted No." *The Spectator* 177 (15 November 1946): 508–9.
Lord Northcliffe. *Newspapers and Their Millionaires: With Some Further Meditations about Us*. London: Associated Newspapers, 1922.
"Lord Northcliffe." *The Nation* 115 (23 August 1922): 180.
Loughlin, J. "Constructing the Political Spectacle: Parnell, the Press, and National Leadership." In *Parnell in Perspective*. Ed. D. G. Boyce and Alan O'Day. 221–41. London: Routledge, 1991.
Lovelace, Colin. "British Press Censorship during the First World War." In *Newspaper History: From the Seventeenth Century to the Present Day*. Ed. George Boyce, James Curran, and Pauline Wingate. 307–19. London: Constable, 1978.

Lucas, Reginald J. *Lord Glenesk and the Morning Post.* London: Alston Rivers, 1910.

Lucy, Sir Henry William. *Sixty Years in the Wilderness: Some Passages by the Way.* London: Smith, Elder, 1909.

Ludlow, J. M., and L. Jones. *The Progress of the Working Class, 1832–1867.* London: A. Strahan, 1867.

Lyons, A. Neil. *Robert Blatchford: The Sketch of a Personality; An Estimate of Some Achievements.* London: Clarion Press, 1910.

Lyons, Charles. *The New Censors: Movies and the Culture Wars.* Philadelphia: Temple University Press, 1997.

Macaulay, Thomas Babington. *Critical and Historical Essays, Contributed to the Edinburgh Review.* 3 vols. London: Longman, 1843.

MacDonagh, Michael. "The Bye-Ways of Journalism." *Cornhill Magazine* 6 (March 1899): 395–406.

———. "The Foreign Correspondent." In *Newspaper Press Directory, 1904.* 14–15. London: Mitchell, 1904.

———. "The Newspaper Interview." In *Newspaper Press Directory, 1900.* 12–14. London: Mitchell, 1900.

———. "Our Special Correspondent." In *Newspaper Press Directory, 1903.* 90–91. London: Mitchell, 1903.

———. *The Reporters' Gallery.* London: Hodder and Stoughton, 1913.

Macdonald, John, ed. *Diary of the Parnell Commission.* London: T. Fisher Unwin, 1890.

Macintosh, Charles A. *Popular Outlines of the Press, Ancient and Modern; or, a Brief Sketch of the Origin and Progress of Printing, and Its Introduction into This Country, with a Notice of the Newspaper Press.* London: Wertheim, Macintosh, and Hunt, 1859.

Mackay, Charles. *Forty Years' Recollections of Life, Literature, and Public Affairs, 1830–1870.* 2 vols. London: Chapman and Hall, 1877.

Mackay, T. "The Unpopularity of the House of Commons." *National Review* 27 (August 1896): 802–15.

Mackie, John. *Modern Journalism: A Handbook of Instruction and Counsel for the Young Journalist.* London: Crosby Lockwood and Son, 1894.

MacKinnon, William. *On the Rise, Progress and Present State of Public Opinion in Great Britain and Other Parts of the World.* London: Saunders and Ottley, 1828.

Maddoux, Marlin. *Free Speech or Propaganda? How the Media Distorts the Truth.* Nashville: Thomas Nelson, 1990.

Madge, Charles. "What Makes News." *The Spectator* 161 (15 July 1938): 100–101.

Mah, Harold. "Phantasies of the Public Sphere: Rethinking the Habermas of Historians." *Journal of Modern History* 72 (March 2000): 153–82.

Mandler, Peter. "The Consciousness of Modernity? Liberalism and the English National Character, 1870–1940." In *Meanings of Modernity: Britain from the Late Victorian Era to World War II.* Ed. Martin Daunton and Bernard Rieger. 119–44. London: Berg, 2001.

Martin, A. Patchett. "Robert Lowe as a Journalist." *National Review* 22 (November 1893): 352–64.

Martin, Kingsley. "British Press and Foreign Affairs." *Political Quarterly* 2 (January 1931): 115–20.

———. "Conservative Press and the Conservative Party." *Political Quarterly* 2 (April 1931): 272–77.
———. *Editor: A Second Volume of Autobiography, 1931–1945*. London: Hutchinson, 1968.
———. *Father Figures: The Evolution of an Editor, 1897–1931*. Chicago: Henry Regnery Co., 1966.
———. *Fascism, Democracy, and the Press*. London: New Statesman and Nation, 1938.
———. "Freedom of the Press." *Political Quarterly* 9 (July 1938): 973–88.
———. "Is Humanism Utopian?" In *Objections to Humanism*. Ed. H. J. Blackham. 79–103. London: Constable, 1963.
———. *The Press the Public Wants*. London: Hogarth Press, 1947.
———. *Propaganda's Harvest*. London: Kegan Paul, Trench, Trubner and Co., 1941.
———. "Public Opinion: Censorship during the Crisis." *Political Quarterly* 10 (January 1939): 128–34.
———. *Truth and the Public*. London: Watts and Co., 1945.
———. "What Is News?" *The Listener*, 10 September 1930, 394–95.
Marvin, Carolyn. *When Old Technologies Were New: Thinking about Electric Communication in the Late Nineteenth Century*. New York: Oxford University Press, 1998.
Massingham, H. W. "The Ethics of Editing." *National Review* 35 (April 1900): 256–61.
———. "Journalism as a Dangerous Trade." *The Spectator* 131 (1 December 1923): 839–40.
———. "The Journalism of Lord Northcliffe." *The Nation and the Athenaeum* 31 (19 August 1922): 674–75.
———. *The London Daily Press*. New York: Fleming H. Revell Co., 1892.
———. "The Modern Press and Its Public." *Contemporary Review* 98 (October 1910): 413–24.
Matheson, Donald. "The Birth of News Discourse: Changes in News Language in British Newspapers, 1880–1930." *Media, Culture, and Society* 22 (September 2000): 557–73.
Matthew, H. C. G. *Gladstone, 1875–1898*. Oxford: Clarendon, 1995.
———. "Gladstone, Rhetoric, and Politics." In *Gladstone*. Ed. Peter J. Jagger. 213–34. London: Hambledon Press, 1998.
———. *The Liberal Imperialists: The Ideas and Politics of a Post-Gladstonian Elite*. London: Oxford University Press, 1973.
———. "Rhetoric and Politics in Great Britain, 1860–1950." In *Politics and Social Change in Modern Britain: Essays Presented to A. F. Thompson*. Ed. P. J. Waller. 34–58. Sussex: Harvester Press, 1987.
Maugham, William Somerset. *Of Human Bondage*. 1915. Harmondsworth: Penguin, 1963.
Maxse, Frederick A. "Anglophobia." *National Review* 28 (October 1896): 180–88.
Mayo, Isabella Fyvie. *Recollections of What I Saw, What I Lived Through, and What I Learned, during More Than Fifty Years of Social and Literary Experience*. London: John Murray, 1910.
McAleer, Joseph. *Popular Reading and Publishing in Britain, 1914–1950*. Oxford: Clarendon, 1992.
McCalman, Iain. *Radical Underworld: Prophets, Revolutionaries, and Pornographers in London, 1795–1840*. Oxford: Clarendon Press, 1993.
McCarthy, Justin. *Reminiscences*. 2 vols. London: Chatto and Windus, 1899.

McCarthy, Justin, and Sir John Robinson. *The Daily News Jubilee: A Political and Social Retrospect of Fifty Years of the Queen's Reign.* London: Sampson Low, 1896.

McCarty, William. "The Press as a Mirror." *The Spectator* 143 (13 July 1929): 42–43.

McChesney, Robert W. *Rich Media, Poor Democracy: Communication Politics in Dubious Times.* Urbana: University of Illinois Press, 1999.

McEwen, John M. "Lloyd George's Acquisition of the *Daily Chronicle* in 1918." *Journal of British Studies* 22 (Fall 1982): 127–44.

———. "The National Press during the First Great War: Ownership and Circulation." *Journal of Contemporary History* 17 (July 1982): 459–86.

———. "Northcliffe and Lloyd George at War, 1914–1918." *Historical Journal* 24 (September 1981): 651–72.

———. "The Press and the Fall of Asquith." *Historical Journal* 21 (December 1978): 863–83.

McGregor, H. "Government, Press, and People." Letter to the editor. *The Spectator* 163 (11 August 1939): 222.

McKibbin, Ross. *Classes and Cultures: England, 1918–1951.* Oxford: Oxford University Press, 1998.

———. *The Ideologies of Class: Social Relations in Britain, 1880–1950.* Oxford: Clarendon Press, 1990.

McLachlan, Donald Harvey. "The Press and Public Opinion." *British Journal of Sociology* 6 (June 1955): 159–68.

McLuhan, Marshall. *The Gutenberg Galaxy: The Making of Typographic Man.* Toronto: University of Toronto Press, 1962.

———. *Understanding Media: The Extensions of Man.* 1964. Cambridge, Mass.: MIT Press, 1994.

McNair, Brian. *News and Journalism in the U.K.: A Textbook.* 3d ed. London: Routledge, 1999.

———. *The Sociology of Journalism.* London: Arnold, 1998.

McQuail, Denis. *Review of Sociological Writing on the Press.* London: Her Majesty's Stationery Office, 1976.

McWilliam, Rohan. "Melodrama and the Historians." *Radical History Review* 78 (Fall 2000): 57–84.

———. *Popular Politics in Nineteenth-Century England.* London: Routledge, 1998.

Merrill, Samuel. *Newspaper Libel: A Handbook for the Press.* Boston: Ticknor and Co., 1888.

Messinger, Gary. *British Propaganda and the State in the First World War.* Manchester: Manchester University Press, 1992.

[Mill, James.] "Liberty of the Press." *Edinburgh Review* 18 (May 1811): 98–123.

Mill, John Stuart. *Autobiography.* 1873. Ed. and intro. Jack Stillinger. Boston: Houghton Mifflin Co., 1969.

———. *The Later Letters of John Stuart Mill, 1849–1873.* Ed. Francis E. Mineka and Dwight N. Lindley. London: Routledge and Kegan Paul, 1972.

———. *On Liberty.* 1869. 4th ed. Ed. and intro. Elizabeth Rapaport. Indianapolis: Hackett Publishing Co., 1978.

———. *The Subjection of Women.* 1869. Ed. and intro. Susan Moller Okin. Indianapolis: Hackett Publishing Co., 1988.

Millar, A. H., ed. *The Dundee Advertiser, 1801–1901: A Centenary Memoir.* Dundee: John Leng and Co., 1901.
Mills, William Haslam. "The *Manchester Guardian:* The Paper and Its Readers, a Century of History." *Manchester Guardian,* 5 May 1921, 36–51.
The Mirrors of Downing Street: Some Political Reflections by a Gentleman with a Duster. New York: G. P. Putnam's Sons, 1921.
"The Misrepresentation of News." *Saturday Review* 151 (7 March 1931): 329.
Mitroff, Ian I., and Warren Bennis. *The Unreality Industry: The Deliberate Manufacturing of Falsehood and What It is Doing to Our Lives.* Oxford: Oxford University Press, 1993.
"The Modern Newspaper." *British Quarterly Review* 55 (April 1872): 348–80.
The Modern Newspaper: How It Is Produced. Manchester: Hulton, 1905.
Montagu, Irving. *Things I Have Seen in War.* London: Chatto and Windus, 1899.
———. *Wanderings of a War Artist.* London: W. H. Allen, 1889.
Montague, C[harles]. E[dward]. *A Hind Let Loose.* London: Methuen, 1910.
Moore, Frank Frankfort. *A Journalist's Note Book.* London: Hutchinson, 1894.
Moore, Henry C. "The Late Joseph Cowen, Esq." In *Newspaper Press Directory, 1901.* 80. London: Mitchell, 1901.
———. "The Late William Lewis, Esq., J.P." In *Newspaper Press Directory, 1901.* 81. London: Mitchell, 1901.
———. "The Sporting Press." In *Newspaper Press Directory, 1903.* 88–89. London: Mitchell, 1903.
Morgan, Kenneth O. *Keir Hardie: Radical and Socialist.* London: Weidenfeld and Nicholson, 1975.
———. "The Boer War and the Media, 1899–1902." *Twentieth Century British History* 13.1 (2002): 1–16.
Morley, John. "Anonymous Journalism." *Fortnightly Review* 8 (September 1867): 287–92.
"Mr. Baldwin and Lord Rothermere." *New Statesman and Nation* 1 (21 March 1931): 136.
"Mr. Cobden and the *Times.*" *Saturday Review* 11 (16 February 1861): 156–7.
"Mr. Lloyd George and Lord Northcliffe." *The Spectator* 122 (26 April 1919): 517–8.
Muggeridge, Malcolm. *The Thirties 1930–1940 in Great Britain.* 1940. London: Collins, 1967.
Murdock, Graham. "Reconstructing the Ruined Tower: Contemporary Communications and Questions of Class." In *Mass Media and Society.* 3d ed. Ed. James Curran and Michael Gurevitch. 7–26. London: Edwin Arnold, 2000.
Murdock, Graham, and Peter Golding. "The Structure, Ownership, and Control of the Press, 1914–76." In *Newspaper History: From the Seventeenth Century to the Present Day.* Ed. George Boyce, James Curran, and Pauline Wingate. 130–48. London: Constable, 1978.
Murray, Alfred Hill. "Libel and the Freedom of the Press." *Quarterly Review* 117 (April 1865): 519–39.
[Murray, E. C. G.] *The Press and the Public Service.* London: Routledge, 1857.
"Muzzled Britain." *New Statesman and Nation* 16 (12 November 1938): 756–57.
National Political Union. *Taxes on Knowledge: Debate in the House of Commons on the 15th June, 1832, on Mr. E. L. Bulwer's Motion.* London: Southwark, 1832.
Negrine, Ralph. *Politics and the Mass Media in Britain.* 2d ed. London: Routledge, 1994.
"The Neurasthenic Press." *The Spectator* 116 (26 February 1916): 278.

"The New Model." *The Spectator* 126 (19 February 1921): 227–28.

"Newspaper Gambling." *The Spectator* 102 (6 March 1909): 367–68.

"The Newspaper of the Future." *The Spectator* 126 (19 February 1921): 226–27.

The Newspaper Stamp and the Duty on Paper, Viewed in Relation to Their Effects upon the Diffusion of Knowledge. London: Charles Knight, 1836.

Nicholas, Siân. "All the News That's Fit to Broadcast: The Popular Press versus the BBC, 1922–45." In *Northcliffe's Legacy: Aspects of the British Popular Press, 1896–1996.* Ed. Peter Catterall, Colin Seymour-Ure, and Adrian Smith. 121–47. London: Macmillan, 2000.

Nicholson, A. P. "Parliamentary Reporting—A Reply." *Contemporary Review* 87 (April 1905): 577–82.

Nicoll, W. Robertson. *James Macdonnell, Journalist.* London: Hodder and Stoughton, 1890.

Nicolson, Harold. "Marginal Comment." *The Spectator* (25 July 1947): 107.

"A Northcliffe Ministry." *The Spectator* 120 (26 January 1918): 76–77.

"Northcliffe on Newspapers." *New Statesman* 19 (13 May 1922): 142–43; (20 May 1922): 179–80.

Northrop, William Bellenger. *With Pen and Camera: Interviews with Celebrities.* London: R. A. Everett, 1904.

Oakeshott, Michael. "Rationalism in Politics." *Rationalism in Politics and Other Essays.* Indianapolis: Liberty Press, 1991.

O'Boyle, L. "The Image of the Journalist in England, France, and Germany, 1815–1848." *Comparative Studies in Society and History* 10 (April 1968): 290–317.

Ockham, David. "Is the Press an Evil? Yes." *Saturday Review* 152 (12 December 1931): 754.

O'Connor, T. P. "The New Journalism." *New Review* 1 (October 1889): 423–34.

Oldcastle, John. *Journals and Journalism: With a Guide for Literary Beginners.* London: Field and Tuer, 1880.

O'Malley, Tom. "The History of Self-Regulation." In *Regulating the Press.* Ed. Tom O'Malley and Clive Soley. 5–141. London: Pluto Press, 2000.

———. "Labour and the 1947–9 Royal Commission on the Press." In *A Journalism Reader.* Ed. Michael Bromley and Tom O'Malley. 126–58. London: Routledge, 1997.

———. "Media History and Media Studies: Aspects of the Development of the Study of Media History in the UK, 1945–2000." *Media History* 8 (December 2002): 155–73.

O'Malley, Tom, and Clive Soley. *Regulating the Press.* London: Pluto Press, 2000.

Onslow, Barbara. *Women of the Press in Nineteenth-Century Britain.* London: Macmillan, 2000.

Orwell, George. *Homage to Catalonia.* 1938. San Diego: Harcourt, Brace, and Co., 1980.

———. *The Road to Wigan Pier.* 1937. San Diego: Harcourt, Brace, and Co., 1958.

———. "Politics and the English Language." In *The Collected Essays, Journalism, and Letters of George Orwell.* Vol. 4, *In Front of Your Nose, 1945–50.* Ed. Sonia Orwell and Ian Angus. 127–43. New York: Harcourt, Brace, and World, 1968.

O'Shea, Captain John Augustus. *Leaves from the Life of a Special Correspondent.* London: Ward and Downey, 1885.

Ostrogorski, Moisei I. *Democracy and the Organization of Political Parties.* New York: Macmillan, 1902.

Owen, Louise. *Northcliffe: The Facts.* London: Owen, 1931.

———. *The Real Lord Northcliffe: Some Personal Recollections of a Private Secretary, 1902–1922*. London: Cassell and C., 1922.

"The Owners of the Press." *The Spectator* 161 (30 December 1938): 1111–12.

Palast, Greg. *The Best Democracy Money Can Buy: The Truth about Corporate Cons, Globalization, and High-Finance Fraudsters*. New York: Plume, 2003.

Parenti, Michael. *Inventing Reality: The Politics of News Media*. New York: St. Martin's Press, 1986.

Parry, Jonathan. *The Rise and Fall of Liberal Government in Victorian Britain*. New Haven, Conn.: Yale University Press, 1993.

Paterson, James. *Autobiographical Reminiscences*. Edinburgh: Maurice Ogle, 1871.

———. *The Liberty of the Press, Speech, and Public Worship, Being Commentaries on the Liberty of the Subject and the Laws of England*. London: Macmillan, 1880.

Pebody, Charles. *English Journalism and the Men who Have Made It*. London: Cassell, Petter, Galpin, and Co., 1882.

Pedersen, Susan, and Peter Mandler, eds. *After the Victorians: Private Conscience and Public Duty in Modern Britain; Essays in Memory of John Clive*. London: Routledge, 1994.

Peel, George. "The Science of Propaganda." *Contemporary Review* 166 (November 1944): 268–74.

Pelling, Henry. *A History of British Trade Unionism*. 5th ed. London: Macmillan, 1992.

———. *Popular Politics and Society in Late Victorian Britain*. London: Macmillan, 1968.

Pendleton, John. *How to Succeed as a Journalist*. London: Grant Richards, 1902.

———. *Newspaper Reporting*. London: Elliot Stock, 1890.

"The People and the Press." *The Spectator* 152 (30 March 1934): 492.

Perkin, Harold. *The Origins of Modern English Society, 1780–1880*. London: Routledge and Kegan Paul, 1969.

———. *The Rise of Professional Society: England since 1880*. London: Routledge, 1989.

———. *The Structured Crowd: Essays in English Social History*. Sussex: Harvester Press, 1981.

Phillipps, E. M. "The New Journalism." *New Review* 13 (August 1895): 182–89.

Phillips, Ernest. *How to Become a Journalist: A Practical Guide for Newspaper Work*. London: Sampson and Low, 1895.

Phillips, John Searles Ragland. "The Growth of Journalism (18th and 19th Centuries)." In *The Cambridge History of English Literature*. Vol. 14. Ed. A. W. Ward and A. R. Walker. 167–204. Cambridge: Cambridge University Press, 1916.

Plunkett, John. *Queen Victoria: First Media Monarch*. Oxford: Oxford University Press, 2003.

Political and Economic Planning. *Report on the British Press: A Survey of Its Current Operations and Problems with Special Reference to National Newspapers and Their Part in Public Affairs*. London: Political and Economic Planning, 1938.

Poovey, Mary. *Making a Social Body: British Cultural Formation, 1830–1864*. Chicago: University of Chicago Press, 1995.

Pope, T. Michael. *The Book of Fleet Street*. London: Cassell and Co., 1930.

"Popular Literature—The Periodical Press." *Blackwood's Edinburgh Magazine* 85 (January 1859): 96–112; (February 1859): 180–95.

Porritt, Edward. "The Value of Political Editorials." In *Sell's Dictionary of the World's Press, 1910*. 508–14. London: Sell, 1910.

Porter, A. N. "Sir Alfred Milner and the Press, 1897–99." *Historical Journal* 16 (June 1973): 323–39.

"The Position of the Prime Minister." *The Spectator* 120 (16 March 1918): 277.

Postman, Neil. *Amusing Ourselves to Death: Public Discourse in the Age of Show Business.* New York: Penguin, 1985.

The Power of the Press: Is It Rightly Employed? Facts, Enquiries, and Suggestions Addressed to Members of Christian Churches. London: Partridge and Oakey, 1847.

The Press and Its Readers: A Report Prepared by Mass-Observation for the Advertising Service Guild. London: Art and Technics, 1949.

"The Press and the Elections." *The Spectator* 131 (1 December 1923): 833.

"The Press and the Public Service." *Fraser's Magazine* 55 (June 1857): 649–62.

"The Press Association." *Chambers's Journal* 74 (14 August 1897): 516–17.

"Press Combinations." *The Spectator* 131 (20 October 1923): 544.

"The Priesthood and the Press." *Bentley's Miscellany* 33 (February 1853): 241–48.

"The Profession of Journalism." *The Spectator* (8 March 1930): 355.

Progress of British Newspapers in the 19th Century, Illustrated. London: Simpkin, Marshall, Hamilton, Kent, and Co., 1901.

Pronay, Nicholas, and D. W. Springs, eds. *Propaganda, Politics, and Film, 1918–45.* London: Macmillan, 1982.

"The Public and the Press." *The Spectator* 177 (9 August 1946): 131–32.

"Public Opinion and Journalists." *Saturday Review* 11 (16 February 1861): 162–63.

Putnam, Robert. *Bowling Alone: The Collapse and Revival of American Community.* New York: Simon and Schuster, 2000.

Raleigh, Sir Walter Alexander. *The War and the Press.* Oxford: Clarendon Press, 1918.

Ransome, Arthur. *Bohemia in London.* Illus. Fred Taylor. London: Chapman and Hall, 1907.

Raymond, E. T. *Uncensored Celebrities.* New York: Henry Holt, 1919.

Read, Donald. *The Power of the News: The History of Reuters, 1849–1989.* Oxford: Oxford University Press, 1992.

———. *The Press and the People, 1790–1850: Opinion in Three English Cities.* London: Edward Arnold, 1961.

Reay, Barry. "The Context and Meaning of Popular Literacy: Some Evidence from Nineteenth-Century Rural England." *Past and Present* 131 (May 1991): 89–129.

"The Reconversion of the Daily News." *Review of Reviews* 23 (1901): 147–53.

Redding, Cyrus. *Fifty Years' Recollectons, Literary and Personal: With Observations on Men and Things.* 3 vols. London: Charles J. Skeet, 1858.

———. *Yesterday and To-day.* 3 vols. London: T. Cautley Newly, 1863.

Reddy, William. "Condottieri of the Pen: Journalists and the Public Sphere in Post-Revolutionary France, 1815–1850." *American Historical Review* 99 (December 1994): 1546–70.

Redlich, Monica. "Marginal Comments." *The Spectator* 156 (10 April 1936): 663.

Reid, Arnot. "How a Provincial Newspaper Is Managed." *The Nineteenth Century* 20 (September 1886): 391–402.

Reid, Fred. "Keir Hardie and the *Labour Leader,* 1893–1903." In *The Working Class in Modern British History: Essays in Honour of Henry Pelling.* Ed. Jay Winter. 19–42. Stanford, Calif.: Stanford University Press, 1983.

Reid, Hugh Gilzean, and P. J. MacDonnell. "The Press." In *The Civilisation of Our Day: A Series of Original Essays on Some of Its More Important Phases at the Close of the Nineteenth Century, by Expert Writers*. Ed. James Samuelson. 276–92. London: Sampson Low, Marston, and Co., 1896.
Reid, Sir [Thomas] Wemyss. *Editors of Today*. London: Griffith and Tarran, 1880.
———. *Memoirs of Sir Wemyss Reid, 1842–1885*. Ed. Stuart J. Reid. London: Cassell, 1905.
———. "Our London Correspondent." *Macmillan's Magazine* 43 (May 1880): 18–26.
———. "Public Opinion and Its Leaders." *Fortnightly Review* 34 (August 1880): 230–44.
Reid, Sir [Thomas] Wemyss, and William Henry Cooke. *Briefs and Papers: Sketches of the Bar and Press by Two Idle Apprentices*. London: H. S. King and Co., 1872.
Report from the Select Committee on Newspaper Stamps. London: House of Commons, 1851.
"A Responsible Press." *The Spectator* 164 (8 March 1940): 317–18.
Richards, Huw. *The Bloody Circus: The Daily Herald and the Left*. London: Pluto, 1997.
Richards, Thomas. *The Commodity Culture of Victorian England: Advertising and Spectacle, 1851–1914*. Stanford, Calif.: Stanford University Press, 1990.
Riddell, Lord. "The Psychology of the Journalist." In *A Journalism Reader*. Ed. Michael Bromley and Tom O'Malley. 110–14. London: Routledge, 1997.
Robbins, Alfred F. "Newspaper Ideals and Individualities: A Retrospect and Review." *Newspaper Press Directory, 1911*. 5–7. London: Mitchell, 1911.
Robbins, Keith. "Public Opinion, the Press, and Pressure Groups." In *British Foreign Policy under Sir Edward Grey*. Ed. F. H. Hinsley. 70–88. Cambridge: Cambridge University Press, 1977.
Robertson, John M. "The Press Fetish." *Contemporary Review* 109 (January 1916): 49–56.
Robinson, Henry Crabb. *Diary, Reminiscences, and Correspondence of Henry Crabb Robinson*. 3 vols. Ed. Thomas Sadler. London: Macmillan, 1869.
Rogers, Edmund Dawson. *The Life and Experiences of Edmund Dawson Rogers, Spiritualist and Journalist, Editor of Light, and President of the London Spiritualist Alliance*. London: Office of Light, 1911.
Rose, J. Holland. "The Unstamped Press, 1815–1836." *English Historical Review* 12 (October 1897): 711–26.
Rose, Jonathan. *The Intellectual Life of the British Working Classes*. New Haven, Conn.: Yale University Press, 2001.
Rosen, Jay. *What Are Journalists For?* New Haven, Conn.: Yale University Press, 1999.
Routledge, James. *Chapters in the History of Popular Progress Chiefly in Relation to the Freedom of the Press and Trial by Jury 1660–1820, with an Application to Later Years*. London: Macmillan and Co., 1876.
Royal Commission on the Press 1947–1949: Report Presented to Parliament by Command of His Majesty, June 1949. London: His Majesty's Stationery Office, 1949.
Rubin, Joan Shelley. *The Making of Middlebrow Culture*. Chapel Hill: University of North Carolina Press, 1992.
Russel, Alexander. "The Newspaper Stamp." *Edinburgh Review* 98 (October 1853): 488–518.
Russell, Sir Edward. *That Reminds Me*. London: T. Fisher Unwin, 1899.
Russell, T. "The Supreme Advertising Medium—The Newspaper." In *Newspaper Press Directory 1907*. 5–6. London: Charles Mitchell, 1907.

Ryan, Alfred. *Lord Northcliffe.* London: Collins, 1953.
Sala, George Augustus. *The Life and Adventures of George Augustus Sala, Written by Himself.* 2 vols. London: Cassell, 1895.
———. *Things I Have Seen and People I Have Known.* London: Cassell, 1894.
Salmon, Lucy M. *The Newspaper and Authority.* New York: Oxford University Press, 1923.
Salmon, Richard. "'A Simulacrum of Power': Intimacy and Abstraction in the Rhetoric of the New Journalism." *Victorian Periodicals Review* 30 (Spring 1997): 41–52.
Sanders, Michael, and Philip M. Taylor. *British Propaganda during the First World War, 1914–18.* London: Macmillan, 1981.
Savage, Gail. "Erotic Stories and Public Decency: Newspaper Reporting of Divorce Proceedings in England." *Historical Journal* 41 (June 1998): 511–28.
Sayers, Dorothy. *Murder Must Advertise.* New York: Harper and Row, 1933.
Schudson, Michael. *Discovering the News: A Social History of American Newspapers.* New York: Basic Books, 1978.
———. *The Power of News.* Cambridge, Mass.: Harvard University Press, 1995.
Schults, Raymond. *Crusader in Babylon: W. T. Stead and the Pall Mall Gazette.* Lincoln: University of Nebraska Press, 1972.
Schwarz, Bill. "Politics and Rhetoric in the Age of Mass Culture." *History Workshop Journal* 46 (Autumn 1998): 129–59.
"The Science of Advertising." *The Spectator* 157 (4 September 1936): 369–70.
The Scotsman. *The Story of The Scotsman: A Chapter in the Annals of British Journalism.* Edinburgh: Printed for Private Circulation, 1886.
Scott, Charles Prestwich. "The Function of the Press." *Political Quarterly* 2 (January–March 1931): 59–63.
———. "A Hundred Years." *Manchester Guardian,* 5 May 1921, 35.
Scott, Patrick, and Pauline Fletcher, eds. *Culture and Education in Victorian England.* London: Associated University Presses, 1990.
Scott-James, R. A. *The Influence of the Press.* London: Partridge and Co., 1913.
———. "Great Provincial Press." *The Spectator* 150 (2 June 1933): 797–98.
Seacole, Mary. *Wonderful Adventures of Mrs. Seacole in Many Lands.* 1858. New York: Oxford University Press, 1988.
Searle, G. R. *Corruption in British Politics, 1895–1930.* Oxford: Clarendon Press, 1987.
———. *The Quest for National Efficiency: A Study in British Politics and Political Thought, 1899–1914.* Berkeley: University of California Press, 1971.
Seaton, Jean. "The Sociology of the Mass Media." In *Power without Responsibility: The Press and Broadcasting in Britain.* 5th ed. Ed. James Curran and Jean Seaton. 264–86. London: Routledge, 1987.
Seaton, Jean, and Ben Pimlott, eds. *The Media in British Politics.* Aldershot: Avebury, 1987.
Seligman, Adam B. *The Idea of Civil Society.* Princeton, N.J.: Princeton University Press, 1992.
Semmell, Bernard. *Imperialism and Social Reform: English Social-Imperial Thought, 1895–1914.* London: G. Allen and Unwin, 1960.
Seymour-Ure, Colin. *The British Press and Broadcasting since 1945.* 2d ed. Oxford: Blackwell, 1996.

———. "Northcliffe's Legacy." In *Northcliffe's Legacy: Aspects of the British Popular Press, 1896–1996*. Ed. Peter Catterall, Colin Seymour-Ure, and Adrian Smith. 9–25. London: Macmillan, 2000.
Shadwell, Arthur. "Journalism as a Profession." *National Review* 31 (August 1898): 845–55.
———. "Proprietors and Editors." *National Review* 35 (June 1900): 592–601.
Shattock, Joanne, and Michael Wolff, eds. *The Victorian Periodical Press: Samplings and Soundings*. Leicester: Leicester University Press, 1982.
Shaw, George Bernard. *Everybody's Political What's What?* London: Constable and Co., 1944.
Shaw, Tony. "The British Popular Press and the Early Cold War." *History* 83 (January 1998): 66–85.
Sheppard, S. T. "In Memoriam: William Howard Russell; The Genesis of a Profession." *United Service Magazine* 155 (March 1907): 569–75.
Siebert, Fred S., Theodore Peterson, and Wilbur Schramm. *Four Theories of the Press: The Authoritarian, Libertarian, Social Responsibility, and Soviet Communist Concepts of What the Press Should Be and Do*. Urbana: University of Illinois Press, 1963.
Simonis, Henry. *The Street of Ink: An Intimate History of Journalism*. London: Cassell, 1917.
Sims, George R. *My Life: Sixty Years' Recollections of Bohemian London*. London: Eveleigh Nash, 1917.
Sinclair, Alexander. *Fifty Years of Newspaper Life, 1845–1895: Being Chiefly Reminiscences of That Time*. Glasgow: Printed for Private Circulation, 1895.
Sinnema, Peter. *Dynamics of the Pictured Page: Representing the Nation in the Illustrated London News*. Aldershot, U.K.: Ashgate, 1998.
Smiles, Samuel. "What Are the People Doing to Educate Themselves?" *People's Journal* 1 (1846): 222–24, 229–30.
Smith, Adrian. *The New Statesman: Portrait of a Political Weekly, 1913–1931*. London: Frank Cass, 1996.
Smith, Anthony. *The Politics of Information*. London: Macmillan, 1978.
Smith, Laura Alex. "Women's Work in London and the Provincial Press." In *Newspaper Press Directory, 1897*. 14–15. London: C. Mitchell and Co., 1897.
Sommerville, C. John. *The News Revolution in England: Cultural Dynamics of Daily Information*. New York: Oxford University Press, 1996.
Sparks, Colin. "Goodbye Hildy Johnson: The Vanishing 'Serious Press.'" In *Communication and Citizenship: Journalism and the Public Sphere*. Ed. Peter Dahlgren and Colin Sparks. 58–74. London: Routledge, 1991.
———. "The Popular Press and Political Democracy." *Media, Culture, and Society* 10 (1988): 209–33.
"A Spectator's Notebook." *The Spectator* 177 (19 July 1946): 56.
Spender, Harold. "Is Public Opinion Supreme?" *Contemporary Review* 88 (September 1905): 411–23.
Spender, John Alfred. *Life, Journalism, and Politics*. 2 vols. London: Cassell, 1927.
———. *The Public Life*. 2 vols. London: Cassell, 1925.
Stansky, Peter. *Ambitions and Strategies: The Struggle for the Leadership of the Liberal Party in the 1890s*. Oxford: Clarendon Press, 1964.

———. *On or About December 1910: Early Bloomsbury and Its Intimate World.* Cambridge, Mass.: Harvard University Press, 1996.

———, ed. *The Victorian Revolution: Government and Society in Victoria's Britain.* New York: Franklin Watts, 1973.

Startt, James D. *Journalists for Empire: The Imperial Debate in the Edwardian Stately Press, 1903–1913.* Westport, Conn.: Greenwood, 1991.

"The State of the Newspaper Press." *The Nation and the Athenaeum* 30 (18 February 1922): 753–54.

Stead, W. T. "The Future of Journalism." *Contemporary Review* 50 (November 1886): 663–79.

———. "Government by Journalism." *Contemporary Review* 49 (May 1886): 653–74.

———. *A Journalist on Journalism.* Ed. Edwin H. Stout. London: John Haddon, 1892.

———. "The Press in the Twentieth Century." *Great Thoughts from Master Minds* 22 (March 1895): 363–64.

———. "Then and Now." *Newspaper Press Directory, 1912.* 5–9. London: Mitchell, 1912.

Steed, Henry Wickham. *The Press.* Harmondsworth: Penguin, 1938.

Steel, Ronald. *Walter Lippmann and the American Century.* Boston: Little, Brown, and Company, 1980.

Stephen, Leslie. "Some Early Impressions—Editing." *National Review* 42 (December 1903): 562–81.

Stephens, Mitchell. *The Rise of the Image the Fall of the Word.* New York: Oxford University Press, 1998.

Stevenson, John. *British Society 1914–45.* Harmondsworth: Penguin, 1984.

St. John, J. A. *The Education of the People.* London: Chapman and Hall, 1858.

Stout, Edwin H. "W. T. Stead: A Character Sketch." In *A Journalist on Journalism,* by W. T. Stead. Ed. Edwin H. Stout. 7–18. London: John Haddon, 1892.

Struther, Jan (Joyce Maxtone Grahame). "On Not Reading the Papers." *The Spectator* 153 (6 July 1934): 12.

Swaffer, Hannen. *Northcliffe's Return (Spiritualistic Communications).* London: Hitchenson and Company, 1925.

———. *Northcliffe's Return.* London: Psychic Press, 1939.

Symon, J. D. *The Press and Its Story: An Account of the Birth and Development of Journalism up to the Present Day, with the History of All the Leading Newspapers: Daily, Weekly, or Monthly, Secular and Religious, Past and Present; Also the Story of their Production from Wood-Pulp to the Printed Sheet.* London: Seeley, Service, and Co., 1914.

Tanner, Duncan. "The Rise of Labour in England and Wales." *Bulletin of the Institute of Historical Research* 56 (November 1983): 205–19.

The Tax on Paper: The Case Stated for Its Immediate Repeal; Published under the Direction of the Committee of the Newspaper and Periodical Press Association for Obtaining the Repeal of the Paper Duty. London: N.p., 1858.

Taylor, A. J. P. *Beaverbrook.* London: Hamish Hamilton, 1972.

Taylor, Antony. *"Down with the Crown": British Anti-Monarchism and Debates about Royalty since 1790.* London: Reaktion, 1999.

———. "*Reynolds's Newspaper,* Opposition to the Monarchy, and the Radical Jubilee:

Britain's Anti-Monarchist Tradition Reconsidered." *Historical Research* 68 (October 1995): 318–37.

Taylor, Frank. *The Newspaper Press as a Power Both in the Expression and the Formation of Public Opinion.* Oxford: Blackwell, 1898.

Taylor, Miles. *The Decline of British Radicalism, 1847–1860.* Oxford: Clarendon, 1995.

Taylor, Philip M. "British Official Attitudes towards Propaganda Abroad, 1918–39." In *Propaganda, Politics, and Film, 1918–45.* Ed. Nicholas Pronay and D. W. Spring. 23–49. London: Macmillan, 1982.

———. *British Propaganda in the Twentieth Century: Selling Democracy.* Edinburgh: Edinburgh University Press, 1999.

Thackeray, W. M. *Pendennis.* 1864. Oxford: Oxford University Press, 1994.

Thomas, Ivor. *The Newspaper.* Oxford Pamphlets on Home Affairs. Oxford: Oxford University Press, 1943.

Thompson, J. Lee. *Northcliffe: Press Baron in Politics, 1865–1922.* London: John Murray, 2000.

———. *Politicians, the Press, and Propaganda: Lord Northcliffe and the Great War, 1914–1919.* Kent, Ohio: Kent State University Press, 1999.

Thompson, John B. *The Media and Modernity: A Social Theory of the Media.* Stanford, Calif.: Stanford University Press, 1995.

Tracey, Herbert, ed. *The British Press: A Survey, a Newspaper Directory, and a Who's Who in Journalism.* London: Europa, 1929.

Trentmann, Frank. "Civilization and Its Discontents: English Neo-Romanticism and the Transformation of Anti-Modernism in Twentieth-Century Culture." *Journal of Contemporary History* 29 (October 1994): 583–625.

Trollope, Anthony. "On Anonymous Literature." *Fortnightly Review* 1 (1 July 1865): 491–98.

———. *The Warden.* 1855. London: Penguin Books, 1986.

Tunstall, Jeremy. *The Media Are American: Anglo-American Media in the World.* New York: Columbia University Press, 1977.

———. *Newspaper Power: The New National Press in Britain.* Oxford: Clarendon Press, 1996.

Tunstall, Jeremy, and David Mackin. *The Anglo-American Media Connection.* Oxford: Oxford University Press, 1999.

Tusan, Michelle. "The Making of the Women's Political Press: Gender and Advocacy Journalism in Britain, 1858–1930." Ph.D. dissertation, University of California at Berkeley, 1999.

Vallance, Aylmer. "Muzzling Democracy." *New Statesman and Nation* 16 (10 December 1938): 958–59.

Vann, J. Don, and Rosemary T. VanArsdel, eds. *Periodicals of Queen Victoria's Empire: An Exploration.* Toronto: University of Toronto Press, 1996.

———. *Victorian Periodicals and Victorian Society.* Toronto: University of Toronto Press, 1994.

Vernon, James. *Politics and the People: A Study in English Political Culture, ca. 1815–1867.* Cambridge: Cambridge University Press, 1993.

———, ed. *Re-reading the Constitution: New Narratives in the History of English Politics.* Cambridge: Cambridge University Press, 1996.
Vicinus, Martha. *The Industrial Muse: A Study of British Working Class Literature.* London: Croom Helm, 1974.
Vickery, Amanda. "Golden Age to Separate Spheres? A Review of the Categories and Chronology of English Women's History." *Historical Journal* 36 (June 1993): 383–414.
Vincent, David. *The Culture of Secrecy: Britain 1832–1998.* London: Oxford University Press, 1998.
———. *Literacy and Popular Culture: England 1750–1914.* Cambridge: Cambridge University Press, 1989.
Vincent, John. *The Formation of the Liberal Party, 1857–1868.* London: Constable, 1966.
Walkowitz, Judith. *City of Dreadful Delight: Narratives of Sexual Danger in Late Victorian London.* Chicago: University of Chicago Press, 1992.
———. "The Indian Woman, the Flower Girl, and the Jew: Photojournalism in Edwardian London." *Victorian Studies* 44 (Autumn 1998/1999): 3–46.
Walsh, Cheryl. "The Incarnation and the Christian Socialist Conscience in the Victorian Church of England." *Journal of British Studies* 34 (July 1995): 351–74.
Walsh, Walter. *The Moral Damage of War.* Boston: Ginn and Co., 1906.
Ward, Mrs. Humphry (Mary Augusta), and Charles Edward Montague. *William Thomas Arnold, Journalist and Historian.* Manchester: Manchester University Press, 1907.
"A Warning." *The Spectator* 120 (6 April 1918): 368–69.
Warren, Samuel. "Public Lectures—Mr. Warren on Labour." *Blackwood's Edinburgh Magazine* 79 (February 1856): 170–79.
"The Waste-Paper Phoenix." *The Spectator* 118 (31 March 1917): 383–84.
Waters, Chris. *British Socialists and the Politics of Popular Culture, 1884–1914.* Stanford, Calif.: Stanford University Press, 1990.
Waugh, Evelyn. *Scoop.* 1937. Boston: Little, Brown and Co., 1999.
Webb, R. K. *The British Working Class Reader, 1790–1848.* London: G. Allen and Unwin, 1955.
Wells, H. G. "Liberalism and the Revolutionary Spirit: Address to the Liberal Summer School at Oxford, July 1932." In *After Democracy.* 1–28. London: Watts and Co., 1932.
———. *The New Machiavelli.* 1911. Ed. Norman MacKenzie. London: J. M. Dent, 1994.
———. *The Salvaging of Civilization: The Probable Future of Mankind.* New York: Macmillan, 1921.
Whorlow, H. *The Provincial Newspaper Society, 1836–1886: A Jubilee Retrospect.* London: Page, Pratt, and Turner, 1886.
Whyte, Sir Frederic. *The Life of W. T. Stead.* 2 vols. London: Jonathan Cape, 1925.
Wiener, Joel H. "The Americanization of the British Press." In *Studies in Newspaper and Periodical History: 1994 Annual.* Ed. Michael Harris and Tom O'Malley. 61–74. Westport, Conn.: Greenwood Press, 1996.
———. "How New Was the New Journalism?" In *Papers for the Millions: The New Journalism in Britain, 1850s to 1914.* Ed. Joel H. Weiner. 47–72. New York: Greenwood Press, 1988.
———. *The War of the Unstamped: The Movement to Repeal the British Newspaper Tax, 1830–1836.* Ithaca, N.Y.: Cornell University Press, 1969.

———. , ed. *Innovators and Preachers: The Role of the Editor in Victorian England.* Westport, Conn.: Greenwood Press, 1985.

———, ed. *Papers for the Millions: The New Journalism in Britain, 1850s to 1914.* New York: Greenwood Press, 1988.

Wiener, Martin J. "The Unloved State: Twentieth-Century Politics in the Writing of Nineteenth-Century History." *Journal of British Studies* 33 (July 1994): 283–308.

Wilkinson, Glenn R. *Depictions and Images of War in Edwardian Newspapers, 1899–1914.* London: Palgrave Macmillan, 2003.

Williams, Francis. *Press, Parliament, and People.* London: William Heinemann, 1946.

Williams, J. B. "The Beginnings of English Journalism: A Study in Personal Forces." In *The Cambridge History of English Literature.* Vol. 7. 343–65. Cambridge: Cambridge University Press, 1911.

———. *A History of English Journalism to the Foundation of the Gazette.* London: Longman, 1908.

Williams, Raymond. *Culture and Society, 1780–1950.* 1958. New York: Columbia University Press, 1983.

———. *The Long Revolution.* 1961. Rev. ed. New York: Harper and Row, 1966.

———. *Marxism and Literature.* Oxford: Oxford University Press, 1977.

———. "The Press and Popular Culture in Historical Perspective." In *Newspaper History: From the Seventeenth Century to the Present Day.* Ed. George Boyce, James Curran, and Pauline Wingate. 41–50. London: Constable, 1978.

Wilson, R. McNair. *Lord Northcliffe: A Study.* Philadelphia: J. B. Lippincott Co., 1927.

Winter, Alison. *Mesmerized: Powers of Mind in Victorian Britain.* Chicago: University of Chicago Press, 1998.

Winter, Jay, ed. *The Working Class in Modern British History: Essays in Honour of Henry Pelling.* Stanford, Calif.: Stanford University Press, 1983.

Wohl, Anthony. "'Dizzi-Ben-Dizzi': Disraeli as Alien." *Journal of British Studies* 34 (July 1995): 375–411.

Wright, Thomas. *Our New Masters.* London: Strahan and Co., 1873.

Yeo, Eileen Janes. *The Contest for Social Science: Relations and Representations of Gender and Class.* London: Rivers Oram Press, 1996.

Yeo, H. *Newspaper Management.* Manchester: J. Heywood, 1891.

Zoonen, Liesbet van. "A Tyranny of Intimacy? Women, Femininity, and the Television News." In *Communication and Citizenship: Journalism and the Public Sphere.* Ed. Peter Dahlgren and Colin Sparks. 217–35. London: Routledge, 1991.

Index

advertising, 33–34, 36, 46n65, 164–65
Altick, Richard, 51, 53
America, 64–65, 92–94, 98, 104n70, 123
Anarchist, The, 68
Angell, Norman: and Labour, 160–63; on Lord Northcliffe, 156; on monopoly and professionalization, 144–45; on readers, 152, 154–55, 158, 169n80
anonymous journalism, 65–69, 70
Arnold, Matthew, 37, 103n28, 132
Arnold, W. T., 79
Astor, J. J., 153
Atkins, J. B., 90
Attlee, Clement, 43

Bagehot, Walter, 139
Baker, Alfred, 89
Baldasty, Gerald, 104n70
Baldwin, Stanley, 149, 157
Barker, Ernest, 164
Barker, Hannah, 25, 37
Barrow, Logie, 76
Beaverbrook, Lord, 42, 167n7
Bell, Walter George, 88
Belloc, Hilaire, 154, 165
Bennett, Arnold, 149–50
bias: in contemporary politics, 3, 15n9; in the nineteenth century, 61, 62, 111; and propaganda, 154–55
Bishop, F. D., 165
Blackwoods Edinburgh Magazine, 58, 60, 62
Blake, George, 153

Blatchford, Robert, 10, 77, 87
Blowitz, Henri de, 77
Boer War, 57, 87, 89, 116
Bohemian Days in Fleet Street, 84
Borthwick, Sir Algernon, 82
Bourne, H. R. Fox, 33, 81, 82, 100
Bradley, F. H., 96–97, 136
Brake, Laurel, 7
Briggs, Asa, 50, 76
Bright, John, 32–33, 64
British Broadcasting Corporation (BBC), 13, 81, 134, 157
Brodrick, George C., 61, 67
Brown, Baldwin, 61
Brown, Lucy, 19, 25
Bulwer, Edward Lytton, 54
Bunce, J. Thackray, 20
Bundock, Clement, 173–74

Canning, Viscount, 64
Carter, Lady Violet Bonham, 176
Catholicism, 53
censorship: and the market, 33–34, 48; and ownership, 3–4, 141, 142, 175; and the state, 30, 43, 140–41, 142, 143
Chalaby, Jean, 40, 41, 46n70, 133, 155
Chamberlain, Neville, 140
chartism, 32
Churchill, Winston, 85, 103n39
circulation, 28, 42
Clarion, The, 87
class: conflict and the media, 159; elite views

of, 5–7, 11, 82–87, 156; and meaning of "knowledge," 108; and reading audiences, 122; and the Reform Act, 32
Cobden, Richard, 32–33, 64
Collins, Wilkie, 59, 82
Conboy, Martin, 179n16
Conrad, Joseph, 20–22
Conservative Party, 11, 56, 61, 131
Contemporary Review, 165
Crawfurd, John, 54
Crimean War, 19, 63, 119
Curran, James: and censorship, 34, 35, 48; and commercialization, 30, 33, 34, 35, 42, 164–65; and the radical press, 33, 139; on readership, 27; on relationship between history and media studies, 2; and social control, 55
Cust, Henry, 87

Daily Herald, 41, 134, 143, 146
Daily Mail: circulation, 28; as a commodity, 40, 41, 42, 123; and the New Journalism, 36, 37, 88
Daily Mirror, 28, 40
Daily Telegraph, 63, 113, 121
Daily Worker, 43, 139–40, 143
Davidson, John, 77–78
Deibert, Ronald, 4, 16n17
Delille, Edward, 93
Dibbley, George Binney, 13, 79–81, 93, 98
Dicey, A. V., 96–97, 139
Dicey, Edward, 83, 89
disinterestedness, 56–57, 62

Economist, The, 19, 60, 64–65
Edinburgh Review, 67, 110
editorial diversity, 10, 61, 62–63, 174
education, 51–54
Education Act (1870), 10, 26, 83–84, 122, 156
educational ideal: definition, 9–10, 50; and John Stuart Mill, 57; persistence of, 132, 135; recedes, 13, 75–76, 81, 94, 101; and representative ideal, 17n33, 62
Edwards, J. Passmore, 57
electorate, 5, 10, 58
Ensor, Robert (R.C.K.), 48–49, 134
Escott, Thomas (T.H.S.), 67
Evans, B. Ifor, 142–43
Ewen, Stuart, 146, 171n129

Falkirk Herald, 117–18
feminization of the press, 12, 119–21

Forster, E. M., 24–25
Fourth Estate. *See* representative ideal.
Fox, Frank, 93
Fry, Oliver, 82

Gardiner, A. G., 89, 135, 149, 151, 152
Gardner, Fitzroy, 87, 122
Gaskell, Elizabeth, 23
George, David Lloyd, 42, 137–38
Gissing, George, 103n28
Gitlin, Todd, 4, 178
Gladstone, W. E., 7, 10, 29, 58, 65
Golding, Peter, 39
Good, E. T., 145–46
Grant, James, 58–59
Graves, Robert, 41, 157
Green, T. H. H., 96, 136, 144
Greenwood, Frederick, 115
Greg, William Rathbone, 67

Habermas, Jürgen, 8, 75, 125, 129n63
Hall, S. Carter, 61
Hall, Stuart, 6, 16n20
Harmsworth, Alfred. *See* Lord Northcliffe.
Harris, Bob, 30, 31
Harrison, J. F. C, 51, 54
Harrisson, Tom, 154
Hayek, F. A., 131
Headlam, Cecil, 100, 120
Hirst, Francis, 81, 88, 122
Hitler, Adolph, 141–42, 146
Hobson, J. A., 87–88, 139, 144
Hoggart, Richard, 119, 133
Hopkin, Deian, 131
Hopkins, Tighe, 69
Hunt, F. Knight, 78

independence, 42, 109, 116
Institute of Journalists (IOJ), 156, 175
irrationality, 13, 94–101, 153, 154–55, 161

Johnson, Richard, 53
Jones, Aled, 1, 19, 78, 94
Jones, Gareth Stedman, 119, 125
Jones, Kennedy, 156

Kaplan, Richard, 104n70
Kay, Joseph, 52–53, 86
Kinnear, A., 84–85
Kinnear, J. Boyd, 58, 68
Knight, Charles, 54, 55
Koss, Stephen, 26

Labour Party, 11, 43, 131–32, 160, 177
Lansbury, George, 156
Laski, Harold, 139, 143, 144, 154
Leavis, F. R., 131
Lee, Alan: and commercialization, 30, 75–76, 139; and liberal ideal, 8, 33, 49–50; and readership, 27–28; and Victorian "golden age," 10, 45n3
legal reform, 30–34
libel, 31, 34, 139
liberal ideal. *See* educational ideal.
Liberal Party, 11, 56, 61, 88
Libertarian theory, 2, 132–33, 146
Liberty of the Press, 9, 143–44, 173
Lippmann, Walter: British influences on, 135, 147; influence on Angell, 160; and stereotypes, 155, 158–59, 163–64
literacy, 26–27
Low, David, 152–53
Lowe, Robert, 131
Lucas, Reginald, 100

Macaulay, Thomas Babbington, 107
Manchester Guardian, 28, 35, 36, 57, 135
Martin, Kingsley: and advertisers, 165; and censorship, 43, 133, 140–41; and educational ideal, 81; and media manipulation, 158, 163–64; rejects knighthood, 116
Massingham, H. W.: and independence, 115–16; and irrationality, 99, 150, 152; and the Market theory. *See* libertarian theory.
mass-observation, 132, 154, 157–58
Matthew, H. C. G., 8, 29, 56
Maugham, William Somerset, 20, 28, 105n92
McLuhan, Marshall, 4
Mill, James, 107
Mill, John Stuart, 12, 57–58, 67–68, 95, 124
Milton, John, 50, 107
Montague, C. E., 79
Morris, William, 127n32
Muggeridge, Malcolm, 157
Murdoch, Rupert, 149, 177
Murdock, Graham, 39
Mussolini, Benito, 43, 151

National Review, 87
National Union of Journalists (NUJ), 42, 43, 173, 176
Nation and Athenaeum, 156–57, 159
Nature, 143
Negrine, Ralph, 2
New Journalism, 36–39, 76, 81, 121, 130

Newnes, George, 49, 128n53
News, 37–38, 41, 76–81
New Statesman and Nation, The, 139, 141–42
Nicolson, Harold, 160
Northcliffe, Lord: and the New Journalism, 37, 41, 88–89, 135–36; on news, 40, 77, 109; political influence, 42, 137, 138–39, 167–68n28; and public opinion, 148–50
Northern Star, 25, 27

O'Connor, Feargus, 25
O'Connor, T. P., 86, 119
Ockham, David, 154
Official Secrets Act, 43, 141
Oldcastle, John, 67
O'Malley, Tom, 144, 173
oral culture, 29
Orwell, George, 25, 155
ownership, 3–4, 142–45, 162, 174, 176

Pall Mall Gazette, 92, 122, 138
Palmerston, Lord, 26, 64
Parker, Sir Gilbert, 153
Parliament and the press, 60, 107, 110, 118
Pebody, Charles, 110–11
Peel, George, 165
Pendleton, John, 89
Penny Magazine, 54, 55, 108
Phillipps, E. M., 119–20
Phillips, J. S. R., 78, 82
Pigott forgery, 90–91
politics by public discussion: and public opinion, 9, 60; and self-government, 8, 57; as a waning ideal, 107, 111, 119
preaching, 60
Press Association, 36, 78, 79
privacy, 38, 93, 121
professionalization, 7, 66, 76, 145
propaganda: fascist and commercial, 141; in nineteenth century, 49, 134–35; overt and hidden, 49, 158; and World War I, 13–14, 60, 136–37, 153
Protestantism, 51, 53
public opinion: as cause of New Journalism, 132, 154–55, 156; and censorship, 4; the press as site of, 111, 129n63, 135; and representative ideal, 108–9, 114, 118, 127n25
public sphere, 8, 13, 29, 100–101, 125

Quarterly Review, 159–60
Quayle, Dan, 5

rationality, 57, 71, 74n67, 108, 124
Raymond, E. T., 149
readers: autonomy of, 6, 156–57
Reform Act (1832), 32
Reform Bill, Second (1867), 131
Reform Bill, Third (1884), 11, 131
Reid, Hugh Gilzean, 78, 109
Reith, John, 13, 81, 134
Representation of the People Act, 11, 131
representative ideal: definition of, 9–10; and educational ideal, 17n33, 62; historical background to, 12, 106–8, 125; twentieth-century legacy of, 130–31, 178
Reuters, 36, 78
Reynolds's News, 27, 28, 35, 36, 49
Riddell, Lord, 156
Roseberry, Lord, 108
Rothermere, Lord, 42, 150, 151, 157
Royal Commission on the Press, 42, 139, 173–76

sales techniques, 41
Salisbury, Lord, 88
Sayers, Dorothy, 40
Schudson, Michael, 177
Schwarz, Bill, 12
science, 143
Scotsman, The, 109–10
Scott, C. P., 10, 57, 116, 135, 140
Scott-James, R. A., 13, 98–99, 122–25, 136
Seacole, Mary, 20
Seligman, Adam, 74n67, 121
Smiles, Samuel, 51, 58
Smith, Anthony, 37
social control, 8, 9, 53, 55, 160–61
Sommerville, John, 50
Spectator, The: on concentration of ownership, 145; and contemporary ideals, 1; on Lord Northcliffe's influence, 137, 138, 166; on readers, 156, 157
speed, 7, 29, 89–90
Stead, W. T.: and "Government by Journalism," 112–14, 132, 137, 138; letter from Norman Angell, 169n80; and "Maiden Tribute of Modern Babylon," 41, 112, 114–15; motivation, 127n18, 126–27n17; and the New Journalism, 76, 92; on power of the press, 42; and prisoners' reading, 85–86; and public opinion, 119, 127n25
Stevenson, John, 39
stunts, 41–42
Symon, J. D., 20, 109

tabloidization, 123
taxes, 27–28, 31, 32, 33, 54, 63–65
Taylor, Frank, 99
Taylor, Philip, 136–37
technology, 34–36
Thackeray, William Makepeace, 22–23
Thomas, Ivor, 154
Thomas, J. H., 134
Times, The: authority of, 67, 90–91, 115, 119; ideals of, 56, 106, 124, 172; influence of, 63, 109; and news agencies, 36; and newspaper taxes, 32; on Royal Commission, 174; and technology, 35; and "views," 37
Trollope, Anthony, 56, 68

Vallance, Aylmer, 142
"views," 37–38
Vincent, David, 26–27, 29

Walsh, Walter, 82–83, 116–17
Warren, Samuel, 62
Watson, Murray, 175–76
Waugh, Evelyn, 154
Wells, H. G., 43, 97, 109, 137, 147–48
Westminster Gazette, 123
Whig interpretation of the press, 30
Wiener, Joel, 37
Wilkes, John, 142
Williams, J. B., 77
Williams, Raymond, 17n34, 37, 122
Wilson, Reginald, 146
World War I, 43, 136–38, 153, 157, 162
World War II, 43, 143
Wright, Thomas, 101

MARK HAMPTON is an associate professor of history at Wesleyan College in Macon, Georgia. He is on the editorial board of *Media History* and has published several articles on the British press. He is currently writing a book on war and journalism in the twentieth century.

The University of Illinois Press
is a founding member of the
Association of American University Presses.

Composed in 10.5/13 Adobe Minion
at the University of Illinois Press
Manufactured by Thomson-Shore, Inc.

University of Illinois Press
1325 South Oak Street
Champaign, IL 61820-6903
www.press.uillinois.edu